See-Through Modelling

The Technical Blueprint to Financial Modelling Using Lessons Learned from PFI

Dominic Robertson

HARRIMAN HOUSE LTD

3A Penns Road
Petersfield
Hampshire
GU32 2EW
GREAT BRITAIN

Tel: +44 (0)1730 233870
Email: enquiries@harriman-house.com
Website: www.harriman-house.com

First published in Great Britain in 2013 by Harriman House.
Copyright © Harriman House Ltd.

The right of Dominic Robertson to be identified as Author has been asserted in accordance with the
Copyright, Designs and Patents Act 1988.

ISBN: 978-0857192-47-9

British Library Cataloguing in Publication Data
A CIP catalogue record for this book can be obtained from the British Library.

 Harriman House

Contents

eBook edition

As a buyer of the print edition of *See-Through Modelling* you can now download the eBook edition free of charge to read on an eBook reader, your smartphone or your computer. Simply go to:

http://ebooks.harriman-house.com/seethroughmodelling

or point your smartphone at the QRC below.

You can then register and download your free eBook.

www.harriman-house.com

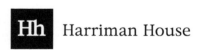 Harriman House

About the author

Dominic Robertson has been modelling since the mid-nineties and is the founding director of Lazuli Solutions, a firm specialised in building financial models that are accessible to both modellers and finance directors.

Lazuli Solutions provides see-through modelling solutions to existing and new infrastructure projects in the UK and Europe, the UK regulated energy distribution market, media-financing slate deals, high speed rail concessions and for shipping & transport.

Prior to this, Dominic was an analyst in the Babcock & Brown infrastructure team working on projects ranging from the development of renewable energy in the UK to defence and utilities PFI projects. Dominic also spent numerous years as a manager in the Arthur Andersen business modelling group in London. During this time, Dominic led the Andersen model audit function across Europe and the Middle East managing the review of 19 large transaction-based models.

Dominic has a degree in Mathematics and Statistics from the University of Bristol and a post-graduate diploma in business administration from ISDA in Rome. Dominic also teaches a post-graduate business modelling course at IPE, a private university in Naples and leads project finance modelling professional accreditation courses at BPP in London.

Dominic grew up in Italy and France and divides his time between London and his farm in southern Italy, where he produces certified organic olive oil.

Contact the author

I welcome feedback from you about this book or about books you would like to see from me in the future.

You can get in contact with me by writing to **dominic.robertson@lazulisolutions.com**. For more information about my work, or for training courses based around the content of this book, please visit **www.lazulisolutions.com** where you will also find a page dedicated to the book.

Preface

WHAT THIS BOOK COVERS

This book aims to provide the reader with a solid theoretical and practical basis for becoming an advanced modeller of see-through financial models in Microsoft Excel. Particular reference will be made to the project finance operating model, and the lessons learned from UK PFI will be drawn upon.

Topics covered by this book include:

- financial theory
- modelling theory
- Excel theory and techniques
- a step-by-step practical guide to building a project finance operating model
- computer setup and efficient use
- keyboard skills
- macro-economic data collection and distribution.

WHO THIS BOOK IS FOR

This book is for finance directors who are looking for a deeper understanding of the dynamics of their enterprise. Above all, this book is for finance directors who want to understand the benefits of adopting a see-through modelling strategy within their enterprise. These benefits are:

- greater strategic vision due to great flexibility of forecast
- lower risk of modelling errors due to standardised modelling
- decreased reliance on individual analysts due to increased ease of model interchange
- clear, detailed and holistic modelling function overview.

This book is also for aspiring financial modellers in general, and UK PFI project finance modellers in particular. Let me explain.

UK PFI has conceived over 900 projects in the UK and has gone a long way towards helping with the evolution of the financial model in Excel. Although there are some fundamental differences between a financial model for a public or private corporation and a model for a project finance operating company, there are also very many similarities.

I initially took knowledge learned from outside of project finance and used it for UK PFI modelling. Subsequently, I have successfully adapted knowledge from my UK PFI models for use in business areas as diverse as regulated energy distribution, media finance funding, telecom spectrum auctions, large container ports, high speed rail, and assorted manufacturing.

Readers of this book should keep in mind that learning to build a UK PFI project finance model is an extremely good place to start to learn financial modelling. UK PFI is like the world in miniature with simplified operations and simplified finance but containing all the accounting and cash elements that are necessary for wider application.

HOW THIS BOOK IS STRUCTURED

The book is divided into three main sections preceded by an introduction and followed by an appendix of useful information.

The introduction outlines:

- the modelling problem
- the possible solutions available.

Part 1 covers the base theory for the professional modeller:

- modelling theory, from mind-set to structure and on to content
- finance theory, from reporting cycles to shareholder returns and banking cover ratios
- FAST theory for Excel coding, from principles to rules and building blocks
- Excel theory, from setup, through useful formulae, to automation and known issues
- computer theory, for ways to optimise the use of the computer.

Part 2 is a practical guide to building a model. It includes:

- building a model in 59 steps
- modelling techniques in practice
- ways of maintaining the modelling investment.

Part 3 is dedicated to further lessons that can be taken from PFI and applied to other industries.

The appendices include:

- links and references
- dictionary of terminology, including abbreviations
- keyboard shortcuts
- Excel functions
- business maps
- the tree analogy.

HOW TO USE THIS BOOK

This guide should be used as a reference. Depending on your role and experience with modelling I would suggest that an efficient approach would be to:

1. Read this preface and the introduction to understand the objectives of the book
2. Skim read Part 2 before doing the same with Part 1, just to familiarise yourself with the overall content
3. Then follow the practical steps of Part 2 while using the theory in Part 1 as a reference guide.

If you are coming to all this without much experience then do not expect to rush through the book in a week. Rather, consider it your companion over time as you learn new ways of looking at and solving the modelling problem.

If you are new to modelling you may want to first concentrate on Part 1 to explore some immediately understandable theoretical concepts. If you are an experienced modeller then you can use this book as a reference.

If you are a finance director then you may want to ensure that someone within the enterprise is tasked with implementing the methods and knowledge contained within this book.

Introduction

The commercial problem

Company directors of PFI projects face some distinct problems:

- How to forecast the future while taking account of the past
- How to properly understand cash in the business
- Is it possible to model the business and learn from past mistakes and experiences?

These are the commercial problems that this book tries to address.

I propose a practical solution called the See-Through Modelling operating model and this book gives you the theory and practical detail necessary to build and maintain this model yourself.

Finance directors and modellers outside of project finance who are dealing with more general financial modelling problems within enterprises other than PFI should consider that the PFI entity is a limited company very similar to other limited companies or even publicly listed companies.

This book is about how to model legal entities that have accounting and cash issues relating to operations, financing from lenders and rewards to shareholders. The project finance operating model is seeded by the last closing balance sheet in exactly the same way that a corporation requires.

OPERATING THE ASSET, AFTER FINANCIAL CLOSE AND POST-CONSTRUCTION

For the purposes of this book I am assuming that there is a PFI project company in which financial close has occurred and the lenders and shareholders have handed over the capital to fund the construction of the asset.

The construction company then delivers the finished piece of infrastructure after the planned construction period and the directors and managers of the project company are left with the maintenance and management of the project for the next 25 years or so.

All companies, whatever industry they operate within, find themselves in an analogous situation to the PFI project company, albeit possibly over longer time horizons.

The maintenance and management of the project leaves the directors with a few problems to overcome, namely:

- Changing commercial objectives
- Limitations of the financial close model
- The practicalities of operating a project
- Balancing the interests of shareholders and lenders
- Reinvention of modelling methods
- What accountants can and cannot do
- Human error.

Let's look at these problems in more detail now.

Changing commercial objectives

At financial close the commercial objective was to close and finance the deal; in other words, to make it happen. During operations the commercial objective is to properly describe the finances in order to satisfy the lenders and directors that the project is performing to plan, and so in turn to be able to reward the shareholders as planned.

Limitations of the financial close model

Let's focus on PFI. The financial close model is limited in a number of ways:

- It can't properly mix actuals and forecast numbers.
- It can't properly deal with the latest closing balances from the last balance sheet.
- It can't deal with indexation actuals.
- It can't deal with a latest tax loss balance.
- It can't adapt the debtors and creditors to the unfolding reality of operations.
- It can't deal with the actuals of construction expenditure if they are different to the financial close expectations.

The practicalities of operating a project company

Excel models need updating, management accounts need to be mapped into the models, the directors and shareholders ask questions about indexation, life cycle expenditure changes, working capital needs to be understood, VAT can cause havoc to the cash flows, and of course the banks require compliant cover ratios to allow distributions to the shareholders.

Balancing the interests of the shareholders and lenders

The lender is the cat that guards the cash and the shareholders are the mice that need small pieces of the cash to survive. Both parties are necessary to begin with and it is also necessary that they can subsequently live with each other.

Reinvention of modelling methods

In every project company, in every bank and at every consultancy there are young modellers reinventing modelling for the umpteenth time. This is risky and unnecessary. Thanks to PFI and the large number of projects in operation there have been some distinct modelling advances in recent times. This book outlines these advances.

What accountants can and cannot do

There is a feeling amongst some project company directors that the management accountants should be able to build and run a financial model to satisfy the banks and reporting process, but I do not think this is the case.

The banks require the model used by the project to be audited. While this is a financial check it is also a logical and technical review. The project company's need for a model audit and the specification of the model audit highlights the fact that models are essentially logical machines with lots of interconnections set within a wider context of fairly straightforward finance.

Logical machines work best when built by expert builders of logic. I believe these expert builders of logic are engineers and mathematicians with knowledge of finance.

Human error

In addition to these difficulties already mentioned, it is also important to recognise another major problem in modelling, which is that financial models tend to be managed by a single person. While this is best practice in terms of focused organisation it is also highly risky in terms of possible human error. Errors in spreadsheets are a well-reported phenomenon and here are some possible reasons why:

- lack of time to double-check analysis
- models create a bottleneck during analysis where only one person can perform the work – this is due to the possibility of important logical changes that need to occur in a single file

- only one person understands the complexities in a model
- managers have no detailed insight into the model logic
- the risk of human error, especially for the lone modeller, is high
- lack of good channels of communication.

This problem of spreadsheet risk is very real and permeates a wide variety of very large companies and industries.

The problem outlined here is thus *financial*, *technical* and *human* so the modelling solution should confront these same issues.

The modelling solution

DIFFERENT APPROACHES IN THE MODELLING MARKET

There are different approaches in the modelling market, varying from the excessively light to the excessively heavy solution. The light approach delivers a skeletal starting model where substantial addition and maintenance may be required over time to satisfy the long-term commercial objectives.

The heavy approach delivers large models with unnecessary duplicate logic, effectively creating a greater need for maintenance, a lack of clarity and higher risk.

The right approach provides the commercially required logical content from the start with the clear understanding that maintenance will always be required.

THE RIGHT APPROACH

The right approach to modelling is a holistic one taking into account all of the issues surrounding the modelling problem – financial, technical and human – and not just some of the financial and technical ones.

The approach I propose in this book covers the following areas:

Financial & legal – dealing with the theoretical financial, commercial and legal issues, and solutions:

- the project characteristics and legal entities involved
- the industry characteristics
- the macro economy
- the government
- strategic or operating solutions

- seeding the future with the past
- the relative importance of cash and accounting.

Technical:

- using Excel
- using a computer
- using other software (the minimum required).

Human:

- managing the build
- managing model control
- managing model delivery
- checking the model for errors.

This approach is illustrated in Figure 1.

FIGURE 1: THE HOLISTIC MODELLING SOLUTION OF SEE-THROUGH MODELLING

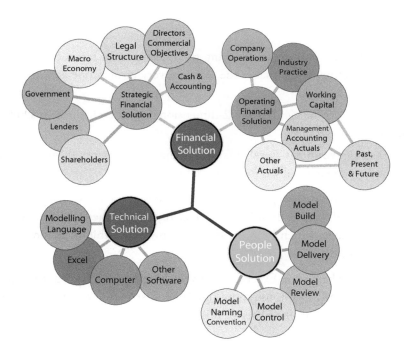

Lessons learnt from PFI

USE OF MICROSOFT EXCEL FOR FINANCIAL MODELLING

Microsoft Excel has become the tool of choice for financial and business modelling, and the UK PFI has gone a long way to prove this. The 900 or so UK PFI projects have required meticulous planning, reporting and human interchange, and this has all been done in Microsoft Excel. This is not withstanding the availability of many other software solutions.

As with most solutions Excel has its strengths and its weaknesses. First the strengths:

- *Flexibility* – Excel is a simple grid across as many sheets as the user needs with the power to add formulae in multiple cells.
- *Grid structure* – this is ideal for organised data such as a financial model.
- *Ubiquity* – all offices are now equipped with Excel so everyone will be able to open the file.
- *Standardisation* – with an increasing drive towards standardisation Excel is proving that it can perform better.

Now the weaknesses:

- *Flexibility* – Excel allows just about anything the user wants in terms of content, formatting and structure which makes the software very error-prone and open to abuse.
- *Grid structure* – this can be rigid as the 2-dimensionality of each sheet precludes multi-dimensional modelling.
- *Ubiquity* – since everyone has Excel this means that experiments in new, more specialised, software are generally doomed to failure.

In order to widen the market as much as possible the original designers of Excel began with the objective of making the software as flexible as possible. To this end they have succeeded as the Microsoft Office package, which includes Excel, is now quasi-ubiquitous amongst the business community worldwide.

As a result of this flexibility, when using Excel for relatively complex tasks such as financial modelling there has been a need to impose some rigidity and structure on the software. The FAST modelling standard – outlined later in this book – does exactly that.

Excel is currently the best solution for financial modelling.

THE STRENGTH OF THE OPERATING MODEL

The financial statements of a strategic operating model contain the perfect mix of actuals plus forecast – past, present and future. This is crucially important for full and easy company reporting.

Operating models have two sets of distinct inputs: *actual historic values* and *future forecast assumptions*. The combination of these two input sets produces results in the form of financial statements with a mix of actuals and forecast. This means that the forecast is being reassessed every time a new set of actuals is added to the operating model, providing the model with a firm foundation in reality.

The vast number of UK PFI projects and the single-minded focus of these projects has opened our eyes to how useful an operating model is. To date, I have not come across a modelling project that would not benefit from a future seeded by the past – from debtor and creditor levels, to growth factors for individual revenue streams.

THE CASH-CENTRIC APPROACH OF PFI

UK PFI is part of project finance. In PFI, as in all project finance, the cash flow waterfall constrains and directs all the cash movements such as payments to suppliers, tax payments, bank debt service, funding of cash reserves and finally the rewarding of shareholders and investors.

From conversations with project developers, bankers and investors it is clear that project finance is all about cash. Above all, everybody involved is asking the question: "How much cash is there?" This is the important question because if properly understood by the company directors and modellers the benefits are enormous.

PFI has made me appreciate the importance of dealing with cash, from the working capital assumptions to the cash flow waterfall. PFI requires an organised cash-centric modelling solution with no duplication. All companies would do well to do the same – even though they may report along more accounting lines.

MACRO-ECONOMIC INDEXATION

Macro-economic indexation has always caused confusion. I have built and rebuilt indices seeded by data from the Office for National Statistics (ONS) for many PFI projects and other businesses and have come to the conclusion that it does matter how indexation is modelled.

See-Through Modelling adopts a simple and effective method of calculating forecast indexation taking into account the very latest actual data from the ONS. I really believe that this method helps shed light on an often misunderstood area of business life.

PART 1
THEORY

I am certain that a minimum of knowledge on the theory of modelling, finance, Excel and the computer is necessary to build a good model. Part 1 will also look at the FAST theory, which is in my view the most complete modelling standard available. My objective here is to give you the core theory of computer and business modelling.

Part 1 is accordingly split into five chapters:

1. Modelling theory
2. Finance theory
3. FAST theory
4. Excel theory
5. Computer theory.

CHAPTER 1
MODELLING THEORY

DEFINITION OF MODELLING

Business modelling includes a variety of different types of modelling. My interpretation of business models is that they are written in Excel with some use of Access and Visual Basic for Applications (VBA) and offer solutions to common business problems.

Models can belong to one or more of the following categories:

- *Financial modelling* – the PFI model is a financial model and a financial model has a P&L (profit & loss), CF (cash flow) and BS (balance sheet) as main results
- *Econometric modelling* – the results vary but the main content is of an econometric nature including any or all of:
    - elasticities to derive volume, supply or demand of goods or services
    - regression analysis or other statistical means to forecast volume, supply or demand of goods or services
- *Deterministic modelling* – where the model derives one set of results
- *Probabilistic modelling* – where the model can derive a distribution of the set of results
- *Simulation modelling* – where the model can be *run* a number of times, while changing one or more variables across a pre-determined range, to derive a distribution of the set of results
- *Operational modelling* – where the model uses management accounting and other actuals to forecast and where the actual updating process happens at regular intervals
- *Strategic financial modelling* – where the model provides the company's senior management with answers to the possible direction of the company's future finances
- *Budget financial modelling* – where the model provides short-term detailed financial variance analysis by comparing actuals data to budget data.

A SHORT HISTORY OF MODELLING

Business modelling began roughly at the time that computers began to find their way into the business and finance workplace. Apparently Deutsche Bank in London had computers in 1987 and actually used them to provide numerical financial analysis.

VisiCalc was the precursor to Lotus 123 and Excel, and had much the same basic grid structure. The initial idea was to provide an extremely flexible grid system rather than attempt to better answer specific questions such as company financial analysis.

Initially the spreadsheet was used to sense check what a person had already calculated using other methods. Compare this to now where the spreadsheet is at the heart of all company finance and any transactions. The complexity of spreadsheets has grown also, largely driven by the technical advances in computing.

Excel has become the leading spreadsheet software in the world. Excel is used to model financial, economic, scientific or other data. However, Excel is also the software of choice for presenting data that may be calculated in other more complex software.

THE FOUR FOUNDING PRINCIPLES OF MODELLING

In my view there are four defining principles of modelling. All modellers would do well to ask themselves if their models abide by these principles.

The four founding principles of modelling are:

1. A model is a model, not reality

The word *model* actually means *a representation of reality that is normally smaller than the original*. This is the essence of a model. Modellers, especially financial modellers, must remember that a model must stop modelling reality at some sensible and optimum point. This is the art of modelling. Just because it can be imagined it does not mean that it should be modelled.

2. A model must be as simple and clear as possible

This sounds obvious but most models do not achieve this goal.

3. A model must answer the commercial needs of the user

The modeller must not get carried away with the exciting technicalities of modelling, but rather remember that the ultimate objective is to answer the commercial questions of the user.

4. As above so below

The model must be see-through to all levels of the organisational structure.

THE MODELLING MIND-SET

Models can look and feel complicated. To build trust in models I propose a three-step process. It boils down to concept, application and maintenance.

These three steps help modellers know, firstly, what state the Excel model is in, secondly, how to make it work properly and thirdly how to maintain this performance. This book will give you the tools to achieve a greater level of trust in your models.

THE BODY OF MODELLING THEORY

In order to describe the important facts about modelling I like to think of the body of modelling theory. The body of modelling theory is divided into five distinct classes:

1. *Structure theory* – the necessary structure of the model
2. *Content theory* – the logic within the model structure
3. *Control theory* – the controls that govern the behaviour of the model
4. *Testing theory* – checking and testing the model
5. *Building theory* – building the model.

Class 1: Model structure theory

The model needs a structure to give it shape. The structure of a model is about organisation, hierarchy and sheet layout, the flow of information and the type of links that best connect the model. These topics are dealt with here, culminating in a discussion of the tree analogy, a visual way of looking at model structure.

ORGANISATION

This is in my view the single most important area of modelling.

Modelling is all about organisation. This includes the names of each and every line item, the units, the choice of row and column to place the line items, the patterns across sheets, the changes in pattern, the order of line items, the hierarchy of all the line items, and the choice the model builder makes about either showing or not showing intermediary line items. This information is either explicitly visible or available for interpretation, or it is implicit and therefore hidden. I am a firm advocate of making this information as open, simple and transparent as possible.

I believe that a model should be organised to represent the entity that is being modelled. If this is a company then the natural organisation follows that of a company: operations, accounting, finance, tax, the financial statements, and the returns and covenants.

A structural look at the model components

The model is made up of both business and modelling components. This represents the first big subdivision within a model. Here is a fuller list of those two types of component particularly referenced to project finance.

Business components

Business components deal with the company finances that are being modelled:

- LIBOR
- macro-economic indexation
- operating revenues
- operating costs
- capital expenditure
- life cycle expenditure
- accounting amortisations, including:
  - fees amortisations
  - fixed asset depreciation
  - finance debtor calculations
- finance, including:
  - debt finance
  - subordinated finance
  - equity finance
- corporation tax
- tax depreciation
- tax losses
- VAT
- profit & loss
- cash flow

- balance sheet

- cover ratio analysis

- investor return analysis

- project return analysis.

Modelling components

Modelling components deal with the necessary modelling technicalities that make a good model work:

- project details

- notes

- macros

- top level outputs

- forecast inputs

- fixed inputs

- management accounting actual inputs

- event flags

- output track

- model checks.

HIERARCHY AND SHEET LAYOUT

This is linked to the previous discussion on organisation. All models should have a deliberate hierarchical organisational structure. This should manifest itself in an accessible layout of the sheets in Excel.

I would suggest allocating the business and modelling components across sheets as shown in Figure 2.

FIGURE 2: BUSINESS AND MODELLING COMPONENTS ALLOCATED ACROSS SHEETS

Sheet name	Type & colour	Description
Cover	Admin	Project details
Notes	Admin	Notes
Control	Control	Macros
	Control	Top level outputs
Inputs	Input	Forecast inputs
Inputs_C	Input	Fixed inputs
Actuals	Input	Management accounting actual inputs
Time	Calculation	Event flags
	Calculation	Macro-economic indexation
Operations	Calculation	Operating revenues
	Calculation	Operating costs
	Calculation	Capital expenditure
	Calculation	Life cycle expenditure
Accounting	Calculation	Fees amortisations
	Calculation	Fixed asset depreciation
Finance	Calculation	LIBOR
	Calculation	Debt finance
	Calculation	Subordinated finance
	Calculation	Equity finance
Tax	Calculation	Corporation tax
	Calculation	Tax depreciation
	Calculation	Tax losses
	Calculation	VAT
Financial_Statements	Outputs	Profit & loss
	Outputs	Cash flow
	Outputs	Balance sheet
Analysis	Calculation	Cover ratio analysis
	Calculation	Investor return analysis
	Calculation	Project return analysis
Track	Admin	Output track
Check	Admin	Model checks

MODEL FLOW

Model flow is defined as the logical direction of information in the model. In much the same way as for that of a book where the reader will read from top to bottom and left to right this is also the model flow across and within sheets.

Model flow is from top to bottom and left to right.

In practice this means that logic in the model will try to use information from above and behind it as far as is possible. This gives the modeller and the user a clear starting point for where to place information and how to perform calculations. Every now and then it is necessary to use information from ahead of the present calculations and I call these *counter flows*.

Model counter flow is any flow of information that travels against the model flow.

For example, when calculating the corporation tax in any period of the model it is necessary to start with the profit before tax line from the financial statements and possibly make some adjustments in order to derive taxable profit. The tax sheet normally resides just before the financial statements sheet since the results of the tax sheet are used in the financial statements, so the profit before tax line used in the tax sheet is defined as a counter flow.

The number of counter flows should be kept to a minimum in order to preserve the conventions and maintain the integrity of the model.

Examples of unavoidable counter flows include:

- profit before tax (PBT) in the corporation tax calculation
- using beginning balances to calculate interest on a loan
- cash available subtotals from the financial statements are used throughout the model to allocate cash down through the cash flow waterfall.

LINKS

A model contains thousands of links between cells sometimes on the same sheet and sometimes across different sheets. These links are called *cell references*. Here I discuss the definitions and implications of at-source cell referencing for best-practice modelling and daisy chain referencing, which is the poor alternative.

At-source cell referencing

Whatever inputs are required for a particular calculation there will exist the optimum at-source location for all the ingredients. In other words, whether the ingredients are raw inputs or other calculations, for each one there will be a single best location source.

At-source referencing means collecting inputs for a calculation from the correct place of first calculation or input rather than from any other location in the model. The overall picture of the references in the model is one where there are no daisy-chains.

Daisy chains referencing

Daisy chains are referenced links in the model that do not go back to the original source. Daisy chains are not good because if a calculation is deleted or changed the repercussions can be difficult and time-consuming to predict and repair.

Example of a daisy-chain

Suppose that the RPI index is used by two different costs as part of the creation of nominal cost lines in the model. Figure 3 shows the trace precedent arrows in Excel showing the two types of references that could be made. Example 1 shows that Cost 2 uses the index from Cost 1, whereas Example 2 shows that in both Cost 1 and Cost 2 the reference to the index is the same.

FIGURE 3: EXAMPLE OF A DAISY CHAIN LINK AND A CORRECT PARALLEL REFERENCE

Example 1: Daisy chain is 'series' referencing	WRONG			Example 2: 'Parallel' referencing	CORRECT		
RPI index	1.0250	1.0506	1.0769	1.1038	RPI index	1.0250	1.0506	1.0769	1.1038
Cost 1					Cost 1				
Cost 1 real	200	220	240	260	Cost 1 real	200	220	240	260
RPI index	1.0250	1.0506	1.0769	1.1038	RPI index	1.0250	1.0506	1.0769	1.1038
Cost 1 nominal	205	231	258	287	Cost 1 nomir	205	231	258	287
Cost 2					Cost 2				
Cost 2 real	100	110	120	130	Cost 2 real	100	110	120	130
RPI index	1.0250	1.0506	1.0769	1.1038	RPI index	1.0250	1.0506	1.0769	1.1038
Cost 2 nominal	103	116	129	143	Cost 2 nomir	103	116	129	143

Example 1 is the wrong way of referencing the index and Example 2 is correct.

Implications of at-source parallel coding

As the model becomes more complex and the number of links reaches the tens of thousands, correct parallel at-source referencing becomes very important for the integrity of the model. Parallel at-source referencing allows for:

- chunks of logic to be deleted or added more freely without risk of errors
- faster tracking to dependents from inputs in cases where this is necessary

THE TREE ANALOGY

The tree analogy is one of the central concepts in this book. The tree analogy (shown in Figure 4) helps explain the structure of a model as well as hinting at the most efficient way of getting around the model.

FIGURE 4: TREE AND ROOT SYSTEM

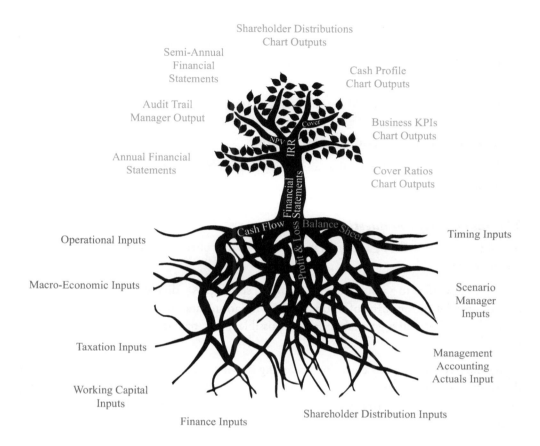

The tree analogy suggests that:

- root ends are the inputs into the model
- roots are the main calculations in the model
- the tree trunk is the financial statements
- the tree's branches are the further results and analysis in the model.

Furthermore, the tree analogy also suggests that:

- further results of the model are made of elements drawn from the financial statements
- financial statements are made of elements drawn from the main calculations and inputs in the model, but not the further results.

Model structure and the tree analogy

Considering the structure of a model the tree analogy also suggests that:

- financial statements are the central element and first main result in a financial model
- further results of the model should be derived by using the financial statements as much as is possible
- the first results to build are the financial statements.

Navigating the model and the tree analogy

To find the appropriate inputs the most efficient path into the model is by starting in the financial statements.

The analysts' typical question

A standard question facing the analyst could be: "What effect will a change in RPI have on the dividends?"

This question refers to a result from the financial statements – dividends – and also an input into the model in the form of a forecast RPI inflation rate. So where should the analyst start? Should the analyst go straight for the possible input, or start somewhere else to ensure the right input is found?

Using the tree analogy it is clear that travelling down a root system from the tree trunk to the roots with intelligence will quickly lead to the input in question. Conversely, testing inputs and tracking up from the roots to the results is by far more time-consuming and inefficient.

The reason is that travelling up a tree diagram in Excel the modeller will be confronted by a trace dependents window like the one in Figure 5.

FIGURE 5: TRACE DEPENDENTS WINDOW

At this point the modeller will have to repeat this step four times to find the best next cell to track to. Alternatively, the modeller can track back from the operating costs in the financial statements using **F5 + Enter** or simply double-clicking the reference and making intelligent choices through the tracking process.

Class 2: Model content theory

Model content deals with the whereabouts of business and modelling components within the model structure. In this section I discuss all the model components including inputs, calculations, outputs, formulae, event flags, switches and macro-economic indexation.

OUTPUTS, CALCULATIONS AND INPUTS

The model can be thought of as an 'i/o' or 'input/output' system. This means a system that takes inputs and produces outputs from those inputs. All computer software is a type of i/o system.

The project finance financial model takes inputs in the form of actuals and forecast inputs and uses coded calculations to produce outputs. The outputs are primarily the company financial statements but also the further calculations thereon, like the shareholder returns and the debt cover ratios. It is clear that to properly drive the model the user needs to at least be able to distinguish between the inputs and the rest.

Since there is a distinction between the inputs, calculations and outputs of a model it is also normal for the modeller to adopt a convention in this regard. For example, a yellow background is the wide-ranging convention for inputs. Calculations are performed on calculation sheets rather than input sheets and output (or report) sheets are marked by colouring the tab green.

A DETAILED LOOK AT THE MODEL COMPONENTS

Below the sheet names are the next level of headings in the model hierarchy. I call these *components* and they are of two generic types: business components and modelling components. Figure 6 shows sheets as boxes and components in the list below the boxes.

FIGURE 6: MODEL HIERARCHY, SHEETS AND COMPONENTS

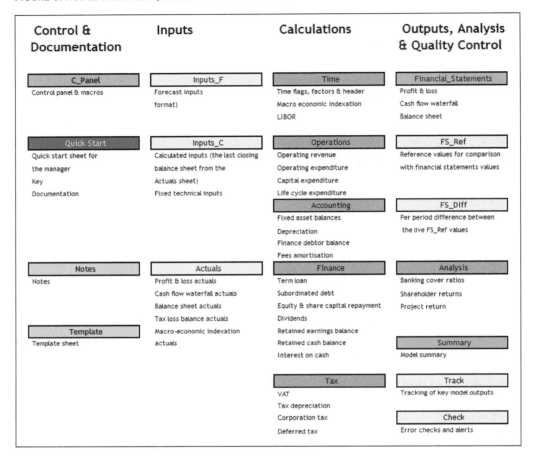

The aggregate of the business components and the modelling components make up all the components in the model. Understanding which components are to be modelled is one of the crucial first steps in building the model.

Business components

As discussed, the business is made up of a series of chunks of logic called components that divide into two classes: business components and modelling components.

Here I discuss each of the components in detail.

LIBOR

The London Interbank Offered Rate often forms part of the basis for the variable interest rate on debt. The most frequently used LIBOR is 3-month or 6-month. If required, the model will need to have an actuals plus forecast LIBOR strip across the timeline of the model.

Macro-economic indexation

The macroeconomics component should contain all calculations relating to the calculation of indices such as RPI and RPIX.

Operating revenues

The operating revenues component deals with all revenues both on an accrued and a cash basis and therefore also the working capital implications of the delay between the accrued and the cash. This can become quite a large component, depending on the type and complexity of the company. Included in this component are:

- revenues accrued and received
- debtor balance calculations.

Operating costs

The operating costs component deals with all costs both on an accrued and a cash basis and therefore also the working capital implications of the delay between the accrued and the cash. This can become quite a large component, depending on the type and complexity of the company. Included in this component are:

- operating costs accrued and paid
- creditor balance calculations
- any prepayments and the prepayments balance.

Capital expenditure

The capital expenditure component deals with all capital expenditure both on an accrued and a cash basis. Normally for a project in operations this has all happened during the construction phase so this component should be empty.

However, for completeness the items included in this component would be:

- capital expenditure accrued and paid (excluding any depreciation calculations)
- creditor balance calculations relating to any assumed or known delay between the accrued expenditure and the paid expenditure.

Life cycle expenditure

The life cycle expenditure component deals with all life cycle costs both on an accrued and a cash basis, and therefore also the working capital implications of the delay between the accrued and the cash. Included in this component are:

- life cycle expenditure accrued and paid (excluding any depreciation calculations)
- creditor balance calculations relating to any assumed or known delay between the accrued expenditure and the paid expenditure.

Accounting amortisations

In the accounting component I deal with all depreciation and amortisation issues that affect the P&L. In particular, these items are:

- depreciation of all assets for accounting purposes
- amortisation of all fees for accounting purposes.

Finance debtor

If the project assets are accounted for by using the finance debtor accounting treatment then this component will contain calculations of:

- finance debtor balance
- finance debtor balance amortisation
- unitary charge control account balance.

Finance

The finance component contains all funding items, non-trading income and high level statement calculations. In particular the items contained are:

- equity and dividends
- subordinated debt, repayments and interest
- mezzanine debt, repayments and interest
- senior debt, repayments and interest
- interest earned and received on reserves and cash balances
- retained earnings balance with net profit in period as a counter flow from the financial statements
- retained cash balance with net cash in period as a counter flow from the financial statements.

Tax

The tax component deals with all government tax issues. In particular:

- VAT or equivalent
- tax depreciation (writing down allowances for assets allowed for tax purposes)
- corporation tax accrued and paid
- tax loss balance.

Financial statements

The financial statements are the P&L, the CFW and the BS.

Actual management accounts

The actual management accounts are made up of a series of actuals that have happened and are fixed and logged. It may be that at some point in the future changes are made but these are rare. For this book, the actual management accounts are made up of:

- P&L actuals to date
- CF actuals to date
- BS actuals to date
- tax loss balance at last actual date
- written down allowance balance for all assets at last actual date
- at cost value of all asset classes (we call this the basis balance) for depreciation calculations.

Analysis

The analysis component deals with all calculations and results that use the financial statements as a source for the data. This component includes calculations carried out with an alternative point of view to that of the company, such as shareholder returns. In particular, the items here are:

- shareholder returns
- present values of shareholder cash flows
- company project return
- present value of company cash flows
- banking cover ratios such as ADSCR, PLCR and LLCR.

Modelling components

Modelling components are necessary to give the model further important functionality beyond core business modelling. These components may or may not also provide a name for the sheet on which they reside.

Inputs

'Inputs' is the abbreviated form for 'forecast inputs' since the historic data is called actuals. These forecast inputs cover all other component titles and are all similar in that they are hard-coded numbers. Inputs can be formatted in a variety of ways, such as %, £k in 0,000, decimals in 0.000 format, and dates in dd-mmm-yy format.

Time

The time component includes all modelling flags that turn calculations on and off throughout the model. The flags are in turn driven mostly by dates from the inputs component.

Quick start

This component provides the manager and the modeller with a single set of navigational links to all parts of the model as well as any documentation on VBA forms.

Control panel

The control panel component is a temporary area where results and inputs can be collected in order to drive the model. Once the analysis has been performed the inputs can be re-instated in their original location and the links to the results deleted.

Financial statement reference

This component has an identical structure to the financial statements except the values are hard-coded, hence the name reference.

Financial statement difference

This component has an identical structure to the financial statements except the values are the difference between the live financial statements and the hard-coded reference financial statements as described in the previous component.

Track

The track component contains hard-coded sets of results derived from changing actuals and changing inputs. Each tracked result set is date and file stamped. This component is the core audit trail in the model.

Check

The check component contains all error checks from throughout the model and summarises these into one single error check.

Header

Each sheet in the model will have a header containing dates, period type labels, sheet name and check & track header (a collection of high-level important information coloured flags). The check & track header is available throughout the model to provide summary information on checks, alerts, and track and input changes.

Template

The template component is a sheet that the modeller can use as a template to create new sheets in the model.

FORMULAE IN MODELLING

I like to keep the formulae as simple as possible.

There is a frequently encountered and often laudable human desire to achieve perfection. When considering Excel formulae it is possible that some combination of formulae will do what we want, so this becomes the end goal. Experience then shows us that the model can suffer in a number of ways that can be hugely detrimental to the purpose of the model. Here is a list of those areas:

- complex formulae are harder to understand and maintain
- complex formulae copied and repeated can substantially add to the file size
- complex formulae can cause unforeseen Excel problems such as inter-sheet link excess that then causes a loss of basic Excel functionality
- complex formulae need to be properly understood to avoid unforeseen behaviour as this can be very time consuming to solve.

Formulae are discussed on page 124.

EVENT FLAGS AND SWITCHES

The simplest way to control when and if calculations happen is through the use of flags and switches.

Event flags are 'on and off' switches mostly governed by input dates that turn calculations on and off for distinct periods of time, ranging from single periods to all periods. Flags are time-dependent. The values that a flag can take are 1 or 0 for each period across the timeline, as in Figure 7.

FIGURE 7: ACTUAL PERIOD FLAG

		E	F	G	H	I	J	K	L	M	N
12		Model Period Beginning					01-Mar-06	01-Sep-06	01-Mar-07	01-Sep-07	01-Mar-08
13		Model Period Ending					31-Aug-06	28-Feb-07	31-Aug-07	29-Feb-08	31-Aug-08
14		Actual vs Forecast					Actuals	Actuals	Actuals	Forecast	Forecast
15		Year # for Current Period's Financial Year End					2,006	2,007	2,008	2,008	2,009
16											
17			Constant	Unit	Total						
18	FLAG										
19											
20		Actuals Period Flag									
21		First Model Column Flag			1	-	1	-	-	-	-
22		Last Closing Balance Flag			1	-	-	-	1	-	-
23		Actual Period Flag		flag	3		1	1	1	-	-
24											

Switches are very similar to flags but they are non-time dependent because they either turn calculations on or off. Switches can take the value 1 or 0 (this is called a Boolean), as in Figure 8.

FIGURE 8: SWITCH

	A	B	C	D	E	F	G
484						Constant	Unit
485							
486			Uplift Switch			1 = on, 0 = off	
487				Uplift Switch		1	switch
488							

INDEXATION

Most PF/PFI models forecast 20 years or so ahead and indexation is an important part of the contractual process. Indexation is also the factor that can most affect a model since any change in rate now has a cumulative effect over time.

Macro-economic indexation is required to inflate real based inputs to nominal values in time. Indexation is based on ONS actual updates (possibly on a monthly basis) to bring the indexation up to date.

Independent and centralised indexation calculations are required in any model that looks to the future.

Class 3: Model control theory

Model control is about directing the model to carry out precise functions in the most efficient way. Here I discuss the optimal format of the inputs, the tracking of outputs, the various points of view described within the model, time as a dimension, the differences between modellers and managers, and overall control during model analysis.

FORECAST INPUTS IN COLUMN FORMAT FOR RUNNING SENSITIVITIES

Advanced control of the model requires a slick sensitivity analysis methodology, structure and content. Arranging the forecast inputs in a column format allows for fast and multiple sensitivity analysis.

The column-format forecast input sheet allows multi-dimensional sensitivity analysis without adding any unnecessary bulk to the model. This is shown in Figure 9.

FIGURE 9: (FORECAST) INPUTS IN COLUMN FORMAT

Inputs			Error chks				[don't del col]	[don't del col]
			Output chgs					
			Input chgs					
			Alerts					
	Active Input Column Label	base					base	
	Comparison Column Label	base					base	
		Constant	Unit		Comment			
Business Rates		-				-		
		-				-		
Consents						-		
		-				-		
Insurance		-				-		
Insurance		-	unesc £k			-		
	31-Aug-2007	-	unesc £k			-		-
	29-Feb-2008	102	unesc £k			-		102
	31-Aug-2008	-	unesc £k			-		-
	28-Feb-2009	102	unesc £k			-		102
	31-Aug-2009	-	unesc £k			-		-
	28-Feb-2010	-	unesc £k			-		-
	31-Aug-2010	102	unesc £k			-		102
	28-Feb-2011	-	unesc £k			-		-
	31-Aug-2011	102	unesc £k			-		102
	29-Feb-2012	-	unesc £k			-		-
	31-Aug-2012	102	unesc £k			-		102
	28-Feb-2013	-	unesc £k			-		-
	31-Aug-2013	102	unesc £k			-		102
	28-Feb-2014	-	unesc £k			-		-
	31-Aug-2014	102	unesc £k			-		102
	28-Feb-2015	-	unesc £k			-		-
	31-Aug-2015	102	unesc £k			-		102

TRACKED OUTPUTS SETS IN COLUMN FORMAT FOR AUDIT TRAIL

Similarly to the column-format forecast inputs, the outputs are also tracked in column-format as in Figure 10. This allows for many recorded sets without adding bulk to the model.

FIGURE 10: TRACK SHEET

	Unit	03a2	Diff	Diff Pct	03a2	03a1	01a
		Error chks					
Track		Output chgs					
		Input chgs					
		Alerts					
Comparison Column Label	Unit	03a2	Diff	Diff Pct	03a2	03a1	01a
COMPARE COLUMN							
Comparison Column Number			3				
Total Comparison Column Differences			-				
Comment					Cover ratio below 1.12 in 2018 after tax on interest earnings as non-trading receipts	Senior debt flag extended into period of Feb 2022, PV of LLCR logic changed, DSRA looks forward 1 year	New Base
[don't delete row]			[range start]				
Date		03-Feb-12			22-Dec-11	21-Dec-11	13-Jul-11
Time		14:59:51			09:25:22	20:17:23	08:33:34
File		pfi_op_model_03a.xls			pfi_op_03a.xls	pfi_op_03a.xls	fi_op_02c.xlsm
KEY METRICS							
COVER RATIOS							
Modified ADSCR (incl DSRA and SDRA Releases)							
Simple Avg ADSCR (incl DSRA & SDRA Release)	ratio	106.3883	4	3.64%	102.6500	101.6500	103.6700
Minimum ADSCR (incl DSRA and SDRA Release)	ratio	1.1298	(0)	-4.25%	1.1800	1.1900	1.2000
Date of Min ADSCR (incl DSRA & SDRA Release)	date	28-Feb-18	731	1.72%	28-Feb-16	28-Feb-16	28-Feb-16

POINTS OF VIEW

Models describe the economics of projects and entities from various points of view. To explain I think it is easiest to consider the example of a project finance company and a model of that company.

The great majority of the model is written from the point of view of the project company or the directors of the project company. There are, however, occasions when other points of view are used:

- rate of return on the investment of shareholders
- positive value of the senior debt repayments
- positive value of the interest paid on the senior debt
- present value of streams of cash flows such as supplier fees (called operating costs by the company)

The shareholder investment cash flows are the clearest example of how the sign flips from positive to negative as the point of view changes. Whereas the equity invested in the project company is a positive for the company accounts, it is a negative for the shareholders. The reverse is true of the dividends that reward the investors for the initial investment; dividends are negative for the company accounts, but most certainly a positive for the investors.

The modeller must beware not to mix up different points of view into the same calculations. In particular, each result will be from one single point of view and all flows and balances that are used to calculate that result must also be from the same point of view.

It is paramount that the modeller is always clear on which point of view is being modelled. This point of view knowledge will make it far easier to carry out precise modelling as the sign of the flows in question will be much more obvious.

THE TIME DIMENSION

The time dimension within a financial model deserves some respect. Excel does not understand the passage of time. Each formula must be coded to deal with time, and formulas can change substantially between a quarterly, semi-annual or annual timeline (this is known as periodicity). In Excel, time creates large amounts of logic and therefore can add substantial bulk and complexity to a model file.

Since each timeline requires all the calculations that form the basis of an individual model it is generally preferable to have only one timeline in a model.

MODELLERS & MANAGERS: HOW THE NEEDS CHANGE

There are possibly two types of users for the model, the modeller and the modeller's manager. In my experience, modellers are quite happy with the technical baggage of the model as well as the business components, as in Figure 11, whereas managers prefer to see the business finances from a business point of view, as in Figure 12.

FIGURE 11: MODELLER VIEW OF MODEL COMPONENTS

Control & Documentation	Inputs	Calculations	Outputs, Analysis & Quality Control
C_Panel	**Inputs_F**	**Time**	**Financial_Statements**
Control panel & macros	Forecast inputs format)	Time flags, factors & header	Profit & loss
		Macro economic indexation	Cash flow waterfall
		LIBOR	Balance sheet
Quick Start	**Inputs_C**	**Operations**	**FS_Ref**
Quick start sheet for the manager	Calculated inputs (the last closing balance sheet from the	Operating revenue	Reference values for comparison with financial statements values
Key	Actuals sheet)	Operating expenditure	
Documentation	Fixed technical inputs	Capital expenditure	
		Life cycle expenditure	
		Accounting	**FS_Diff**
		Fixed asset balances	Per period difference between
		Depreciation	the live FS_Ref values
		Finance debtor balance	
		Fees amortisation	
Notes	**Actuals**	**Finance**	**Analysis**
Notes	Profit & loss actuals	Term loan	Banking cover ratios
	Cash flow waterfall actuals	Subordinated debt	Shareholder returns
	Balance sheet actuals	Equity & share capital repayment	Project return
	Tax loss balance actuals	Dividends	
Template	Macro-economic indexation	Retained earnings balance	
Template sheet	actuals	Retained cash balance	**Summary**
		Interest on cash	Model summary
		Tax	**Track**
		VAT	Tracking of key model outputs
		Tax depreciation	
		Corporation tax	**Check**
		Deferred tax	Error checks and alerts

FIGURE 12: MANAGER VIEW OF MODEL COMPONENTS

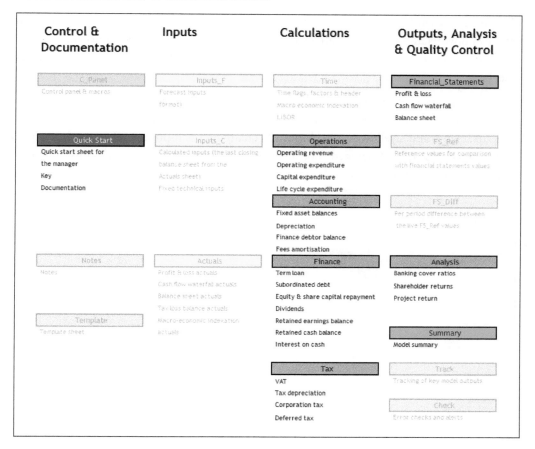

If modellers and managers place emphasis on different elements of the model, then how does the emphasis change and how should the model adapt to these different needs? The answers lie in the view point of each.

Managers look for the business components, while modellers start by looking for the modelling components. Since the model structure is fine for modellers it is sufficient to display an alternative entry structure that satisfies the manager. The Quick Start sheet is my answer to the manager's needs.

See Appendix 5 for a detailed look at the Quick Start sheet.

OVERALL CONTROL OF MODEL ANALYSIS

As the analyst works with the model they are sure to be carrying out changes to inputs to discover how related outputs are affected. If these changes become repetitious and involved there grows a need to see both the inputs and the results in a single place rather than across sheets.

My normal way of dealing with this is to temporarily bring the inputs and outputs to a sheet called the *control panel*. Figure 13 shows a simple control panel with a mixture of outputs, charts and a yellow-shaded input. By changing the input the effect on the outputs and charts can be quickly gauged. The analyst can build up a feeling for the movements in model outputs and thus better understand the dynamics of the project or company finances.

FIGURE 13: SIMPLE CONTROL PANEL

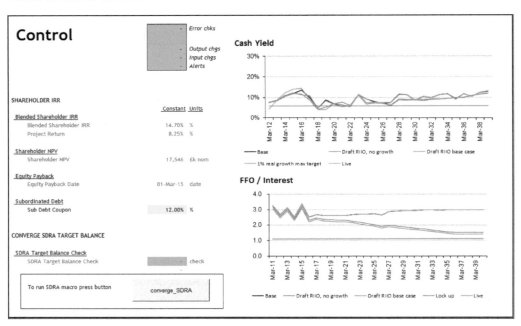

Class 4: Model testing theory

Checking the model during the build and prior to delivery is a core part of modelling. This section on testing theory is divided into seven sections.

1. Ongoing modeller tests, performed during the component build process
2. Ongoing financial statement tests, carried out while compiling the financial statements or reviewing them for errors

3. Tests prior to delivery
4. End user actual update and re-forecast testing
5. Three fundamental financial statements checks
6. End user acceptance tests, carried out by the end user after delivery
7. Auditor tests, carried out during a professional model review process.

1. ONGOING MODELLER TESTS

As each modelling and business building block and result is prepared the modeller needs to be satisfied that the logic is accurate and working to specification. There are various techniques for this and here is a list of these:

- *Use all inputs test* – make sure that all inputs that have a value of zero are actually tested with a non-zero value.

- *Greatly simplify the inputs test* – use simple rounded numbers as inputs and then seek the local results in expectation of simple results.

- *Zero the opening balance test* – if the opening balance has a value try temporarily setting this to zero and then checking the results.

- *Zero the inputs test* – temporarily set non-zero inputs to zero to test the results.

- *Value the opening balance test.*

- *Check dependents test* – press Alt + T + D to check the dependents of a cell to visually check where it is used.

- *Check precedents test* – press Alt + T + T to check precedents of a cell to visually check where it came from.

- *Map the logic test* – use mapping software (such as Excel Savvy as described in 'Excel add-ins and dashboards' on page 113) to map the sheet or workbook.

- *Check the sums test* – use a calculator to check that the sums are referencing all the rows above that they should be referencing.

- *Paint the result into financial statements test* – add sets of results to the financial statements as described on page 232.

- *Colour code dependent test* – go through each dependent of a cell and colour-code the dependent cells with a distinct colour in order to check that there is no repetition.

2. ONGOING FINANCIAL STATEMENTS TESTS

Adding the step results to the financial statements is a big test in itself. If this fails then the modeller needs to perform other tests to find out where the error is. An example is the large number test.

Large number test

Once the results have been painted into the financial statements the modeller expects to see a balanced set of statements. If this is not the case then some part of the double-entry has not been carried out or is not working correctly. By increasing the inputs of the painted results to very large numbers the modeller can better see where the double-entry has failed on the financial statements and then track and repair the error.

3. TESTS PRIOR TO DELIVERY

The modeller should also perform a series of checks for proper delivery. These are:

1. check the look-forward and look-backward formulae

2. check for white text

3. check for proper capitalisation

4. check that counter flows are appropriately marked

5. check there are no external links

6. check units for each line item

7. check all inputs have been compiled in the inputs sheet

8. check spelling

9. home cursor and set view at 100% for all sheets

10. save the model on the cover sheet.

4. END USER ACTUAL UPDATE AND RE-FORECAST TESTING

Updating and re-forecasting an operating model consists of two updates:

1. update actuals inputs

2. update forecast inputs.

To update the actuals it is important that the actual financial statements that form the basis of this update demonstrate complete integrity. This means that the three fundamental checks of any set of financial statements hold true.

5. THREE FUNDAMENTAL FINANCIAL STATEMENTS CHECKS

The three fundamental checks of financial statements are:

- Retained Profit Balance in the balance sheet is the same as the Retained Profit Balance shown in the Profit & Loss and as a function of the constituent parts of the Profit & Loss.

- Retained Cash Balance in the balance sheet is the same as the Retained Cash Balance shown in the Cash Flow Waterfall and as a function of the constituent parts of the Cash Flow Waterfall.

- Balance Sheet balances.

6. END USER ACCEPTANCE TESTING

There are various tests that the end user has to perform in order to properly acceptance test the model. The tests coincide with the various phases of delivery, of which the first is the shadow delivery. To progress to the update stage of the build process the user has to populate the model with 'real' update inputs.

7. AUDITOR TESTS

Model auditors carry out a variety of tests to make sure of the accuracy of the model. To be precise, the model auditors are normally tasked with carrying out tests with the following scope.

Model auditor example of scope arrangement

An independent evaluation and review of the Model is proposed to provide reasonable assurance that:

- The Model does not contain material arithmetic or logical errors in either its base case or when used for two further agreed data sensitivity sets (the Construction Delay set, and the Availability Deductions set).

- The principal accounting assumptions in the Model are materially consistent with UK Generally Accepted Accounting Principles (UK GAAP).

- The tax charge liabilities and payments calculated in the Model are materially consistent with the assumptions made regarding certain tax matters, as stated on pages 11 and 12 of the Data Book.

- There are no material inconsistencies between the assumptions as set out in a document prepared by <office> and provided to <model auditors> ("the Data Book") and the Model.

The review specifically excludes examination of, or comment on, any aspect of the following:

- appropriateness, accuracy or adequacy of any financial, contractual or other structures and arrangements.

- input data and assumptions used other than as set out above.

- achievability or appropriateness of outputs.

- appropriateness of the assumptions made in relation to certain tax matters on pages 11 and 12 of the Data Book and their compliance with UK legislation and practice.

Model auditor example approach arrangement

The assignment will be carried out by following Model Review Methodology, which has been used previously on a wide variety of projects.

In outline, the methodology involves the following steps:

- familiarisation – discussions with modellers and preparation of a block diagram documentation of the Model together with documentation describing its operation
- low level review, including:
  - checking that SUM/total formulae appear valid
  - checking that all ranges in formulae, especially lookup functions (e.g. VLOOKUP, INDEX), appear valid
  - checking formulae exceptions from a map of the spreadsheet formulae (e.g. a unique formula embedded in the middle of a row of copied formulae)
  - following through all unique formulae to test for logical errors
  - checking formulae for consistent use of correct units (e.g. currency, tonnes, cubic metres, etc.)
  - checking that all lookup formulae seek an exact match (in Excel: the fourth parameter is set to FALSE), or if not that the range it references is sorted
  - checking that references in IF formulae appear valid
  - checking that all range names appear to cover the appropriate cell ranges
  - checking any ROUND functions to ensure that material accuracy is not lost
  - reviewing any #REF/#ERR, etc., cells to establish the cause
  - checking any array formulae
  - checking macro/program code
- issue a list of queries and errors
- it will be the modeller's responsibility to correct any errors identified within the Model
- once the errors have been corrected a re-review (maximum of four) will be performed to ensure that these changes have been made satisfactorily
- after the Base Case Model has been reviewed sensitivities will be tested.

In order that the review is completed as effectively as possible access to someone who is familiar with the Model is needed at all times.

Model auditor example reports arrangement

After completing the preliminary investigation, a list of queries and exceptions will be issued. Any disagreements or concerns regarding the appropriateness or significance of the findings may be discussed. Once changes have been made as a result of these discussions, a final check will be carried out to review that the changes made are satisfactory. After this final check, the final report will be issued report, which it is anticipated will substantially take the form of the draft pro-forma report attached.

Model auditor example error/query categories

Model auditors produce reports with categorised queries as shown in Figure 14.

FIGURE 14: MODEL REVIEW ERROR CATEGORIES

Colour	Category Colour Key
AE	Actual error
PE	Potential error
F	Formatting / label query
C	Clarification
N	Numerical assumption
Inf	Information

Model auditors are most often required to check the arithmetic accuracy of the formulae and they do this in one of two ways. Classically this was the cell-by-cell audit, but more recently the re-performance method has gained followers and increased credibility. Both methods aim to bring out the potential arithmetic errors in the model formulae, and the auditors compile a list of queries for the modeller to answer based upon their analysis.

Model auditor example test – the forecast balance sheet test

Model auditors also perform a simple but effective test to find accounts that may not be dealt with properly. The test is called the forecast balance sheet test and consists of using the first forecast balance sheet as the last actual balance sheet in the model to see if the overall results are the same.

Another way to understand the mechanics of this test is to think of the update process where a new last closing balance sheet of actuals is added to the model and the model then creates a new forecast based upon this update.

For this test a new set of actuals is not used, but instead the first forecast numbers from the model all the way from profit and loss statement, the cash flow and the balance sheet, as well as the tax loss balance and any other actuals required to run the new forecast, are used.

The expectation is that the financial statements of the 'updated' model will be precisely the same as those of the model prior to the 'update'. If this is not the case then each difference must be examined, understood and repaired.

In most cases the differences, and therefore errors, will relate to how the modeller is dealing with the last closing balance for any particular account, particularly with respect to accruals and creditors.

The FS_ref and FS_Diff sheets are essential for this test and subsequent analysis.

Class 5: Model build theory

To build a model the modeller should follow the well-trodden software development path of rapid application development. In this section I discuss the five categories of modelling work:

- Specification
- Design
- Build
- Test
- Deliver.

1. SPECIFICATION (S)

Specification means 'the specification of the content and structure of the model'. The model content is made up of a logical machine into which data is input. This logical machine will use this input data to calculate defined outputs. The model structure is made up of organised content set in a specific timeframe.

The first step in building a new model is to define the timeframe of the model. By this I mean start dates, end dates, reporting dates and periodicity. The second step is to define and specify the main outputs in the model; these main outputs are the financial statements of the legal entity or company being modelled.

After these two steps each line of the financial statements is used to further define the content of the model.

2. DESIGN (D)

The design of a model is about the structure, organisation and choice of logic. So model design is also about the choice of formulae. For a project finance company in operations there is limited design left to do given the sheer quantity of projects out in the market. In other words, there is a clear template that can be used.

However, there will always be occasions when some further design is necessary to overcome particular difficulties. These might arise from projects with more complicated operations, such as waste water projects. Or they might arise from more complicated finances, with more tranches of junior debt, such as mezzanine finance. Essentially the model is a pragmatic expression of a series of contracts between various parties and the project company. So design also means the nitty-gritty logic that describes these contracts.

There is good design and bad design.

Good design:

- achieves the objectives in an elegant and transparent solution
- knows its limitations – it is not the intention to build a model that can withstand a 100-year storm
- flags errors and requires further design later as required
- employs clear organisation and structure
- has no duplication or repetition
- minimises logical counter flows
- minimises the number of reports
- understands the importance of model maintenance for the success of a model
- above all, is simple.

Bad design:

- is over-complicated logic
- is massive formulae
- is changing timelines on the same sheet
- is disorganised and has a lack of structure
- is repetitive and duplicative
- has no respect for hierarchy
- creates endless rehashed versions of the financial statements that will require constant maintenance, and
- is the use of un-auditable formulae like OFFSET.

Basic model structure

For a modeller, the basic structure of a PPP/PFI model is well established. This structure was shown in Figure 6 on page 14.

The operating model will contain most or all of these sheets in the order shown in Figure 6 and with the components as listed. Since this design is well-tested the modeller can concentrate on the design of the calculations, which will be particular to the project in hand.

Business map of the model

The manager may not want to see the model in the same overall structure as the modeller. However, we can't change the order of the building blocks to suit the manager as some important benefits derived from the modelling structure would be lost and this would complicate life for the main user of the model. Instead the manager is offered the Quick Start sheet which allows direct navigation to those areas of interest to the manager.

See Appendix 5 for the Quick Start sheet.

3. BUILD (B)

Shadow phase

The objective is to re-perform the results of the old FC model. Most of the model build takes place during this phase. During this phase there are three important steps.

Step 1 – Update:

The objective is to update with actuals and make any further requested/specified changes.

Step 2 – Test:

The objective is to test the model after the updated changes.

Step 3 – Audit:

- The updated and tested model now goes for audit where a reputable firm of model auditors review both the integrity and usability of the new model according to a set specification.
- This phase is important for the lenders as it creates an audit trail between the financial close model and the new operating model.
- This phase validates the logic that has been built and asks a whole series of questions about the model logic that the builder has to respond to – these are called queries and are normally categorised:
  - Actual error, Potential error, Formatting/label query, Clarification, Numerical assumption, Information.

4. TEST (T)

Testing a model is a vital part of the build process. In fact, it is so vital that I have dedicated a section within the body of modelling theory to testing; see 'Class 4: Model testing theory' on page 26.

5. DELIVER (V)

Model delivery is the act of passing a model over to the end user. This happens at various stages during the build process.

There are various strategic moments when this is best done and certainly moments when it is not best done. In general it is better to lower delivery expectations by adding some delay rather than delivering a sub-standard product. However, this is something that comes with experience.

There are three main model delivery events in the production of a UK PFI project finance operating model, listed and described here:

1. Shadow delivery
2. Update delivery
3. Final delivery.

During each of these delivery events the model will undergo a whole raft of ongoing tests during the build (page 27) and also pre-delivery tests (page 28). It is also important that the client carries out end-user acceptance testing (page 29) after Update delivery. The topic of testing will be dealt with in greater detail in a future eBook.

1. Shadow delivery (V1)

The user requires a model that re-performs the results from financial close (FC). This is an important milestone in the audit trail from the FC model to the operating (OP) model.

2. Update delivery (V2)

The objective is to deliver a model with a new forecast based upon the latest actuals and the new forecast inputs.

3. Final delivery (V3)

The model will have been audited by a reputable firm of model auditors. The objective is to deliver an audited model with the latest actuals and best forecast assumptions.

Non-project finance delivery events

The equivalent three delivery events for a non-project finance model are:

1. Shadow delivery is all modelling prior to a new actual update
2. Update delivery is all modelling after a new actual update
3. Final delivery is after a possible model audit and after final changes driven by client acceptance testing.

CHAPTER 2
FINANCE THEORY

CHARACTERISTICS OF A PROJECT FINANCE PFI DEAL

The public-private deal and the history of PFI

The private finance initiative (PFI) is a way of creating public–private partnerships (PPPs) by funding public infrastructure projects with private capital. PFI was initially invented by the Australians in the 1980s and controversially started in the UK by the Conservatives during the early 1990s. However, it was the Labour government after 1997 that implemented PFI on a large scale. There are now more than 900 PFI projects in construction or operation in the UK across a wide spectrum of business sectors.

In simple terms the objective of PFI was to create extensive amounts of public infrastructure without the need to advance the whole capital investment at the start. Instead the government or authority would pay a long-term unitary charge over the agreed life of the project. The private sector would be left to shoulder the upfront finance costs while being allowed to take a market return for the risk over the life of the project.

The private finance most often consists of a very small portion of equity with a larger portion of subordinated debt as the equity-risk element, and one or more tranches of senior debt in the form of loans or bonds as the lower-risk debt portion. Since the projects were effectively government-backed the debt to equity weighting at financing reached highly-leveraged rates of 97.5% in some cases.

Financial modelling has greatly benefited from the number of PFI projects since each one requires at least a financial close model to aid the transaction and an operating model to manage the post-construction phase.

PFI finance debtor accounting treatment

The coming adoption of International Financial Reporting Standards in the UK is forecast to have a significant impact on financial reporting for UK PFI.

The application of IFRIC 12 Service Concession Arrangements looks likely to reclassify most UK PFI infrastructure assets along the financial assets model rather than the fixed assets version. Although some UK PFI projects, notably schools projects and some hospitals, are already being recorded using finance debtor accounting, the effects could be felt in terms of tax and dividends.

However, the objective of this book is not to discuss detailed reasons for the accounting treatments of UK PFI projects. So I will simply discuss how to apply the finance debtor treatment to an existing project treated on a fixed asset basis.

For a current review of the PFI accounting situation see the helpful 'Accounting for PFI' PDF available for download from Mazars (**www.mazars.co.uk/Home/News/Our-publications/Advisory-publications/Project-finance-publications/Accounting-for-PFI**).

FINANCE DEBTOR TREATMENT

From a modelling point of view the change from fixed asset to finance debtor treatment has the following accounting effects and modelling implications.

Accounting effects of the finance debtor treatment

- On the P&L the operating revenues are replaced and reclassified into an amount of revenue based on two elements:
  1. Finance debtor interest revenue = interest at chosen rate on the finance debtor amortising balance
  2. Net Service Income = a function of the total operating revenue over the concession and the operating costs profile in the current period
- The balance sheet replaces the fixed assets balance with two balances:
  1. Finance debtor balance
  2. Unitary charge control account balance.

Modelling implications of the finance debtor treatment

- The export line-items from the Accounting sheet of the model for the finance debtor treatment are:
  - Finance Debtor Balance to balance sheet
  - Unitary Charge Control Account Balance to balance sheet

- Net Service Income to profit and loss
- Finance Debtor Interest Revenue to profit and loss
- The fixed assets are re-classified as financial assets called a finance debtor
- A finance debtor interest rate is chosen to suit – around 5.00% per annum is the norm. See Figure 15.

FIGURE 15: FINANCE DEBTOR INTEREST RATE

Finance Debtor Interest Rate		
Finance Debtor Interest Rate	5.000%	% pa
Quarterly Periods in a Year	4	periods
Finance Debtor Interest Rate	1.25%	% pqtr

- The finance debtor balance is amortised over the life of the concession by the principal component of an annuity calculation with the finance debtor interest rate. This is shown in Figure 16.

FIGURE 16: FINANCE DEBTOR PRINCIPAL AMORTISATION

Finance Debtor Amortisation						
Finance Debtor Interest Rate	1.250%	% pqtr				
Forecast Period Flag	-	flag	30	-	1	1
Remaining FD Op Periods	-	counter	-	-	30	29
Finance Debtor Balance BEG	-	nom £ k	-	-	18,940	18,416
Finance Debtor Amortisation		nom £ k	18,940		524	531

- The finance debtor interest revenue is calculated as the interest portion of the annuity calculation with the same finance debtor interest rate, as in Figure 17.

FIGURE 17: FINANCE DEBTOR INTEREST REVENUE

Finance Debtor Interest Revenue						
Finance Debtor Interest Rate	1.250%	% pqtr				
Finance Debtor Balance BEG	-	nom £ k	-	-	18,940	18,416
Forecast Period Flag	-	flag	30	-	1	1
Finance Debtor Interest Revenue	PL	nom £ k	3,889		237	230

- A unitary charge control account (UCCA) balance is set up to account for the difference between the sum of the two new profit and loss line items (Net service income, Finance debtor interest revenue) and the principal component, the amortisation of the finance debtor balance, and what they replaced, the operating revenues. This is shown in Figure 18.

FIGURE 18: UNITARY CHARGE CONTROL ACCOUNT (UCCA)

Unitary Charge Control Account Balance						
Unitary Charge Control Account - Opening Balance		-	nom £ k			
Last Closing Balance Flag		-	flag	1	-	-	-
Unitary Charge Control Account Balance BEG			nom £ k		-	(501)
Plus: Op Revenue Post-Finance Debtor		-	nom £ k	126,373	-	3,683	3,549
Less: Operating Revenue Accrued	PL		nom £k	126,373	-	4,184	4,184
Unitary Charge Control Account Balance	BS	nom £ k			(501)	(1,135)

- The unitary charge control account balance must come to zero by the end of the concession and takes into account the following changes:
  - Add the sum of (Net service income, Finance debtor interest revenue, Finance debtor amortisation)
  - Take away the operating revenues before reclassification.
- The Net service income is probably the most complicated calculation to perform as it is a function of the operating costs incurred by the project to provide the services and the operating revenue over the life of the concession. The calculations are:
  - Sum the operating costs and the life cycle expenditure and call this Opex total, as in Figure 19.

FIGURE 19: OPEX TOTAL

Operating Cost Accrued POS		-	nom £k	61,254	-	1,769	1,722
Life Cycle Expenditure POS		-	nom £k	5,407	-	112	73
Opex Total			nom £ k	66,660		1,881	1,795

- Calculate a period-by-period profile percentage of the period Opex total over the total concession Opex total (the sum of these percentages should be 100%). Call this the Current Period Opex as % of Remaining Project Life Opex, shown in Figure 20.

FIGURE 20: CURRENT PERIOD OPEX AS % OF REMAINING PROJECT LIFE OPEX

Opex Total		-	nom £ k	66,660	-	1,881	1,795
Opex To End Of Concession			nom £ k			66,660	64,779
Current Period Opex as % of Remaining Project Life Opex						2.82%	2.77%

- On a period-by-period basis take the finance debtor amortisation and the Finance debtor interest revenue from the period operating revenue – call this Op Revenue Post-Finance Debtor, Pre-Revenue Recognition, as in Figure 21.

FIGURE 21: OP REVENUE POST-FINANCE DEBTOR, PRE-REVENUE RECOGNITION

Operating Revenue Accrued	PL	nom £k	126,373	-	4,184	4,184
Less: Finance Debtor Amortisation	-	nom £ k	18,940	-	524	531
Less: Finance Debtor Interest Revenue	PL	nom £ k	3,889	-	237	230
Op Revenue Post-Finance Debt, Pre-Revenue Recognition	PL	nom £ k	103,543		3,423	3,423

- Find the total Op Revenue Post-Finance Debtor, Pre-Revenue Recognition over the remaining life of the concession for each period – call this the Total Operating Revenue Over Remaining Project Life, as in Figure 22.

FIGURE 22: TOTAL OPERATING REVENUE OVER REMAINING PROJECT LIFE

Op Revenue Post-Finance Debt, Pre-Revenue Recognition	PL	nom £ k	103,543	-	3,423	3,423
Forecast Period Flag	-	flag	30	-	1	1
Total Operating Revenue Over Remaining Project Life		nom £ k			103,543	100,121

- Multiply the Current Period Opex as % of Remaining Project Life Opex by the (Total Operating Revenue over Remaining Project Life less UCCA Balance BEG) to arrive at a Net service income, as in Figure 23.

FIGURE 23: NET SERVICE INCOME

Total Operating Revenue Over Remaining Project Life	-	nom £ k	-	-	103,543	100,121
Less: Unitary Charge Control Account Balance BEG	-	nom £ k	-	-	-	(501)
Current Period Opex as % of Remaining Project Life Opex	-	-	-	-	2.82%	2.77%
Net Service Income	PL	nom £ k	103,543		2,922	2,788

- Sum the (Finance debtor amortisation, Finance debtor Interest revenue, Net service income) and call this Op Revenue Post-Finance Debtor. See Figure 24.

FIGURE 24: OP REVENUE POST-FINANCE DEBTOR

Finance Debtor Amortisation	-	nom £ k	18,940	-	524	531
Finance Debtor Interest Revenue	PL	nom £ k	3,889	-	237	230
Net Service Income	PL	nom £ k	103,543	-	2,922	2,788
Op Revenue Post-Finance Debtor		nom £ k	126,373		3,683	3,549

Effectively the finance debtor treatment reclassifies the unitary charge and uses the UCCA to make sure that the total revenue over the concession is actually recognised by the end of the concession. The reclassified revenue that is recognised in the profit and loss is profiled in accordance with the operating and life cycle spend, which is normally more back-ended.

Hence the overall effect of the finance debtor treatment is to:

- lessen revenue, hence lessen profit in the earlier part of the life of the concession
- tax may be affected, but it is difficult to predict if for the better or for the worse
- dividends may also be affected due to the altered distributable profits profile.

PROJECT FINANCE: INTERESTED PARTIES AND THEIR NEEDS

The directors

The directors want to avoid unnecessary risks and make sure the project operates as close to the forecast as possible while maximising shareholder value.

The lenders

The lenders want to be assured that they will get their money back, with interest. In order to be sure of this the bank will monitor cover ratios and use the audited financial model as the calculation tool.

The government and the authority

The government, or authority, requires value for money for the taxpayer from the project. This can be verified using the financial model and making comparisons to alternatives.

The shareholder

The shareholder objective is to maximise the return on the investment from the project. This also can be analysed from the financial model using standard techniques in finance.

The suppliers

The suppliers want to make a margin on their supplies to the project.

Other parties

Other parties include:

- SPV (Special Purpose Vehicle – the project company) management companies that manage the project company
- financial and tax consultants
- auditors
- technical advisors.

THE BUSINESS

It is useful to consider the underlying company and business as the core elements of the project finance deal. These are:

- operations
- accounting
- finance
- tax
- financial statements
- analysis: ratios and returns
- management accounting actuals
- the macro-economy.

THE BUSINESS REPORTING CYCLE

From a purely financial point of view the project goes through a business cycle over the reporting period of the project. The business reporting cycle starts with the logging of invoices and ends with the distributions to shareholders. The reporting period is usually semi-annual or quarterly.

There are three phases to the business reporting cycle:

1. From invoice codes to management accounts

- Revenue and cost invoices are logged into the management system by the management accountants as and when they occur.
- Sometime before the reporting date the management accountants then collect the actuals from the management system and re-compile these to make management accounts for the project in the form of PL, CF and BS.

2. From management accounts to signed off financial statements

- Closer to the reporting date the financial controllers that manage the project accounts use these management accounts in a reconfigured format to update the financial statements in the model.
- The updated financial statements are then discussed by the board of directors of the project company and the board signs off the update.

3. From compliant cover ratios to distributions

- The model and cover ratios are then submitted to the bank for approval.
- Finally, on favourable bank approval, distributions to the shareholders can be made.

THE MACRO-ECONOMY

The impact of the macro-economy on the project model is felt through finance interest rates and inflation.

The variable finance interest rates are mostly swapped for fixed rates so this risk is mostly taken care of. Although some projects are also inflation-neutral through the use of indexed-linked bonds, the effect of changing inflation still needs to be reported in most projects.

I use the RPI example to illustrate the format of the data.

RPI data from ONS site

RPI data from the ONS website comes in the form of Excel tables and to one decimal place (see Figure 25). The data table also has a name, in this case CHAW, to name the RPI data from the last base month in January 1987, when the index was 100.

The data can be found under the Data tab on the ONS website homepage (**www.ons.gov.uk**). After this follow these steps to access the data:

1. Use the search box to query the archive – that will take you to the list of data tables
2. Press the data table name that refers to your index
3. Press the blue writing 'Excel' over on the right under Download options to download the XLS file with the data
4. The downloaded data file in Excel will probably contain many pages, so look for the most relevant result, which in the case of RPI is Table 20, as shown in Figure 25.

The monthly RPI rate that changes the index can be found on another table or simply calculated. For example, the November 2011 rate was 238.5 and the October 2011 rate was 238.0, so the rate of retail price inflation in the UK for the month of October was roughly 0.21%, calculated by:

= „238.5–238.0.–1.0.*100 ~ 0.21%

FIGURE 25: RPI DATA TABLE FROM ONS TABLE 20

Table 20	RPI all items: 1947 to 2011		Annual average	Jan	Feb	Mar	Apr	May	Jun	Jul	Aug	Sep	Oct	Nov	Dec
CHAW	January 1987=100														
		1987	101.9	100.0	100.4	100.6	101.8	101.9	101.9	101.8	102.1	102.4	102.9	103.4	103.3
		1988	106.9	103.3	103.7	104.1	105.8	106.2	106.6	106.7	107.9	108.4	109.5	110.0	110.3
		1989	115.2	111.0	111.8	112.3	114.3	115.0	115.4	115.5	115.8	116.6	117.5	118.5	118.8
		1990	126.1	119.5	120.2	121.4	125.1	126.2	126.7	126.8	128.1	129.3	130.3	130.0	129.9
		1991	133.5	130.2	130.9	131.4	133.1	133.5	134.1	133.8	134.1	134.6	135.1	135.6	135.7
		1992	138.5	135.6	136.3	136.7	138.8	139.3	139.3	138.8	138.9	139.4	139.9	139.7	139.2
		1993	140.7	137.9	138.8	139.3	140.6	141.1	141.0	140.7	141.3	141.9	141.8	141.6	141.9
		1994	144.1	141.3	142.1	142.5	144.2	144.7	144.7	144.0	144.7	145.0	145.2	145.3	146.0
		1995	149.1	146.0	146.9	147.5	149.0	149.6	149.8	149.1	149.9	150.6	149.8	149.8	150.7
		1996	152.7	150.2	150.9	151.5	152.6	152.9	153.0	152.4	153.1	153.8	153.8	153.9	154.4
		1997	157.5	154.4	155.0	155.4	156.3	156.9	157.5	157.5	158.5	159.3	159.5	159.6	160.0
		1998	162.9	159.5	160.3	160.8	162.6	163.5	163.4	163.0	163.7	164.4	164.5	164.4	164.4
		1999	165.4	163.4	163.7	164.1	165.2	165.6	165.6	165.1	165.5	166.2	166.5	166.7	167.3
		2000	170.3	166.6	167.5	168.4	170.1	170.7	171.1	170.5	170.5	171.7	171.6	172.1	172.2
		2001	173.3	171.1	172.0	172.2	173.1	174.2	174.4	173.3	174.0	174.6	174.3	173.6	173.4
		2002	176.2	173.3	173.8	174.5	175.7	176.2	176.2	175.9	176.4	177.6	177.9	178.2	178.5
		2003	181.3	178.4	179.3	179.9	181.2	181.5	181.3	181.3	181.6	182.5	182.6	182.7	183.5
		2004	186.7	183.1	183.8	184.6	185.7	186.5	186.8	186.8	187.4	188.1	188.6	189.0	189.9
		2005	192.0	188.9	189.6	190.5	191.6	192.0	192.2	192.2	192.6	193.1	193.3	193.6	194.1
		2006	198.1	193.4	194.2	195.0	196.5	197.7	198.5	198.5	199.2	200.1	200.4	201.1	202.7
		2007	206.6	201.6	203.1	204.4	205.4	206.2	207.3	206.1	207.3	208.0	208.9	209.7	210.9
		2008	214.8	209.8	211.4	212.1	214.0	215.1	216.8	216.5	217.2	218.4	217.7	216.0	212.9
		2009	213.7	210.1	211.4	211.3	211.5	212.8	213.4	213.4	214.4	215.3	216.0	216.6	218.0
		2010	223.6	217.9	219.2	220.7	222.8	223.6	224.1	223.6	224.5	225.3	225.8	226.8	228.4
		2011		229.0	231.3	232.5	234.4	235.2	235.2	234.7	236.1	237.9	238.0	238.5	

Key: - zero or negligible   .. not available

Source:
Office for National Statistics
Prices Division
1.227 Cardiff Road
Newport
South Wales
NP10 8XG
Tel: 01633 456900

www.ons.gov.uk

The process is similar for all other indices gathered from the ONS site. Here is a list of the most frequently used:

- RPI, retail price index, CHAW, last based in January 1987

- CPI, consumer price index, D7BT, last based in June 2005

- PPI, producer price index – there are many relating to all parts of the economy.

Beware that the ONS has a habit of changing names, website and data format fairly frequently, so each visit will require special attention. Furthermore, the indices are re-based every certain number of years so make sure the model is aware of this if it is relevant.

FLOWS AND BALANCES

A financial model contains flows and balances.

Flows can be accounting flows or cash flows and take time to occur. This means that flows are produced between a start date and an end date, normally over each period in a model whether that is monthly, quarterly, semi-annual or annual. For example, a salary is an accounting flow that then becomes a cash flow and takes time, normally a month, to accrue and then pay.

Balances are snapshots at the start and the end of the period and tell us how much of the flow in question is either owned or owed to another party. An individuals' bank account is the simplest example where a positive balance at the period end date means the individual owns the cash that the bank is keeping. An overdraft means the individual owes the bank instead.

The financial statements of the model are full of flows, sums of flows, balances and sums of balances. In particular, the profit and loss is made up of:

- flows
- sums of flows
- flows and more sums of flows
- finally the retained earnings brought forward, which is a balance
- the retained earnings carried forward, which is also a balance.

The cash flow is made up of:

- flows
- sums of flows
- flows and more sums of flows
- finally the retained cash brought forward, which is a balance
- the retained cash carried forward, which is also a balance.

The balance sheet is made up of:

- balances
- sums of balances.

Every line in the model is either a flow or a balance. It is flows that change a balance from one period to the next, so to calculate the balances at one single date in time the step elements are:

- balance brought forward
- add the flows that increase the balance
- take away the flows that decrease the balance
- balance carried forward.

I like to call this four-step balance calculation a corkscrew because as it is repeated over time the calculations in Excel look very like a corkscrew, as shown in Figure 26.

FIGURE 26: BALANCE CORKSCREW

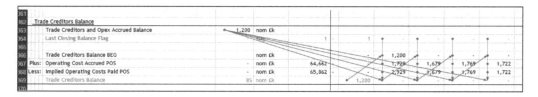

ACCRUED AND CASH: THE IDEA OF WORKING CAPITAL

To understand working capital it is necessary to consider all flows that may have receipt or payment delays. This mainly means revenues and operating costs, and here we concentrate only on these flows. The core concept is simply about the passage of time, and the receipts or payments in cash.

The accrual concept

For a revenue or cost to be accrued it needs to remain unpaid.

The cash concept

When the revenue or cost is received or paid in cash, this is the cash flow.

The working capital concept

It can take some time for the accrued revenue flow to become a revenue cash flow. The same is true for the conversion from accrued cost flow to cost cash flow. This can be caused by a variety of reasons ranging from administrative to technical. The time lag between the accrued flow and the cash flow creates working capital implications for the project company.

Working capital balances created by the delay in payment

Accrued revenues that are as yet unpaid are added to the debtors balance in current assets on the BS.

Accrued costs that are as yet unpaid are added to the creditors balance in current liabilities on the BS.

INFORMAL DEFINITION OF THE FINANCIAL STATEMENTS (FOR MODELLING PURPOSES)

Purely for modelling purposes it is useful to have an informal definition of the financial statements. This helps the modeller to understand where all of the accounts should be placed within the financial statements.

The informal modeller definitions of the financial statements are:

- The P&L is nearly the tax calculation, but not quite – so the modeller's objective is to make sure that all income and all costs are put through the P&L. I like to think that this is in an effort to reduce the profit as much as possible. So, for example, depreciation is put through the P&L as it is the nearest you get to being allowed to put all capital costs through.

- The CF is what you have in your pocket – or bank account. Cash is an easy concept to understand for all of us as we are used to it from an early age.

- The BS is a repository for all financial things – except, strangely, the tax loss balance which is not shown on the balance sheet although it is worth money. So, for the modeller, there should be a place for all accounts on the balance sheet.

There are some other interesting ways of looking at the three statements that can help the modeller to understand more about them without necessarily being an accountant. Here they are:

- P&L can be thought of as the theoretical statement of income and expenditure because it only contains accrued flows.

- CF can be thought of as the actual statement of income and expenditure because it only contains cash flows.

- P&L is *faster* than the CF because the revenues and costs hit the P&L first.

- CF is *slower* than the P&L due to the lag in the cash flow effect.

- Conversely, the P&L is *slower* than the CF because not all expenditure is allowed to hit the P&L straight (such as capital expenditure) but only in amortised form (as depreciation).

- If time is allowed to pass then eventually the CF gets to where the P&L got to.

- P&L and CF are full of flows and these are the values that change the balances in the BS.

- P&L is full of flows and sums of flows, with a balance corkscrew at the bottom (the retained earnings balance).

- CF is full of flows and sums of flows, with a balance corkscrew at the bottom (the retained cash balance).

- BS is full of balances and sums of balances.

THE HIDDEN FINANCIAL STATEMENT: THE TAX CALCULATION

The corporate tax calculation is the hidden financial statement that does not appear on the financial statements sheet in the model. This statement uses the remaining actuals that the rest of the statements do not use, namely the tax loss balance and the various written down values for tax purposes.

The tax calculation uses most of the P&L by starting with the profit before tax line. Since this line is a sum of all the previous P&L flows it also includes accounting depreciation so this drives the first adjustment to the tax calculation.

Adjustments to the tax calculation

Here is a list of adjustments that are made to the tax calculation to derive the taxable profit for the project company:

- Adjustment 1: Add back the accounting depreciation and deduct tax depreciation
- Adjustment 2: Add back the amortisation of any capitalised development, issue and upfront finance fees
- Adjustment 3: Deduct capital allowances.

There may be other adjustments due to the individual project company situation and these can be assessed by tax experts.

Effective tax rate

The effective tax rate of the project can be calculated by using aggregate values from the P&L. The calculation is shown in Equation 1.

EQUATION 1: THE EFFECTIVE TAX RATE

$$\text{Effective tax rate (as a \%)} = \frac{Aggregate\ corporation\ tax\ due}{Aggregate\ profit\ before\ tax} \times 100$$

Deferred tax

Deferred tax is an accounting concept that takes account of future tax assets or liabilities arising from timing differences between the rates at which expenses can be written off for tax purposes as opposed to accounting purposes.

In the UK PFI world there are two situations that give rise to deferred tax charges/credits and resulting deferred tax asset and liability balances:

1. When the tax depreciation of the assets is faster than the accounting depreciation of the same assets this will give rise to a deferred tax charge and a resulting increase in the deferred tax liability balance.

2. Increases in the tax losses that a PFI project can carry forward give rise to deferred tax credits and a resulting increase in the deferred tax asset balance.

THE CASH FLOW WATERFALL; POWER AT YOUR FINGERTIPS AND EASY NAVIGATION

The cash flow waterfall (CFW) is at the heart of the model.

One of the greatest failings of a lot of project finance operational models is the complication around how the cash is dealt with.

The CFW as the only cash allocation engine

Cash is central to project finance as it drives the calculation of cover ratios, which if compliant allow the senior lenders to authorise shareholder distributions, as shown in Figure 27. To this extremely important end there has to be a cash payment priority calculation system in the model that calculates the availability of cash for the calculation of cover ratios and for the distributions to shareholders. This is called a cash flow waterfall.

It is my strong view that this cash flow waterfall is the project cash flow financial statement. Furthermore, there should be no duplication of the cash flow waterfall as this calculation can also serve as one of the key results in the model.

FIGURE 27: CASH FLOW WATERFALL CENTRAL POSITION IN PROJECT FINANCE MODEL

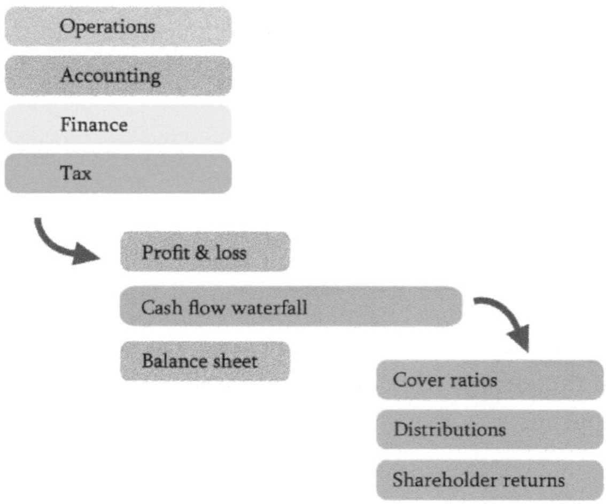

In detail, here is how to make the cash flow waterfall the central cash allocation engine in the model:

1. Replace the project cash flow with the cash flow waterfall financial statement.

2. Make the cash flow waterfall a step-by-step cash allocation engine with all flows in priority order.

3. For each cash payment in the cash flow waterfall after the operating cash flow first calculate the cash available for that payment by summing all previous payments.

4. For each cash payment, such as repayments of loans and payments of interest, collect the cash available for that payment from the cash flow waterfall as a counter flow and then cap the payment in question by the cash available on a period-by-period basis.

The CFW as the central navigation and model entry point

The CFW can also be used in another fundamental way as the navigation and entry point into the model.

By using our understanding of the tree analogy (as in Figure 4), the most efficient entry point into any model is through the main results, in this case the financial statements. Since the most important statement in project finance is the cash flow it makes sense to enter the model from this statement.

The outline payment priority in the CFW

I find the modeller benefits from summary and outline information that relates the actual practical workings of the project finance deal. These help to understand the workings of the model.

The priority of payments in the CFW follows a logical and sensible order:

- first the revenues are received
- then the operating costs are paid, because without this the company cannot operate
- then the assets are maintained, because this ensures that the basic viability of the company is assured into the future
- then the government taxes are paid, because it is the company's duty to pay these and it is illegal not to
- at this point the cash is available for servicing the senior debt lenders
- then any mezzanine finance is serviced
- and then the subordinated debt is serviced
- then finally the shareholders are rewarded through the payment of dividends.

So the outline priority of payments is:

- company operating costs
- company maintenance costs
- government taxes
- senior lender debt service
- junior debt service
- shareholder reward.

BANKING COVER RATIOS

Banking ratios as a fraction

Project finance banking cover ratios are essentially covenants imposed on the project by the lender to make sure the project retains more than enough cash at any one time in order to service the repayments and interest on the senior debt from the lender.

The extent of the cash the project retains as part of the covenant is specified as a multiple, normally in the region of 1.10x to 1.50x. The ratios are negotiated before the initial transaction and stipulated in the contract between the lender and the project, called the credit agreement.

As part of the credit agreement the project provides the lenders with periodic information regarding the ratios, normally in the form of an updated and previously audited financial model in Excel – this is normally called lender reporting. The periodicity of the lender reporting is defined by the credit agreement and normally follows the payment dates, which are the dates when the project is required to make debt repayments to the lender.

All the banking ratios are calculated using a fraction with a denominator on the bottom and a numerator on top. An example is shown in Equation 2.

EQUATION 2: BANKING RATIO

$$banking\ ratio = \frac{f(cash\ available)}{f(debt\ service)} \equiv \frac{'numerator'}{'denominator'}$$

The denominators are a function of the debt service (senior debt repayments and interest) and the numerators are a function of the cash available to service the debt. In simple terms this means that the bank is looking for a ratio that is greater than 1 to make sure that there is more cash than absolutely required to service the debt.

The three standard banking cover ratios: ADSCR, LLCR and PLCR

The three standard ratios for a project finance deal are:

- *ADSCR* – Annual Debt Service Cover Ratio calculated by referencing a year of cash flows for both the denominator and the numerator by:
  - looking forward including the current period
  - looking forward excluding the current period
  - looking backward including the current period
- *LLCR* – Loan Life Cover Ratio calculated using cash flows over the life of the loan only
- *PLCR* – Project Life Cover Ratio calculated using cash flows over the whole life of the project.

Each of the three standard ratios has a particular calculation method, outlined below.

CFADS or cash available for debt service

CFADS is one of the most important elements in the project finance model because it aggregates all free cash flows that are available to service the debt in any given period. In a similar fashion to the tax calculation it is sensible to try to use one central calculation engine rather than make for duplicate logic. CFADS is calculated in the CFW.

The core elements of CFADS are those that reside higher in the priority of payments and are:

- Operating revenues received
- Operating costs paid
- Life cycle expenditure paid
- Corporation tax paid.

ADSCR in detail

The ADSCR is calculated on each payment date and takes into account a full year of cash flows for both the numerator and the denominator. The denominator is made up of the debt service and this is made up of repayments plus interest. The numerator is a function of the cash available for debt service which can be calculated using the CFW. This is shown in Equation 3.

EQUATION 3: ANNUAL DEBT SERVICE COVER RATIO (ADSCR)

$$ADSCR = \frac{\Sigma_{over\ year\ in\ question}\ CFADS}{\Sigma_{over\ year\ in\ question}(senior\ debt\ repayments + senior\ debt\ interest\ paid)}$$

LLCR in detail

The LLCR is calculated on each payment date and takes into account all future CFADS during the life of the loan and the current period end outstanding debt balance. In particular the LLCR numerator is the present value of all CFADS during the loan life discounted at the effective senior debt all-in interest rate, while the denominator is the senior debt outstanding balance at the end of the period. This is shown in Equation 4.

EQUATION 4: LOAN LIFE COVER RATIO (LLCR)

$$LLCR = \frac{\Sigma_{for\ i=1\ to\ n}\ \frac{CFADS_i}{(1 + all\_in\ debt\ interest\ rate_i)}}{Senior\ Debt\ balance}$$

Where:

i = 1 is the current period, and

n = the last period in the life of the loan

PLCR in detail

The PLCR is calculated in exactly the same way as the LLCR, except it includes CFADS over the life of the project. Depending on the amount of *tail* at the end of the project after the debt is repaid, the PLCR includes more cash flows for the same debt balance and is therefore higher than the LLCR.

So, the PLCR is calculated on each payment date and takes into account all future CFADS during the life of the project and the current period end debt balance. In particular the PLCR numerator is the present value of all CFADS during the project life discounted at the effective senior debt all-in interest rate, while the denominator is the senior debt outstanding balance at the end of the period. This is shown in Equation 5.

EQUATION 5: PROJECT LIFE COVER RATIO (PLCR)

$$PLCR = \frac{\sum_{for\ i=1\ to\ m} \frac{CFADS_i}{(1 + all\_in\ debt\ interest\ rate_i)}}{Senior\ Debt\ balance}$$

Where:

i = 1 is the current period, and

m = the last period in the project concession

Project return

The project return is a fundamental measure for the success of a project. By the time the project reaches operations it is no longer a widely used measure but before financial close and particularly during the initial development of the project it is very important.

The project return gives the project developer a rough estimate of the feasibility of the project by looking only at pre-tax and operational cash flows before financing.

Project cash flows

The project return looks only at unleveraged cash flows and does not include any corporation tax. In a relatively crude way, the project return only considers four streams of cash:

1. *Operating revenues* – this will be a +
2. *Operating costs* – this will be a -
3. *Capital expenditure* – this will be a -
4. *Life cycle expenditure* – this will be a -

For each period, from the start of construction to the end of the concession, these four streams of cash are added together. The result is a stream of cash flows that start with negatives representing the capital expenditure and then become positive as the project stretches through operations, as represented in Figure 28.

FIGURE 28: TYPICAL SIGN AND SIZE OF INVESTOR CASH FLOWS

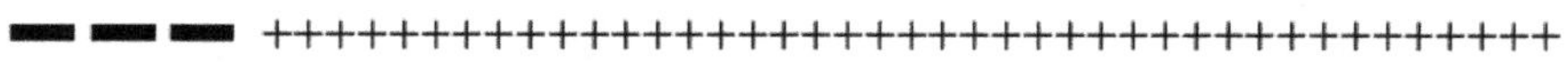

Internal rate of return

Much has been written on the Internal Rate of Return (IRR) calculation so I will limit this study to the basics.

PROJECT IRR

The project IRR is the rate that if used to discount the project cash flows will yield a sum of zero. Effectively, this means that the project IRR is a measure of the overall yield on the investment, given it starts with the negative cash flows and leads to a long stream of positive cash flows.

> Project Return (known as Project IRR) = IRR of the project cash flows

PROJECT IRR VALUES

In a past incarnation I worked in the infrastructure team of an investment bank in London. During this time we were intrigued about the actual value of project returns across the market from PFI, to big infrastructure project finance, to wind farms. This was around 2002.

The reference debt interest rates at the time were:

- merchant project reference debt interest rate of just under 7.00%
- wind farm project reference debt interest rate of around 6.00%
- PFI project reference debt interest rate of around 5.40%

We came to some fundamental conclusions about the value of project returns:

- over all projects from PFI to merchant project finance the project return varied from around 7.20% to 12.00% for projects in development and close to financial close
- average project return was around 8.50%
- lowest project return of 7.2% was for a huge infrastructure project that was atypical, therefore possibly not to be considered
- projects' returns started their life high and came down the closer they got to financial close
- average project return of around 8.50% (and an average debt rate of around 6.20% at the time) gave a differential of over 2.30%
- 2.30% gross of tax differential equates to around 2.30% *(1 - 30%) ~ 1.60% net of tax differential
- 1.60% differential net of tax gave ample room for the effect of leverage on shareholder returns given the assumed debt to equity ratios of from 60:40 to 95:5 at that time.

In any case, the project return is a fundamental stepping stone for a successful project.

INVESTOR RETURN CALCULATIONS

The investors in the project have some standard ways of measuring the return on their investment. These standard measures use cash flows from the CFW and basic financial theory.

Blended equity return

Equity investors inject their capital into PFI projects in the form of a minimal equity and more substantial subordinated debt in order to take advantage of the tax deductibility of the interest on the subordinated debt. It is therefore more meaningful to calculate the shareholder return by aggregating the equity and subordinated debt as a blended calculation.

The blended equity cash flows are:

- equity invested
- equity redemption
- dividends paid
- subordinated debt invested
- subordinated debt interest paid
- subordinated debt repayments.

The blended equity return calculation is:

Blended Equity Return (IRR) = IRR of the blended equity cash flows

READING THE PROJECT MODEL

It is important to be able to read the model and discuss the project.

How to read the cash flow waterfall

Being able to read the cash flow waterfall is key to understanding the project. Much like the direction of model flow, the cash flow waterfall should be read from left to right and top to bottom, like a book.

The story of the cash flow waterfall is the story of the project as the events unfold from construction through operations.

FIGURE 29: CASH FLOW TOTALS

15	E	F	G	H	J	K	L	M	N	O
16										
17	Turnover Received	£k	155,682		320	-	-	598	2,293	2,320
18	Operating Costs Paid	£k	(46,557)		(3,544)	(406)	(394)	(510)	(739)	(710)
19	Capital Expenditure Paid	£k	(37,665)		(8,232)	(15,265)	(10,724)	(3,074)	(370)	-
20	VAT Net Funding Requirement	£k	-		(643)	(737)	655	576	149	-
21	Land Sale Proceeds Received	£k	27,283		-	-	220	-	-	-
22	Life Cycle Expenditue Paid	£k	(11,230)		-	-	-	-	(76)	(1)
23	Equity & Subordniated Debt Drawdown	£k	2,599		2,599	-	-	-	-	-
24	Mezzanine Finance Drawdown	£k	1,242		1,242	-	-	-	-	-
25	Operating Cash Flow	£k	91,354		(8,258)	(16,407)	(10,243)	(2,409)	1,257	1,609
26										
27	Interest on Free Cash Balance & Reserves	£k	2,660		2	0	0	4	15	31
28	Tax (Paid)/Received	£k	(13,989)		(113)	0	0	0	(0)	(0)
29	Cash Flow Available for Debt Service	£k	80,025		(8,369)	(16,407)	(10,243)	(2,405)	1,271	1,641
30										
31	Drawdown on Senior Debt Facility	£k	38,164		8,371	16,407	10,243	2,409	733	-
32	Interest And Fees on Senior Loan/Bond Paid	£k	(40,302)		-	-	-	-	(774)	(1,160)
33	Principal on Senior Loan/Bond Paid	£k	(41,059)		-	-	-	-	-	(172)
34	Cash Flow Available for Reserves	£k	36,828		2	0	0	4	1,231	308
35										
36	Cashflow (To)/From TRA	£k	0		(0)	(0)	(0)	0	-	-
37	Cashflow (To)/From DSRA	£k	-		-	-	-	-	(667)	2
38	Cashflow (To)/From MRA	£k	-		-	-	-	-	-	-
39	Cashflow (To)/From Asset Renewal Reserve	£k	76		(1)	(0)	(0)	(4)	-	(19)
40	Cash Flow Available for Mezzanine Finance	£k	36,904		1	(0)	0	0	564	292
41										
42	Mezzanine Finance Interest And Fees Paid	£k	(2,401)		-	-	-	-	(46)	(69)
43	Mezzanine Finance Repayment	£k	(1,491)		-	-	-	-	-	(5)
44	Cash Flow Available for Sub Debt Interest	£k	33,012		1	(0)	0	0	518	218
45										
46	Subordinated Loan Stock Interest And Fees Paid	£k	(7,263)		-	-	-	-	(138)	(207)
47	Cash Flow Available for Sub Debt Repayment	£k	25,749		1	(0)	0	0	380	11
48										
49	Subordinated Loan Stock Repayment	£k	(3,307)		-	-	-	-	-	(12)
50	Cash Flow Available for Dividends	£k	22,442		1	(0)	0	0	380	(1)
51										
52	Dividends Paid	£k	(22,442)		-	-	-	-	-	-
53	Net Cash Flow	£k	0		1	(0)	0	0	380	(1)
54										
55	Retained Cash Balance BEG	£k			-	1	1	1	1	382
56	Net Cash Flow	£k	0	#	1	(0)	0	0	380	(1)
57	Retained Cash Balance	£k			1	1	1	1	382	381

Let's take VAT as an example of part of this story and use the values from Figure 29. As row 19 shows an increasing and then decreasing amount of capital expenditure being spent to construct the project, so row 20 shows the project also paying VAT on that expenditure. However, we know that a company will receive the VAT back from HMRC on a quarterly basis, so the net VAT effect should be zero, which is the value in row 20, column H. Furthermore, the cash effect of VAT flips from column K to column L as the company receives the initial VAT back from HMRC.

Now let's take sources and uses at financial close as another example. Sources and uses describe all the cash inflows and outflows up to the end of construction. These cash flows are covered by the deal struck at financial close and need to be explicit. These cash flows will necessarily form the first part of the cash flow waterfall before operations but may include some operating-type cash flows if the project can start some operations before the end of construction.

The sources of finance are equity and subordinated debt, mezzanine debt, and senior bank debt. Looking at Figure 29 again, these values can be seen in column H, row 23, 24 and 31 respectively. Adding these up we get around £42m. So I would expect there to be a roughly equal amount of uses on the other side, given that there may be some operational cash flows to account for as well.

The capital expenditure is £37.6m in column H, row 19. So there is a portion of costs incurred during construction that do not seem to be accounted for to the value of around £43m less £37.6m ~ £5.4m. These costs could be the interest during construction and my guess is that these have been accounted for in the Operating Costs in row 18.

In fact if you add up the operating costs in row 18 from column J to column N you get £5.6m, after which point the capital expenditure stops.

Project dimensions

In order to talk sensibly about a project it is very useful to have some basic facts at your fingertips. It is my view that these facts come from the cash flow waterfall. In particular they come from the row total column.

In Figure 29, it is plain to see that the totals column shows an Operating Cash Flow of more than £91m for this project, with an initial capital expenditure of nearly £38m. The tax paid is nearly £14m and VAT shows a zero net effect, which is to be expected. £36.9m is used to reward the mezzanine, subordinated debt and equity investors. The various reserves show ins and outs but a nearly net effect of zero, which again is to be expected.

Effective tax rate

The effective tax rate of a project can be calculated by using the totals column on the P&L. Divide the Corporation Tax total as a positive number by the Profit before Tax total number.

CHAPTER 3
THE LANGUAGE OF MODELLING THEORY

All modellers in Excel effectively have to speak a language to communicate the finances of a business to users of the model. Some languages are very particular to the individual modeller and some are extremely flexible, sometimes so flexible that they are difficult to understand.

I advise readers to use a simple and clear language called FAST. FAST is a modelling standard. This means that FAST is a way of coding a spreadsheet to make financial models. In any sphere of activity there are obvious benefits to speaking the same language and so with FAST.

FAST stands for *flexible, appropriate, structured and transparent*.

I have adopted the FAST standard because it makes sense, but I am not wedded to rigidly sticking to only what FAST mediators say is possible. Any language should be able to cope with organic and somewhat uncontrolled change in different quarters; just like variations in the English language.

In this book I write about the FAST standard as a user and not as one of the FAST standard mediators or as a FAST creator. Therefore, this section on FAST theory is written as much as possible in my own words and as my personal interpretation. For a full interpretation by the creators and mediators of FAST visit their website (**www.fast-standard.org**).

As in any language, the FAST modelling standard offers model builders a set of initial principles followed by rules and then examples of ways of doing things. This does not mean that the individual modeller cannot explore adaptations but rather that FAST will improve if adopters make suggestions to the FAST mediators. However, since the language is in its infancy and since the world of modellers is large, the true benefits of using FAST will only be apparent many years from now.

I have also created a slight adaptation to the basic FAST structure called FAST + 2, discussed later in this chapter.

There are six distinct benefits to using FAST, so this chapter on FAST is accordingly split into six parts:

1. The modelling language principles
2. The modelling language rules
3. The sheets
4. The modelling building blocks
5. The FAST + 2 adaptation
6. The benefits of using FAST.

1. THE MODELLING LANGUAGE PRINCIPLES

By understanding and agreeing to the principles that underpin the FAST modelling standard the reader can go a long way to learning the rules that follow.

Simple but no simpler

The objective is to create logic which is simple to build, understand and maintain. However, just as Einstein said, there is an optimum level of simplicity that is appropriate for any given situation. The objective is to achieve something which is *simple but no simpler*.

The corollary of this principle is that each situation deserves individual attention and that blanket rules cannot always be applied.

My advice is to be patient, as achieving the correct level of simplicity comes with practice.

Transparency

The FAST standard is all about greater transparency.

Greater transparency means others outside of the modeller can access and understand the model. Transparency lowers the risk of error and aids the maintenance of the model by making it easier to understand.

Ordered bite-size pieces of logic

All logic is broken up into small, bite-size pieces and assembled in an order that makes progressive sense.

Smaller pieces of logic are easier to understand and repair if necessary. Smaller pieces of logic are also easier to build in the first place.

Classification

As much as possible all line items in the model should be classified by name, type, size, sign, provenance, destination and adherence to flow.

Proper classification allows the modeller to easily refer to and deal with line items.

Row is the minimum transferrable item

A whole row is the minimum transferable item in the model.

Each non-empty row in the model will have a name, units, one or many values and possibly a text comment. If this row is referenced somewhere in the model then all of these properties will need to travel, rather than only the value as is often the case. This implies what FAST calls *live labelling* whereby the name of a line item is also part of the formula. In practice this means that the whole row is part of the formula.

Standard size and shape

As much as possible all sheets in the model should have the same basic structure.

Keyboard shortcuts

The advanced use of keyboard shortcuts greatly enhances modelling efficiency.

Keyboard shortcuts are an *elegant* way of using the computer and therefore modelling on the computer. Elegant is a term borrowed from mathematics as a way of describing solutions that are not only correct but beautiful and most efficient at the same time.

The 2-dimensional approach

The 2-dimensional approach is a simple block-by-block interpretation of how to calculate and deal with data groups that span multiple classes. As an example multiple repetitions are preferred to complex lookup formulae.

The overall objective is to avoid complex formulae and to keep the *dimensions* to a minimum. Dimensions will inevitably exist within the operations of the project, the financing, and the general organisation and hierarchy of the model.

For example, consider a set of costs that can be classified as variable or fixed, expensed or capitalised, operating or financial, allocated across many operating categories and allocated across many finance categories. The multi-dimensional approach is to list these once and then pick them for further calculation using a SUMIF or VLOOKUP. The 2-dimensional approach is to never search across the same base group, however inviting this is. Instead we prefer to re-compile the list over and over for each new individual cut, using more rows but keeping the dimensions and use of lookup formulae to a minimum.

Each situation deserves individual attention

Although FAST proposes a series of rules, the modeller must remain flexible and consider the individual merits of each situation. The structure and time rule should never be broken, however.

Tracked changes

Models should contain functionality to track changes when inputs or logic is changed.

Model checks

Models should contain a centralised repository for all model checks readily available to the modeller at all times.

Model flow

As much as possible, the model should flow from top to bottom and left to right.

Model flow uses the classic flow of a book by emulating the concept of a story, starting with the inputs, through the calculations and finally to the results.

2. THE MODELLING LANGUAGE RULES

Some of the rules are direct interpretations of the FAST modelling principles, others follow indirectly. In order to properly learn these rules I would advise the reader to first fully understand and agree to the principles in the preceding section.

Line-item properties: name, units & values

All rows in the model are referred to as line-items. Each line item should have three properties: a name, the units and either a non-time dependent value or a series of time dependent values.

See the example in row 18 of Figure 30 where the 'Term Loan Initial Loan Amount' is defined with a non-time dependent value of 40,853 and units of nominal £k. Similarly, row 22 is a calculation called 'Term Loan Repayment' with a series of time-dependent values and units of nominal £k.

FIGURE 30: LINE-ITEM CLASSIFICATION AND COLOUR-CODING

	E	F	I	J	K	L	M	N	O	P	Q
Finance			Error chks								
2	Model Period Beginning		Output chgs			01-Sep-10	01-Mar-11	01-Sep-11	01-Mar-12	01-Sep-12	01-Mar-
3	Model Period Ending		Input chgs			28-Feb-11	31-Aug-11	29-Feb-12	31-Aug-12	28-Feb-13	31-Aug-
4	Actual vs Forecast		Alerts			Actuals	Actuals	Forecast	Forecast	Forecast	Forec
5	Year # for Current Period's Financial Year End					2,011	2,012	2,012	2,013	2,013	2,0
6											
7		Constant	Unit	Total							
8											
9	**SENIOR DEBT**										
10											
11	**TERM LOAN**										
12											
13	Term Loan Repayment										
14	Model Period Ending		date	-	-	28-Feb-11	31-Aug-11	29-Feb-12	31-Aug-12	28-Feb-13	31-Aug-
15	Term Loan Repayment (As % Of Initial Loan)	VLOOKUP	%			-	-	2.42%	2.82%	2.86%	2.9
16	Term Loan Repayment (As % Of Initial Loan)		%			-	-	2.42%	2.82%	2.86%	2.9
17											
18	Term Loan Initial Loan Amount	40,853	nom £k								
19	Term Loan Repayment (As % Of Initial Loan)	-	%	-	-	-	-	2.42%	2.82%	2.86%	2.9
20	Term Loan Repayment		nom £k	26,920		-	-	987	1,153	1,167	1,1
21											
22	Term Loan Repayment	-	nom £k	26,920	-	-	-	987	1,153	1,167	1,1
23	Term Loan Balance BEG	-	nom £k	-	-	-	-	26,920	25,934	24,781	23,6
24	Forecast Period Flag	-	flag	30	-	-	-	1	1	1	
25	Term Loan Repayment POS		nom £k	26,920		-	-	987	1,153	1,167	1,1
26	Term Loan Repayment	CF	nom £k	(26,920)		-	-	(987)	(1,153)	(1,167)	(1,1
27											
28	Term Loan Balance										
29	Term Loan Balance	26,920	nom £k								
30	Last Closing Balance Flag	-	flag	1	-	1	-	-	-	-	
31											
32	Term Loan Balance BEG		nom £k			-	26,920	25,934	24,781	23,6	
33	Plus:										
34	Less: Term Loan Repayment POS	-	nom £k	26,920	-	-	987	1,153	1,167	1,1	
35	Term Loan Balance	BS	nom £k			-	26,920	25,934	24,781	23,613	22,4
36											
37	Check										
38	Term Loan Balance	BS	nom £k	-	-	-	26,920	25,934	24,781	23,613	22,4
39	Last Forecast Period Flag	-	flag	1	-	-	-	-	-		
40	Term Loan Balance Last Forcst Pd	0	nom £k								
41	Term Loan Balance Check	-	check								

Line-item classification and colour-coding

This rule follows directly from the FAST principle of classification.

Line-items should be classed according to two fundamental criteria and colour-scheme:

- where they come from or go to (called imports and exports)
- black font – nether an import nor an export
- blue font – import from another sheet
- red font – export to another sheet
- whether their provenance is with or against the model flow
- white background fill – with the flow
- grey background fill – against the flow, or counter flow.

See the example in row 18 of Figure 30 where the 'Term Loan Initial Loan Amount' is defined in a blue font which means it is an import to this sheet from another sheet previous to it in the model flow. Similarly row 26 of Figure 30 shows the 'Term Loan Repayment' colour-coded as an export and with negative time-dependent values.

For an example of a counter flow see the example in row 23 of Figure 30 where the 'Term Loan Balance BEG' is defined with a grey background fill.

It can also be the case that line-items are classified by both criteria. For example, a line-item can be both an import and a counter flow and can therefore have blue font and a grey background fill thus:

> Import from a sheet to the right

Sheet classification and colour-coding

Sheets in the model are colour coded according to their primary purpose, as in Figure 31.

FIGURE 31: EXCEL SHEET COLOUR-CODING

Light Yellow	Input sheets
Light Grey	Documentation and calculation sheets
Dark Grey	Monthly calculation sheets
Green	Key output sheets
Light Green	Graph and charts
Light Blue	Cover sheet
Turquoise	Quality control
Gold	Macro and control sheets

Structure and time are sacred

The sheet and column structure are a sacred part of the model and should be respected in all cases.

In the example 'Finance' sheet in Figure 30 the sheet structure shows column L with the first time period and the columns previous to it are defined in the standard way. All other sheets are structured in an identical way.

From this example it is clear that if all sheets are the same then it makes absolute sense to always use these columns in this way throughout the model. The modeller is then assured of always finding the units in column I, the name in column E and the first time dependent value in column L, and a serious risk of error has been removed.

The only exceptions to this are the sheets that have no timeline, like the Track sheet, the Inputs sheet, the Check sheet and the Control sheet.

Live labelling

All ingredients to a calculation, whether an input or a previous calculation, are collected by referencing the whole row each time, thereby ensuring that the three line-item properties always travel together. This is called live labelling.

For example, consider the 3-month LIBOR strip as an input for the calculation of an all-in rate of interest for a tranche of debt. LIBOR is normally calculated at the top of the Finance sheet. Further down the same Finance sheet a reference is made to the LIBOR strip at the top of the sheet. The formula in column E references the same column E as does the whole row to the right, thereby collecting not only the value but also all the other properties such as name and units.

For an example of live labelling refer to Figure 30 where the 'Term Loan Repayment' calculated in row 20 is again reported in row 22 and the whole row is referenced.

FAST column structure

All sheets in the model have the same basic structure that allows for the three basic properties of each line item to be clearly visible and always in the same position. Specifically, the line-item name is always in the cell in column E, the units are always in the cell in column G and the non-time dependent value in the cell in column F, while the time dependent values start in the cell in column J, as in Table 1. Refer to Figure 32 for an example of this structure.

TABLE 1: FAST COLUMN STRUCTURE

Column	Designation
A, B, C	3 levels of heading
D	For use of 'Less:', 'Add:' 'Addbk:'
E	Line-item name
F	Value if non time-dependent
G	Units
H	Totals, min or max as applicable
I	Empty
J	Values start here if time-dependent

FIGURE 32: FAST SHEET AND COLUMN STRUCTURE

							Constant	Unit		Total				
			ABCD	E		F	G	H	I	J	K	L		
1		**Finance**				-	Error chks							
2		Model Period Beginning				-	Output chgs			01-Sep-10	01-Mar-11	01-Sep-11	01-A	
3		Model Period Ending				-	Input chgs			28-Feb-11	31-Aug-11	29-Feb-12	31-A	
4		Actual vs Forecast				-	Alerts			Actuals	Actuals	Forecast	Fe	
5		Year # for Current Period's Financial Year End								2,011	2,012	2,012		
6														
7						Constant	Unit		Total					
8														
9		SENIOR DEBT												
10														
11		TERM LOAN												
12														
13		Term Loan Repayment												
14		Model Period Ending				-	date		-	-	28-Feb-11	31-Aug-11	29-Feb-12	31-A
15		Term Loan Repayment (As % Of Initial Loan)				VLOOKUP	%			-	-	2.42%		
16		Term Loan Repayment (As % Of Initial Loan)					%			-	-	2.42%		
17														
18		Term Loan Initial Loan Amount				40,853	nom £k							
19		Term Loan Repayment (As % Of Initial Loan)				-	%		-	-	-	-	2.42%	
20		Term Loan Repayment					nom £k		26,920		-	-	987	

In summary:

- name is always in the cell in column E
- units are always in the cell in column G
- non-time dependent value in the cell in column F
- time dependent values start in the cell in column J.

Column input sheet

I recommend using a column input sheet for all forecast inputs. A column input sheet fits with the FAST standard and enables fast, easy and virtually endless scenario testing and recording. See Figure 33 for an example of a column input sheet. The formulae used to code this type of sheet are explained in the practical section of this book under '5. Build the Inputs sheet' on page 156.

FIGURE 33: INPUT SHEET IN COLUMN FORMAT

Inputs		-	Error chks	[don't del col]	[don't del
		-	Output chgs		
		-	Input chgs		
		-	Alerts		
Active Input Column Label	base			base	
Comparison Column Label	base			base	
	Constant Unit		Comment		
Total Comparison Column Differences		-			
Comment				Base Case	
				01a	
[don't delete row]				[range start]	
TIME		-			
First Modelling Column Date	31-Aug-2006	date		-	31-Aug-2006
Last Forecast Date (Model Period End)	31-May-2026	date		-	31-May-2026
First Modelling Column Financial Year Number	2,006	year #		-	2,006
Financial Year End Month Number	2	month #		-	2
LAST ACTUAL CLOSING BALANCE SHEET & INDEXATION DATES		-			
Last Actual Period End Date	31-Aug-2010	date		-	31-Aug-2010
Last Indexation Actual Period End Date	31-Aug-2011	date		-	31-Aug-2011

At-source referencing

The ingredients for any calculation should be referenced from source.

At the heart of the FAST standard is the collection of ingredients for each calculation. These ingredients may be raw inputs or calculations already performed previously, or later if a counter flow.

Tracked changes

Tracked changes over time are one of the FAST principles. Tracked changes show, in a tabulated format, how a selection of important results has changed over time. See Figure 34 for an example.

FIGURE 34: TRACK SHEET

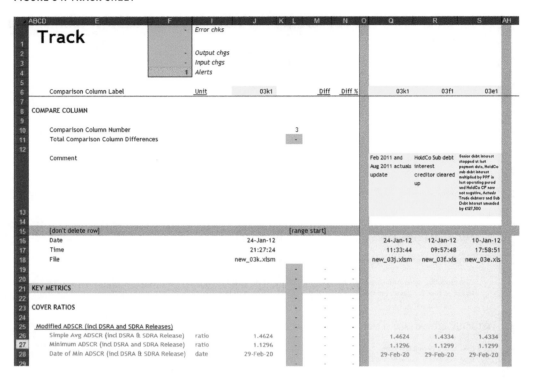

Model checks

Model checks are one of the FAST principles. The Check sheet in the model collects all the checks from around the model and produces one global check that is then reported on all sheets. See Figure 35.

FIGURE 35: CHECK SHEET

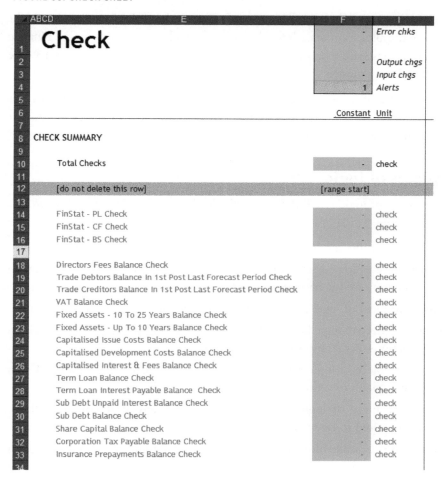

Model flow

Model flow is one of the principles of FAST. The model should flow from start to finish in a progressive manner. This means that any calculations should use ingredients either from above or from a previous sheet.

There are some notable exceptions to this rule that cannot be avoided. FAST calls these counter flows:

- The tax calculation on the tax sheet uses profit before tax from the financial statements, which is a sheet in front of it and therefore a counter flow.
- Balance calculations normally reside at the end of a section. Hence, debt repayments and similar balance amortisations use the brought forward balance from the balance calculation which is normally below it and is therefore a counter flow.

- The cash flow waterfall on the Statements sheet produces a series of sub-totals that start with the words "Cash available for …". These sub-totals are indispensable for calculating the allocation of cash for the finance tranches that reside on the Finance sheet. Using these sub-totals is a counter flow, albeit an extremely necessary one that I allow in my models.

Sometimes it is possible to have to choose between one counter flow and another. In this case the counter flows that have already been used are preferred to a new type of counter flow, although each situation deserves individual attention.

Bite-size pieces of logic

To use bite-size pieces of logic is a FAST principle. To help define *bite-size pieces of logic* here are some properties:

- All calculations in the model are made up of one or more bite-size pieces of logic.
- A bite-size piece of logic is the smallest level of calculation in the model – much the same as atoms are the basic unit of matter.
- Each bite-size piece of logic contributes towards calculating a higher level result.
- Each bite-size piece of logic has inputs that are called ingredients that can be either other calculations, actual inputs or forecast inputs.
- Each bite-size piece of logic performs a defined task and is allowed a blank row before it and a blank row after it.
- Each bite-size piece of logic is internally self-sufficient as it contains all the ingredients required to carry out the calculation.
- In as much as is possible bite-size pieces of logic are laid out in a progressive order to minimise the number of counter flows or to allow one type of counter flow rather than another.
- The creation and scope of each bite-size piece of logic is at the discretion of the modeller – therein lies the art of modelling.

Figure 36 shows an example of bite-size logic in the term loan repayment from a series of percentages and a total debt amount.

FIGURE 36: PROGRESSIVE LOGIC EXAMPLE

ABCD	E	F	I	J	K	W	X	Y
Finance			Error chks					
Model Period Beginning			Output chgs			01-Sep-11	01-Mar-12	01-Sep-12
Model Period Ending			Input chgs			29-Feb-12	31-Aug-12	28-Feb-13
Actual vs Forecast			Alerts			Forecast	Forecast	Forecast
Year # for Current Period's Financial Year End						2,012	2,013	2,013
		Constant	Unit	Total				
SENIOR DEBT								
TERM LOAN								
Term Loan Repayment								
Model Period Ending		-	date	-	-	29-Feb-12	31-Aug-12	28-Feb-13
Term Loan Repayment (As % Of Initial Loan)		VLOOKUP	%			2.42%	2.82%	2.86%
Term Loan Repayment (As % Of Initial Loan)			%			2.42%	2.82%	2.86%
Term Loan Initial Loan Amount		40,853	nom £k					
Term Loan Repayment (As % Of Initial Loan)		-	%	-	-	2.42%	2.82%	2.86%
Term Loan Repayment			nom £k	28,787		987	1,153	1,167
Term Loan Repayment			nom £k	28,787	-	987	1,153	1,167
Forecast Period Flag		-	flag	30	-	1	1	1
Term Loan Repayment POS			nom £k	26,920		987	1,153	1,167
Term Loan Repayment		CF	nom £k	(26,920)		(987)	(1,153)	(1,167)

Calculation sign convention

All calculations are carried out in the positive and flipped to suit at the last minute before export to the financial statements.

Operating costs are the best example of this. They are calculated as positives in whatever way is necessary. However, they will exist as negative numbers in the financial statements and so are multiplied by -1 as a last step before export to the financial statements.

See the example of a flipped sign for export in row 25 the term loan repayment in Figure 36.

Number formatting

FAST specifies how numbers and text are formatted in Excel. Table 2 shows the list of FAST number formats in Excel language.

TABLE 2: FAST NUMBER FORMAT DEFINITIONS

Format name	Example	Excel Format Cells definition
Comma format	45	#,##0_);(#,##0);"";" "@
Factor format	45.0023	#,##0.0000_);(#,##0.0000);"";" "@
Percentage format	45.00%	0.00%_);0.00%_);"";" "@
Date format	14-Jun-20	dd mmm yy_);;"";" "@

In order to define the formats shown above, use the Format > Format Cells command in the old Excel menus, or alternatively press 'CTRL + 1' to bring up the same window, as in Figure 37. Then choose a custom format as shown in Figure 37. Then use the space under the word 'Type:' to place the format in question from Table 2. Press OK and your new format will have been created.

FIGURE 37: FORMAT CELLS WINDOW IN EXCEL

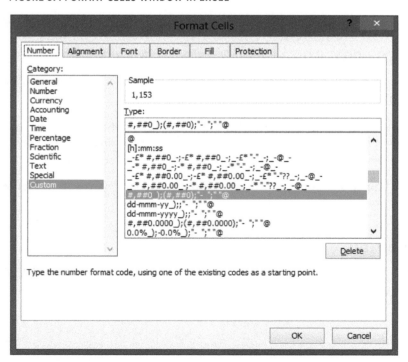

3. THE MODELLING SHEETS

There are two core types of sheet in FAST:

1. calculation sheet – see FAST column structure on page 67
2. input/track sheet – see Figure 10 and Figure 33.

Both these sheets permit the user to access non time-dependent line items by referencing columns E to H, however the calculation sheet allows users to access the whole timeline as well.

4. THE MODELLING BUILDING BLOCKS

The Excel modelling building blocks are the actual pieces of logic that make up the model. This section is by no means exhaustive as all modellers create their own building blocks as well as using versions of the ones below. In general, the modelling building blocks can be divided into 15 types:

1. Sums
2. Division & sign-flip
3. Multiplication
4. Balance corkscrew
5. Flags
6. Dateline
7. Indexation
8. Uplift
9. Choice & lookup
10. Conditional sums of flows & balances
11. Caps & floors
12. Allocators
13. IRRs & cover ratios
14. Track, checks & error-trapping
15. Text manipulation & truncation.

1. Sums

In Excel, the SUM formula is very frequently used. Here I show a slightly more complicated use of the formula with particular reference to financial applications.

SIMPLE SUM

While using the SUM formula is relatively simple there is a dimensional decision to make when it is used to find the total of a whole row. The specific case in question is when the modeller is required to find the total of a whole row that is itself the total of individual columns.

FIGURE 38: SIMPLE SUM

	A B C D	E	F	G	H	I	J	K
12							31-Aug-06	28-Feb-07
13	SIMPLE SUM							
14			Constant	Unit	Total			
15	Revenue							
16		Band 1 Revenue		nom £k	671,240		7,751	7,971
17		Band 2 Revenue		nom £k	460,639		5,167	5,323
18		Band 3 Revenue		nom £k	39,437		-	27
19		Band 4 Revenue		nom £k	450,109		5,038	5,191
20		Band 5 Revenue		nom £k	313,218		3,359	3,470
21		Revenue		nom £k	1,934,043		21,314	21,982
22								

There are two cases:

1. Using SUM to find the total of an individual row
2. Using SUM to find the total of a whole row which is itself the total of a number of rows above.

The solution to type 1 is simply to reference the whole row. The solution to type 2 is to do the same. For type 2, this may not sound like an important solution. However, the modeller has the choice of referencing the rows above or the whole row and the latter is by far the most efficient for these reasons:

- ease and simplicity of writing
- can be copied from other similar constructs without inadvertently referencing incorrect rows.

COMPLEX SUM

A slightly more complex use of the SUM formula shows all rows to be added or added back and uses a '- SUM' for the rows that are to be deducted. The example in Figure 39 shows the beginning of the tax calculation, in particular the taxable profit or loss calculation.

The formula in K33 is:

= SUM(K29:K30) - SUM(K31:K32)

FIGURE 39: COMPLEX SUM

			E	F	G	H		J	K
25								31-Aug-06	28-Feb-07
26	COMPLEX SUM								
27				Constant	Unit	Total			
28	Taxable Profit								
29			Profit / (Loss) Before Tax		nom £k	368,192		4,033	4,161
30		Add:	Depreciation POS		nom £k	8,885		109	112
31		Less:	Capitalised Issue Costs Amortisation POS		nom £k	1,215		27	27
32		Less:	Capitalised Interest & Fees Amortisation POS		nom £k	585		13	13
33			Taxable Profit		nom £k	375,277		4,102	4,233
34									

CUMULATIVE SUM

Sometimes, particularly for the calculation of event flags, a cumulative total is required. Effectively this is a balance, except that it is carried out in non-financial situations where using a balance corkscrew is deemed to be excessive. An example could be when looking for a stream of values to exceed a certain value, such as in a payback calculation.

While still referring to Figure 39 the syntax for a cumulative sum from J33 to column K would be:

= SUM($J33:K33)

2. Division & sign-flip

DIVISION WITHOUT ERRORS

Mathematically, dividing by zero gives infinity. In Excel dividing by zero returns a #DIV/0! error, which is unusable.

Figure 40 shows a cost allocation example where the number of divisions to allocate costs to is zero at some point. This may be because at that point it is beyond the scope of the model or for a variety of other reasons. In any case the modeller can prevent errors by wrapping the division with an IF statement. By testing the denominator of the fraction for a value of zero, the result is effectively trapped.

FIGURE 40: DIVISION WITHOUT ERRORS

	A B C D	E	F	G	H	I	J	K	L
47							31-Aug-06	28-Feb-07	31-Aug-07
48	DIVISION WITHOUT ERROR								
49			Constant	Unit	Total				
50	Cost Apportionment								
51		Operating Cost POS		nom £k	8,885		109	112	115
52		Number Of Divisions	5				5	5	-
53		Cost Apportionment		nom £k	44		22	22	-
54									

Logically, if the denominator is not equal to zero then carry out the division, otherwise return a zero. Hence the test and the two cases for the IF statement are:

- test is if denominator is not zero
- case if TRUE is to carry out division
- case if FALSE is to return a value of zero.

Here is the syntax for L53:

= IF(L52 <> 0, L51 / L52, 0)

SIGN FLIP

The sign flip finds the opposite sign of a single value or a stream of values. The sign flip is best exemplified in J44 of Figure 41.

FIGURE 41: SIGN FLIP

	A B C D	E	F	G	H	I	J	K
39							31-Aug-06	28-Feb-07
40	SIGN FLIP							
41			Constant	Unit	Total			
42	Depreciation POS							
43		Depreciation		nom £k	(8,885)		(109)	(112)
44		Depreciation POS		nom £k	8,885		109	112
45								

The syntax is:

= - 1 * J43

3. Multiplication

While the multiplication of two rows is self-evident, the multiplication of a line-item by a single fixed percentage is a key building block.

PERCENTAGE MULTIPLICATION

The percentage multiplication building block is a standard piece of code that is repeated many times in a financial model. The example in Figure 42 shows how this is applied to the calculation of the interest on a tranche of senior debt. The multiplication is simple and requires the multiplication of the brought forward senior debt balance in row 63 by the senior debt interest rate in F64. The calculation should only take place while the debt flag is turned on.

The syntax of the formula in K66 is:

= IF(K65 = 1, K63 * $F64, 0)

FIGURE 42: PERCENTAGE MULTIPLICATION SHOWN WITH SENIOR DEBT INTEREST EXAMPLE

	A	B	C	D	E	F	G	H	I	J	K	L
59										31-Aug-06	28-Feb-07	31-Aug-07
60	% MULTIPLICATION											
61												
62				Senior Debt Interest								
63					Senior Debt Balance BEG		nom £k			25,934	24,781	23,613
64					Senior Debt Interest Rate	4.78%	%					
65					Senior Debt Flag	-	flag	8	-	-	1	1
66					Senior Debt Interest	7,801	nom £k			-	1,185	1,129
67												

4. Balance corkscrew

The Balance Corkscrew is the fundamental building block for all balances in the model. As shown in Figure 43 this is a 7-line construct that adds and subtracts positive flow values and creates both a starting balance and a closing balance for each period.

FIGURE 43: THE BALANCE CORKSCREW

	A	B	C	D	E	F	G	H	I	J	K	L
72										31-Aug-06	28-Feb-07	31-Aug-07
73	TRADE DEBTORS											
74												
75				Trade Debtors Balance								
76					Trade Debtors Balance	1,209	nom £k					
77					Last Closing Balance Flag	-	flag	1		-	1	-
78												
79					Trade Debtors Balance BEG		nom £k				-	1,209
80		Plus:			Indexed Operating Revenue		nom £k	73,393		-	-	8,061
81		Less:			Operating Revenue Received		nom £k	72,128		-	-	7,850
82					Trade Debtors Balance	BS	nom £k			-	1,209	1,420
83												

The flag in row 77 of Figure 43 allocates the last closing balance from F76 into the corkscrew in row 82.

Rows 79 to 82 are the balance corkscrew, with row 79 as the opening balance, denoted with the letters BEG, and row 82 as the closing balance.

Rows 80 and 81 are the two flows that add and detract respectively from the closing balance calculated in row 82.

The syntax of the formula in K82 is:

= IF(K77 = 1, $F76, K79 + K80 – K81)

And for completeness the syntax of L79 is:

= K82

The check for the balance corkscrew is described in 'The Check building block' on page 104.

5. Flags

Flag building blocks create event flags that can be used throughout the model. Event flags are on and off switches in that they have a Boolean value which is either one or zero. One means the event is happening and zero means the event is not happening.

SINGLE PERIOD EVENT FLAG

The single period event flag takes a value of 1 in a single period and zero in all other periods, thus flagging the occurrence of an event that only occurs in one time period. Examples of a single period event flag are the Start Date Flag and End Date Flag.

This building block uses the IF statement to check that a timeline date is the same as an input fixed date, in which case it returns a 1. Otherwise it returns a zero.

One of the most important single period event flag building blocks in an operating model is the Last Closing Balance Flag, as in Figure 44.

FIGURE 44: LAST CLOSING BALANCE FLAG

A B C D	E	F	G	H	I	J	K	L
88						31-Aug-06	28-Feb-07	31-Aug-07
89 SINGLE PERIOD EVENT FLAG								
90								
91	Last Closing Balance Flag							
92	Last Actual Period End Date	28-Feb-2007	date					
93	Period End Date	-	date		- -	31-Aug-06	28-Feb-07	31-Aug-07
94	Last Closing Balance Flag		flag	1		-	1	-
95								

The syntax of the formula in K94 is:

= IF($F92 = K93, 1, 0)

The End Date Flag is an example of a single period event flag. The End Date Flag defines the end period for a particular event. This building block uses the IF statement to check that a timeline date is the same as an input fixed date, in which case it returns a 1. Otherwise the End Date Flag returns a zero.

MULTIPLE PERIOD EVENT FLAG

A multiple period event test flag creates a flag that defines a series of periods over which a particular event occurs. These flags require the use of one or more single period event flags such as a Start Date Flag and an End Date Flag.

Two examples are shown in Figure 45. The first uses one single event flag to create the Forecast Period Flag and the syntax in K106 is:

= IF(SUM($J105:K105) > 0, 1, 0)

The second example uses two single event flags to create the Debt Repayment Flag and the syntax in L113 is:

= SUM($J111:L111) − SUM($J112:K112)

FIGURE 45: MULTIPLE PERIOD EVENT FLAGS

	E	F	G	H	I	J 31-Aug-06	K 28-Feb-07	L 31-Aug-07	M 29-Feb-08
102	MULTIPLE PERIOD EVENT FLAG - 1 FLAG								
104	Forecast Period Flag								
105	First Forecast Period		flag	1	-	-	1	-	-
106	Forecast Period Flag		flag	8		-	1	1	1
108	MULTIPLE PERIOD EVENT FLAG - 2 FLAGS								
110	Debt Repayment Flag								
111	Debt Repayment Start Date Flag		flag	1	-	-	1	-	-
112	Debt Repayment End Date Flag		flag	1	-	-	-	1	-
113	Debt Repayment Flag		flag	2		-	1	1	-

INTERSECTION AND EXCLUSION EVENT FLAG

Sometimes it is necessary to find flags to highlight events that require one or more other events to occur first. Conversely, some events occur when others don't occur.

Examples include the intersection of the forecast periods of a model with a number of other events like debt repayment, shareholder distribution or the calculation of operating revenues.

Examples of mutually exclusive events include:

- actual and forecast periods of a model
- construction and operating periods of a project finance model
- shareholder distributions lock-up periods and dividends.

By using the logical functions OR, AND and NOT the modeller can combine intersections and exclusions. Here is a discussion of those three flags:

OR event flag

An OR flag construct uses the logical function OR to check that *any* of a multiple set of tests are returned as TRUE. If one is TRUE, then OR returns a TRUE, if all are FALSE, the OR returns a FALSE. When checking that a value is TRUE it is not necessary to add '= 1', as TRUE and the value 1 are synonymous.

The OR Event Flag is used, for example, to create a flag for the event that the model is either in the actuals period or the forecast period of the project, as in Figure 46.

FIGURE 46: OR EVENT FLAG

	A B C D	E	F	G	H	I	J	K	L
100							31-Aug-06	28-Feb-07	31-Aug-07
101	OR EVENT FLAG								
102									
103	Actual & Forecast Flag								
104		Actual Period Flag	-	flag	1	-	1	-	-
105		Forecast Period Flag	-	flag	8	-	-	1	1
106		Actual & Forecast Flag		flag	9		1	1	1
107									

The syntax in K106 is:

```
= IF( OR ( K104, K105 ), 1 , 0 )
```

AND event flag

An AND flag construct uses the logical function AND to check that *all* of a multiple set of tests are returned as TRUE. AND will only return a TRUE if all are TRUE. If one is FALSE then AND returns a FALSE.

The AND Event Flag is used, for example, to create a flag for the event that the model is both in the operations period and in the forecast period of the project, as in Figure 47.

FIGURE 47: AND EVENT FLAG

	A B C D	E	F	G	H	I	J	K	L
110							31-Aug-06	28-Feb-07	31-Aug-07
111	AND EVENT FLAG								
112									
113	Operations & Forecast Flag								
114	Operations Period Flag		-	flag	9	-	1	1	1
115	Forecast Period Flag		-	flag	8	-	-	1	1
116	Operations & Forecast Flag			flag	8		-	1	1
117									

The syntax in K116 is:

= IF(AND (K114, K115), 1 , 0)

NOT event flag

A NOT flag construct uses the logical function NOT to check a single test. NOT returns the opposite of the test. NOT returns a TRUE when the test returns a FALSE and returns a FALSE when the test returns a TRUE.

The NOT Event Flag is used, for example, to create a flag for the event that the model is not in the actuals period of the project. Another way of looking at this is that the model is in either the forecast or the post-forecast periods of the project, as in Figure 48.

FIGURE 48: NOT EVENT FLAG

	A B C D	E	F	G	H	I	J	K	L
120							31-Aug-06	28-Feb-07	31-Aug-07
121	NOT EVENT FLAG								
122									
123	Not In Actuals Period Flag								
124	Actual Period Flag		-	flag	1	-	1	-	-
125	Not In Actuals Period Flag			flag	8		-	1	1
126									

The syntax in K125 is:

= IF(NOT (K124), 1 , 0)

6. Dateline

A dateline is a standard first step in a model. A dateline is made up of a period start date and a period end date and normally resides in the top rows of each sheet. It is easier to define the period end date first by defining, as an input, the date for the first period end in the model.

MODEL PERIOD END

To define the Model Period End you require three pieces of information:

1. A flag defining the first date column in the model
2. A date defining the first period end date in the model
3. The periodicity of the model (this could be daily, weekly, monthly, quarterly, semi-annual or annual).

The Period End Date is calculated with a combination of an IF statement and the EOMONTH standard Excel function.

The EOMONTH function requires two variables; a date and the periodicity in months. The function looks for the last day of the month, in a number of months after the date, set at the value of the periodicity (in months).

The IF statement is used to seed the resulting period end dateline with the first period end date, which is an input.

There is no need to separate out the periodicity of the model as an input as in most cases it will not be possible to change the periodicity given the increased complexity that would demand of almost all logic in the model.

FIGURE 49: MODEL PERIOD END AND MODEL PERIOD START

	A B C D	E	F	G	H	I	J	K
132							31-Aug-06	28-Feb-07
133	DATELINE BUILDING BLOCKS							
134								
135		Model Period End						
136		First Model Column End Date	31-Aug-2006	date				
137		First Model Column Flag	-	flag	1 -		1	-
138		Model Period End		date			31-Aug-06	28-Feb-07
139								
140		Model Period Start						
141		Model Period End	-	date	- -		31-Aug-06	28-Feb-07
142		First Model Column Flag	-	flag	1 -		1	-
143		Model Period Start		date			01-Mar-06	01-Sep-06
144								

The syntax in K138 of Figure 49 is:

```
= IF( K137 = 1, $F136, EOMONTH( J138, 6 ) )
```

MODEL PERIOD START

The start date for each period in a model is easily calculated from the Period End Date, again using the combination of an IF statement and the EOMONTH function.

The IF statement's two cases are:

1. Case 1 is when we require the first model period start date (and use the EOMONTH function to find it).
2. Case 2 is when we require any other model period start date (and simply add one day to the preceding Model Period End).

The EOMONTH function with the Model Period End date and the periodicity as variables finds the previous period end last day in the month date for case 1, in the first period.

Wrapping this result in an IF statement will pick out all the cases when it is not the first period, and to find the period start date it is sufficient to add 1 day to the last period end date.

Again referring to Figure 46, the syntax for the formula in K143 is:

= IF(K142 = 1, EOMONTH(K141, – 6) + 1, J141 + 1)

The idea with this use of the EOMONTH function is to pick the last day of the last month of the preceding semi-annual period and then simply add 1 day to bring the date to the first day of the current semi-annual period.

7. Indexation

Indexation building blocks deal with macro-economic and real inflation, and are not entirely straightforward. It is my view that this is the simplest and clearest way of modelling indexation. However, it does require an annual timeline.

ACTUAL + FORECAST INDEXATION

An index is created with a base or actual index and a forecast index change rate. This building block constitutes the heart of an indexation system within a financial model, as shown in Figure 50. There are various parts to this building block, not least the yellow shaded actuals from the ONS and the white shaded forecast values, which require monthly updating.

There are three different formulae to know, as well as an update routine, but the whole is well worth knowing as indexation is a classic area of confusion in many models.

The first formula in row 181 at the bottom of the indexation block is used to forecast the index in December of each year. This formula takes the last December index and inflates it by the forecast index growth rate in row 166. The syntax of the formula in L181 is:

= K181 * (1 + L166)

The second formula in row 170 is identical in function to the third formula but cannot be copied down, so is an original formula. This second formula plots a straight-line path between the previous December index and the current year December index. The syntax of the formula in N170 is:

= M181 + (N$181 – M$181) / (12 – N$167)

The third formula is used in all the white shaded cells in the middle section from rows 171 to 180 inclusive. The syntax of the formula in P171 is:

= P170 + (P$181 – O$181) / (12 – P$167)

FIGURE 50: ACTUAL + FORECAST INDEXATION

	E	G	J	K	L	M	N	O	P
162			31-Mar-10	31-Mar-11	31-Mar-12	31-Mar-13	31-Mar-14	31-Mar-15	31-Mar-16
163	INDEXATION								
164									
165	RPI Growth								
166	December To December RPI Growth (Forecast)	% pa			5.00%	2.80%	2.75%	2.75%	2.75%
167	Months of Actual Data		12	12	11	-	-	-	-
168									
169	Month to Month RPI Index								
170	January RPI Index	index	217.9000	229.0000	234.2000	239.8200	247.0999	253.8952	260.8773
171	February RPI Index	index	219.2000	231.3000	239.9000	239.8200	247.6649	254.4757	261.4738
172	March RPI Index	index	220.7000	232.5000	241.3350	239.8200	248.2299	255.0562	262.0703
173	April RPI Index	index	211.5000	222.8000	234.4000	239.8200	248.7949	255.6367	262.6667
174	May RPI Index	index	212.8000	223.6000	235.2000	239.8200	249.3598	256.2172	263.2632
175	June RPI Index	index	213.4000	224.1000	235.2000	239.8200	249.9248	256.7977	263.8597
176	July RPI Index	index	213.4000	223.6000	234.7000	239.8200	250.4898	257.3783	264.4562
177	August RPI Index	index	214.4000	224.5000	236.1000	239.8200	251.0548	257.9588	265.0526
178	September RPI Index	index	215.3000	225.3000	237.9000	239.8200	251.6197	258.5393	265.6491
179	October RPI Index	index	216.0000	225.8000	238.0000	239.8200	252.1847	259.1198	266.2456
180	November RPI Index	index	216.6000	226.8000	238.5000	239.8200	252.7497	259.7003	266.8421
181	December RPI Index	index	218.0000	228.4000	239.8200	246.5350	253.3147	260.2808	267.4385
182									
183	February RPI Index								
184	Model Period End	date	31-Mar-10	31-Mar-11	31-Mar-12	31-Mar-13	31-Mar-14	31-Mar-15	31-Mar-16
185	February RPI Index	index	219.2000	231.3000	239.9000	239.8200	247.6649	254.4757	261.4738
186									
187	December RPI Index								
188	Model Period End	date	31-Mar-10	31-Mar-11	31-Mar-12	31-Mar-13	31-Mar-14	31-Mar-15	31-Mar-16
189	December RPI Index	index	218.0000	228.4000	239.8200	246.5350	253.3147	260.2808	267.4385
190									

For this actual + forecast indexation system to work the modeller needs to keep the yellows updated at regular intervals. The update process consists of adding yellow actuals to the indexation block as well as updating the number of months of actuals data in row 167 at each update.

For example, the next update will be to add the December 2012 RPI index from the ONS website to L181. To do this write over the formula with the actual index and make sure the cell is coloured yellow and change the value of L167 to 12.

To draw month-on-month indexation from the indexation block for particular contractual indexation calculations use versions of rows 185 or 189 in conjunction with a HLOOKUP function on the date.

In a semi-annual model and on the semi-annual Time sheet with end periods 31 Mar, 30 Sep, use the HLOOKUP formula and an IF statement to create a semi-annual index.

In Figure 51 the formula in J497 is:

= HLOOKUP(J496, 'Index(A)'!$L$28:$R$29, 2, FALSE)

And to stretch the index into the semi-annual timeline, the formula in L502 is:

= IF(L501 = 1, L500, K502)

FIGURE 51: INDEXATION ON TIME SHEET

			E		Constant	Unit	G		H	Total	I	J	K	L	M	N	O	P
493						Constant	Unit			Total								
494																		
495		RPI																
496			Model Period End				date					31-Mar-10	30-Sep-10	31-Mar-11	30-Sep-11	31-Mar-12	30-Sep-12	31-Mar-13
497			February RPI Index			W/ ERROR	Index					219.2000	#N/A	231.3000	#N/A	239.9000	#N/A	239.8200
498			February RPI Index				Index					219.2000	-	231.3000	-	239.9000	-	239.8200
499																		
500			February RPI Index			-	index					219.2000	-	231.3000	-	239.9000	-	239.8200
501			March Period End Flag				flag		5			1	-	1	-	1	-	1
502			February RPI Index				index					219.2000	219.2000	231.3000	231.3000	239.9000	239.9000	239.8200
503																		

REBASED INDEX

In order to apply indexation to the model it is necessary to know the base date for the indexation and the index at that base date. Dividing the RPI index (of actuals + forecast) by the base index will yield an indexation factor that can be used multiplicatively within the model.

Figure 52 shows the rebased factor in row 197 that can be used multiplicatively in the model. The syntax of the formula in K197 is:

= K195 / $F196

FIGURE 52: REBASING THE INDEX TO CREATE A MULTIPLICATIVE INDEX FACTOR

	A	B	C	D	E	F	G	H	I	J	K	L	M
191										31-Aug-06	28-Feb-07	31-Aug-07	29-Feb-08
192	INDEXATION												
193													
194				Rebased February RPI Index									
195					February RPI Index	-	index	-	-	219.2000	231.3000	239.9000	240.9392
196					Base Index	219.2000	index						
197					Rebased February RPI Index		index			1.0000	1.0552	1.0944	1.0992
198													

SIMPLE INDEXATION

Multiplying a real modelling flow by the appropriately rebased index factor creates a nominal modelling flow. Consider the example of Band 1 operating revenues as in Figure 53. The units of row 206 are real and un-escalated so they require to be multiplied by a multiplicative factor in row 207 to become nominal operating revenues in row 208.

The syntax of the formula in L208 is:

= L206 * L207

FIGURE 53: SIMPLE INDEXATION IMPLEMENTED

	A	B	C	D	E	F	G	H	I	J	K	L	M
202										31-Aug-06	28-Feb-07	31-Aug-07	29-Feb-08
203	INDEXATION												
204													
205				Band 1 Revenue Indexation									
206					Band 1 Revenue	unesc £k		53,491		7,751	7,554	7,490	7,669
207					Rebased February RPI Index	-	index	-	-	1.0000	1.0552	1.0944	1.0992
208					Band 1 Revenue	nom £k		59,089		7,751	7,971	8,198	8,430
209													

8. Uplift

Uplift building blocks return decimal factors and percentages and deal with simple percentage or factor uplift, as well as the reverse – decay. These are useful building blocks for adding sensitivities to the model.

% UPLIFT

The % Uplift building block uplifts a time dependent or non-time dependent value or values by an input % if the event flag has value 1, using an IF statement.

Figure 54 shows the % Uplift building block. The syntax in K173 is:

= IF(K172 = 1, K170 * (1 + $F171), 0)

FIGURE 54: % UPLIFT EXAMPLE

	A B C D	E	F	G	H	I	J	K	L
166							31-Aug-06	28-Feb-07	31-Aug-07
167	% UPLIFT								
168									
169		Band 1 Revenue Uplifted							
170		Band 1 Revenue	-	nom £k	671,240	-	7,751	7,971	8,198
171		Band 1 Reneue Uplift	3.00%	%					
172		Forecast Period Flag	-	flag	8	-	-	1	1
173		Band 1 Revenue Uplifted		nom £k	72,547		-	8,211	8,444
174									

LINEAR FACTOR

The linear factor is identical to the % Uplift except that it is first calculated as a factor and then applied wherever it is required. It is a multiplicative factor, meaning that it can be used even when the uplift is set to 0%.

Figure 55 shows the Linear Uplift building block with the syntax in cell K184:

= IF(K183 = 1, (1+ $F182), 1)

FIGURE 55: LINEAR FACTOR EXAMPLE

	A B C D	E	F	G	H	I	J	K	L
178							31-Aug-06	28-Feb-07	31-Aug-07
179	LINEAR FACTOR								
180									
181		Band 1 Revenue Uplift Factor							
182		Band 1 Revenue Uplift	3.00%	%					
183		Forecast Period Flag	-	flag	8	-	-	1	1
184		Band 1 Revenue Uplift Factor		nom £k			1.0000	1.0300	1.0300
185									

COMPOUND UPLIFT FACTOR

The compound uplift factor building block is used to uplift based on one or more step changes defined by a percentage strip over time.

Figure 56 shows the Compound Uplift building block with a % Uplift strip over time in row 12 and the syntax in cell L195:

= IF(L194 = 1, 1, K195 * (1 + L193))

FIGURE 56: COMPOUND UPLIFT FACTOR EXAMPLE

	A B C D	E	F	G	H	I	J	K	L
189							31-Aug-06	28-Feb-07	31-Aug-07
190	COMPOUND UPLIFT FACTOR								
191									
192		Band 1 Revenue Compound Uplift Factor							
193		Band 1 Revenue Uplift	%					3.00%	2.50%
194		First Model Column Flag	-	flag	1	-	1	-	-
195		Band 1 Revenue Compound Uplift Factor	nom £k				1.0000	1.0300	1.0558
196									

9. Choice & lookup

INDEX AND MATCH FOR SCENARIO CHOICE

The combination of the INDEX and MATCH functions in Excel produces the simplest scenario choice building block.

Referring to Figure 57, the input scenarios are stored in column format between columns M and N, with the name of each scenario in row 7. Column F contains the input value of the chosen scenario.

The user chooses the scenario to run in cell F7 by copying the name of the scenario from M7 or N7. The formula in J11 chooses the column reference of the active scenario by referring to cell F7 and looking for a match in cells K7:O7.

Notice there is a hidden column L which contains the formatting required by a new input scenario – to the left of a new column if it is added by highlighting column M.

The syntax in cell J11 is:

```
= MATCH( F7, K7:O7, FALSE )
```

Notice that the third parameter is set to FALSE, equivalent to a value of zero, in order to require the function to find an exact match.

FIGURE 57: MATCH EXAMPLE FOR SCENARIO CHOICE

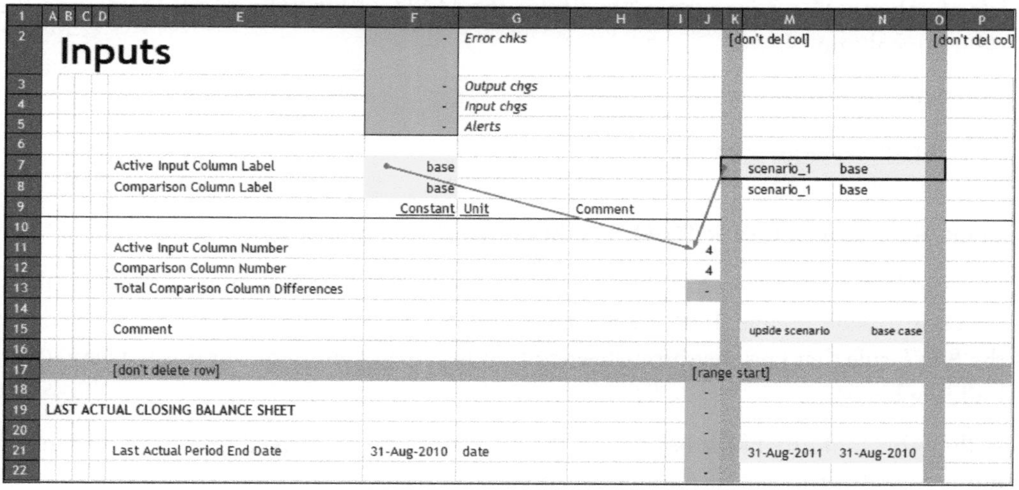

Figure 58 shows the use of the INDEX function to choose the correct input from the active input column set. F21 is an example of an input that is used in the model and M21 and N21 are examples of the two values this input can take from each of the two scenarios.

FIGURE 58: INDEX EXAMPLE FOR SCENARIO CHOICE

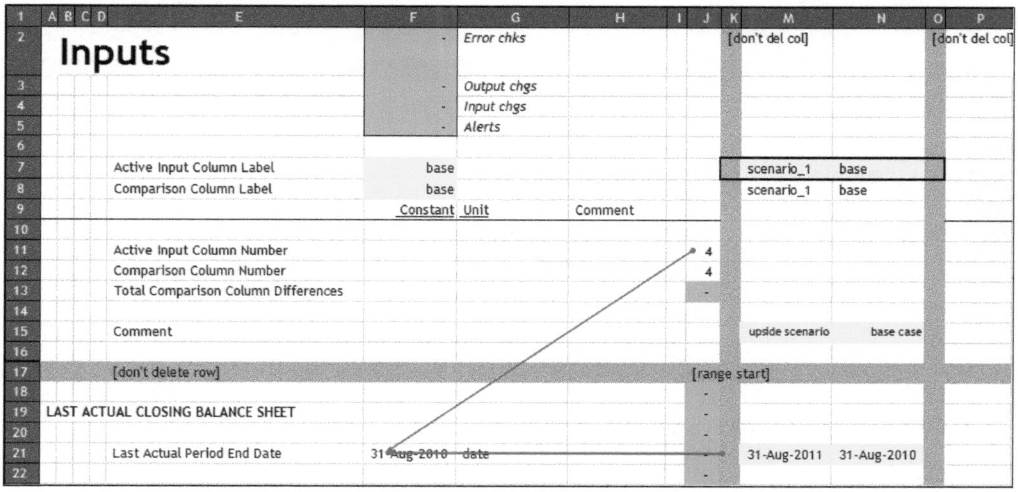

The formula in F21 chooses the input from the chosen column by referring to cell J11 and looking for a match in cells K21:O21. Notice that there is a hidden column L that contains the formatting from column M that is used by Excel when a new column is inserted to the left of column M – hence the value 4 from the MATCH function in cell J11 to find the values in column N.

The syntax in cell F21 is:

= INDEX(K21:O21, $J$11)

VLOOKUP COLLECTOR TO FLIP VERTICAL INPUTS

The VLOOKUP Collector is a building block that collects vertical inputs and places them on a horizontal timeline. In this sense the VLOOKUP Collector is a luxury and also defies the FAST rule that says that intra-sheet collections are not allowed. But this is a very useful building block.

I allow this building block because of the immense benefit derived from vertical forecast inputs, notably the ease of running sensitivities.

Firstly the VLOOKUP Collector looks in two limited column sections of the Inputs sheet to collect the date and value arrays, as in Figure 59. The fourth parameter of the VLOOKUP function should be set to FALSE in order to drive out an error of type '#N/A' when no value corresponds to a tested date. The syntax in M207 of Figure 60 is:

= VLOOKUP(M206, Inputs!$E$42:$F$60, 2, FALSE)

FIGURE 59: INSURANCE (FORECAST) INPUTS IN COLUMN FORMAT

	A B C D	E	F	G	H	I J K	M	N	O P
37						·			
38	VLOOKUP COLLECTOR - INPUTS					·			
39						·			
40	Insurance					·			
41	Insurance			unesc £k		·			
42		31-Aug-2007	-	unesc £k		·	-	-	
43		29-Feb-2008	102	unesc £k		·	102	102	
44		31-Aug-2008	-	unesc £k		·	-	-	
45		28-Feb-2009	102	unesc £k		·	102	102	
46		31-Aug-2009	-	unesc £k		·	-	-	
47		28-Feb-2010	102	unesc £k		·	102	102	
48		31-Aug-2010	-	unesc £k		·	-	-	

In J208 of Figure 60 the syntax of the error-trapping formula is:

= IF(ISNA(J207), 0, J207)

The rest of row 208 and row 207 have relatively identical functions.

FIGURE 60: VLOOKUP AND ERROR-TRAPPING FOR VLOOKUP COLLECTOR

				E	F	G	H	I	J	K	L	M	N
202									31-Aug-06	28-Feb-07	31-Aug-07	29-Feb-08	31-Aug-08
203	VLOOKUP COLLECTOR - CALCULATIONS AND ERROR TRAPPING												
204													
205		Insurance Prepayment											
206			Model Period End		-	date		-	-	31-Aug-06	28-Feb-07	31-Aug-07	29-Feb-08	31-Aug-08
207			Insurance		W / ERROR	unesc £k		-	#N/A	#N/A		102	-
208			Insurance			unesc £k	508		-	-	-	102	-
209													

DATA VALIDATION (LOCAL)

Excel Data Validation is a simple solution for choosing the scenario in cell F7 of Figure 57. Data validation allows the user to click into cell F7 and pick the scenario name from a drop-down list as in Figure 61.

FIGURE 61: DATA VALIDATION DROP-DOWN LIST

				E	F	G
1	A	B	C	D		
2					**Inputs**	-	Error chks
3						-	Output chgs
4						-	Input chgs
5						-	Alerts
6							
7					Active Input Column Label	base ▼	
8					Comparison Column Label		
9						scenario_1	hit
10						base	
11					Active Input Column Number		

To define the list in the data validation drop-down choose Data Validation from the Data tab as in Figure 62.

FIGURE 62: DATA VALIDATION ON EXCEL MENU

Then define the list as the cells K7:O7 from Figure 58 and as shown in Figure 63.

FIGURE 63: DATA VALIDATION WINDOW AND DEFINED SOURCE

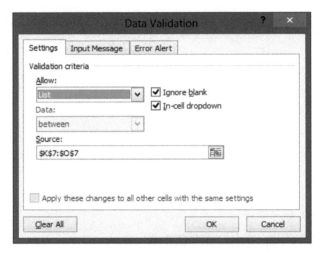

10. Conditional sums of flows & balances

SUMIF COLLECTOR FOR FLOWS TO ANNUAL PERIODICITY

The SUMIF collector is used sparingly as I call this a multi-dimensional function. Multi-dimensional functions look into other sheets and collect values according to criteria such as time.

FIGURE 64: SEMI-ANNUAL FINANCIAL STATEMENT LINE ITEM

				E	F	I	J	K	L	M	N	O	P
				Financial Statements - Semi-Annual									
				Model Period Start					01-Jan-09	01-Jul-09	01-Jan-10	01-Jul-10	01-Jan-11
				Model Period End					30-Jun-09	31-Dec-09	30-Jun-10	31-Dec-10	30-Jun-11
				Actual vs Forecast					Forecast	Forecast	Forecast	Forecast	Forecast
				Year # for Current Period's Financial Year End					2,009	2,009	2,010	2,010	2,011
	CONDITIONAL SUMS OF FLOWS												
	Profit & Loss Item												
				Operating Revenue	PL	nom 0k	25,513		-	2,178	2,205	2,233	2,261

One of the very few uses of this SUMIF function is to summarise the semi-annual financial statement flows into annual time periods from the semi-annual example in Figure 64 to the annual example in Figure 65.

FIGURE 65: USING SUMIF TO SUMMARISE SEMI-ANNUAL FLOWS TO AN ANNUAL TIMELINE

				E	F	I	J	K	L	M	N
2				**Financial Statements - Annual**							
3				Model Period Start					01-Jan-09	01-Jan-10	01-Jan-11
4				Model Period End					31-Dec-09	31-Dec-10	31-Dec-11
5				Actual vs Forecast					Forecast	Forecast	Forecast
6				Year # for Current Period's Financial Year End					2,009	2,010	2,011
7											
8		CONDITIONAL SUMS OF FLOWS									
9											
10		Profit & Loss Item									
11				Operating Revenue	PL	nom £k	25,513		2,178	4,438	4,550
12											

The formula in M11 of Figure 65 is:

= SUMIF(FS_Semi_Annual!$L$6:$P$6, 'FS_Annual'!M$6, FS_Semi_Annual!$L11:$P11)

Where:

- row 6 of the FS_Semi_Annual sheet, shown in Figure 64, contains the year of allocation
- row 6 of the FS_Annual sheet, as in Figure 65, contains the year of allocation
- row 11 of the FS_Semi_Annual sheet contains the flow to summarise.

In the example shown here the year of allocation is the year value 2,010 and this is given to every time period in the semi-annual model. The annual model also has the year of allocation, and hence the result in cell M11 of the annual model in Figure 65; the SUMIF function adds together flows that correspond to the annual time period.

LOOKUP COLLECTOR FOR BALANCES TO ANNUAL PERIODICITY

The LOOKUP collector is used sparingly as this is also a multi-dimensional function.

The only use for this function is to summarise the quarterly or semi-annual financial statement balances into annual time periods.

The formula in M24 of Figure 67 is:

= LOOKUP(M$17, FS_Semi_Annual!$J$17:$EO$17, FS_Semi_Annual!$J24:$EO24)

Where:

- row 17 of the FS_Annual sheet, as in Figure 67, contains the annual period end date
- row 17 of the FS_Semi_Annual sheet, as in Figure 66, contains the period end dates
- row 24 of the FS_Semi_Annual sheet, as in Figure 66, contains the balance to summarise.

FIGURE 66: SEMI-ANNUAL FINANCIAL STATEMENTS BALANCE SHEET ITEM

Financial Statements - Semi-Annual									
Model Period Start						01-Jan-09	01-Jul-09	01-Jan-10	01-Jul-10
Model Period End						30-Jun-09	31-Dec-09	30-Jun-10	31-Dec-10
Actual vs Forecast						Forecast	Forecast	Forecast	Forecast
Year # for Current Period's Financial Year End						2,009	2,009	2,010	2,010
CONDITIONAL BALANCE									
Balance Sheet Item									
Fixed Assets - 25 Years & Over Balance	BS		nom £k	1,229		109	218	327	436

FIGURE 67: ANNUAL FINANCIAL STATEMENTS BALANCE SHEET ITEM

Financial Statements - Annual								
Model Period Start						01-Jan-09	01-Jan-10	01-Jan-11
Model Period End						31-Dec-09	31-Dec-10	31-Dec-11
Actual vs Forecast						Forecast	Forecast	Forecast
Year # for Current Period's Financial Year End						2,009	2,010	2,011
CONDITIONAL BALANCE								
Balance Sheet Item								
Fixed Assets - 25 Years & Over Balance	BS		nom £k	2,088		218	436	655

Note also that the LOOKUP function finds the balance that corresponds to the annual period end date and does not aggregate balances. Note also that the LOOKUP function has no fourth parameter and will return a '#N/A' error when no match is found.

FORWARD & BACKWARD COLLECTOR

The forward and backward collectors look forward or backward along a test line-item. The important thing about these building blocks is that the look forward or backward aspect is reported as part of the line-item description, as in Figure 68. Here the annual future Term Loan Service is labelled with '2 PD LK FW' in column F to show that the function looks forward by two periods.

This particular example is used to calculate future annual rolling debt service for cover ratio calculations.

FIGURE 68: FORWARD-LOOKING COLLECTOR

A B C D	E	F	G	H	I	J	K	L
						31-Aug-06	28-Feb-07	31-Aug-07
278	FORWARD LOOKING COLLECTOR							
279								
280	Term Loan Service							
281	Term Loan Repayment		nom £k	(24,658)		(896)	(971)	(987)
282	Term Loan Interest Paid		nom £k	(7,291)		(602)	(584)	(565)
283	Term Loan Service		nom £k	(31,949)		(1,499)	(1,555)	(1,552)
284	Term Loan Service	2 PD LK FW	nom £k pa			(3,106)	(3,249)	(3,387)
285								

11. Caps & floors

Caps and floors are building blocks that either:

- cap a calculation to a certain value
- floor a calculation to a certain value
- both cap and floor a calculation to an upper and lower boundary.

SIMPLE FLOOR

Use the MAX function to floor the values of a calculation, as in Figure 69. Row 232 is the operating cost value before the floor in row 233 has been applied. In this case the operating cost cannot be lower than £800k in each period.

K234 provides the formula that satisfies this criteria and the syntax is:

= MAX(K232:K233)

FIGURE 69: SIMPLE FLOOR

A B C D	E	F	G	H	I	J	K	L
						31-Aug-06	28-Feb-07	31-Aug-07
229	FLOOR							
230							(1)	
231	Simple Floor							
232	Operating Cost Calculation		nom £k	23,097		896	765	802
233	Operating Cost Floor		nom £k	15,200		800	800	800
234	Operating Cost		nom £k	23,256		896	800	802
235								

FLOOR AND POSITIVE

As a sensible precaution the operating cost after flooring should not be less than zero. Use the same MAX function to floor a calculation, while ensuring the result is never negative. While referring to Figure 70, the formula in K244 is:

= MAX(K242:K243, 0)

FIGURE 70: FLOOR AND POSITIVE

	A B C D	E	F	G	H	I	J	K	L
238							31-Aug-06	28-Feb-07	31-Aug-07
239	FLOOR								
240								(1)	
241		Floor & Positive							
242			Operating Cost Calculation		nom £k	22,060		896	765	(235)
243			Operating Cost Floor		nom £k	15,200		800	800	800
244			Operating Cost		nom £k	23,254		896	800	800
245									

Alternatively, this same use of the MAX function can be used to simply find the positive values of a calculation. Referring to Figure 71, the formula in L253 is:

= MAX(0, L252)

FIGURE 71: POSITIVE VALUE USING MAX

	A B C D	E	F	G	H	I	J	K	L	M
248							31-Aug-06	28-Feb-07	31-Aug-07	29-Feb-08
249	FLOOR									
250										
251		Positive								
252			Operating Cost Calculation		nom £k	22,060		896	765	(235)	862
253			Operating Cost		nom £k	22,295		896	765	-	862
254										

SIMPLE CAP

To cap a calculation value use the MIN function, as in Figure 72. The syntax for the formula in K263 is:

= MIN(K261:K262)

FIGURE 72: SIMPLE CAP

	A B C D	E	F	G	H	I	J	K	L
257							31-Aug-06	28-Feb-07	31-Aug-07
258	CAP								
259									
260		Simple Cap							
261		Operating Revenue Calculation		nom £k	52,122		1,062	1,760	1,845
262		Operating Revenue Cap		nom £k	31,350		1,650	1,650	1,650
263		Operating Revenue Cap		nom £k	30,671		1,062	1,650	1,650
264									

NEGATIVE AS A POSITIVE

To restrict the result to only negative values of a calculation, use the MIN function and multiply the result by a '- 1'. In Figure 73, the syntax of the formula in L272 is:

$$= - 1 * MIN(0, L271)$$

FIGURE 73: NEGATIVE AS A POSITIVE VALUE (POS)

	A B C D	E	F	G	H	I	J	K	L
267							31-Aug-06	28-Feb-07	31-Aug-07
268	CAP								
269									
270		Negative As Positive							
271		Interest (Paid)/Received		nom £k	(20,965)		(18)	340	(654)
272		Interest Paid POS		nom £k	21,305		18	-	654
273									

Note that the negative value that is found is converted to a positive value and the letters POS are added to the label. Effectively this calculation reports a negative value in the cases where the calculation is negative but as a positive value. In the cases where the calculation is not negative the result is simply zero.

CAPPED & FLOORED

There is sometimes the need to cap and floor in the same calculation and this is achieved by the combined use of MAX and MIN functions in Excel, as in Figure 74.

This building block is best shown as an example. The chosen case requires calculation of the cash deposits to the debt service reserve account (DSRA). These deposits are a function of two elements:

1. The target deposit as defined by the amount the reserve needs to be topped up by to reach the required level in a period.

2. The amount of cash that is available in the project at the time of calculation.

FIGURE 74: CAPPED & FLOORED

	A B C D	E	F	G	H	I	J	K	L
285							31-Aug-06	28-Feb-07	31-Aug-07
286	CAPPED & FLOORED								
287									
288	DSRA Deposits								
289		DSRA Target Deposits		nom £k	646	-	105	12	-
290		Cash Available For DSRA		nom £k	-	-	3,292	(93)	3,096
291		DSRA Deposits POS		nom £k	646		105	-	-
292		DSRA Deposits	CF	nom £k	(646)		(105)	-	-
293									

So the formula in K291 of FIGURE 72 is:

= MAX(0, MIN(K289, K290))

This ensures that the amount to be deposited is both the minimum of the target deposit in row 289 and the amount of cash available in row 290, but at the same time is never a negative value. Only once this final deposit amount is found do we flip the value to a negative in preparation for its export to the financial statements cash flow waterfall in row 292. The syntax of the formula in J292 is:

= - 1 * J291

12. Allocators

Allocator building blocks collect values and allocate them to flagged periods.

SIMPLE ALLOCATOR

The Simple Allocator collects a non-time dependent value and allocates it to a flagged period on the timeline.

The syntax in K302 of Figure 75 is:

= IF(K301 = 1, $F300, 0)

FIGURE 75: SIMPLE ALLOCATOR EXAMPLE

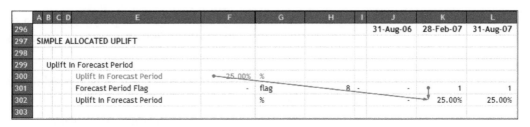

	A B C D	E	F	G	H	I	J	K	L
296							31-Aug-06	28-Feb-07	31-Aug-07
297	SIMPLE ALLOCATED UPLIFT								
298									
299	Uplift In Forecast Period								
300		Uplift In Forecast Period	25.00%	%					
301		Forecast Period Flag	-	flag	8	-	-	1	1
302		Uplift In Forecast Period		%			-	25.00%	25.00%
303									

FACTOR ALLOCATOR

The Factor Allocator collects a value that is non-time dependent and allocates it at a factored rate to flagged periods on the timeline.

The syntax in K314 of Figure 76 is:

= IF(K313 = 1, (1– $F312), 1)

FIGURE 76: FACTORED ALLOCATOR EXAMPLE

	A	B	C	D	E	F	G	H	I	J	K	L
308										31-Aug-06	28-Feb-07	31-Aug-07
309	FACTOR ALLOCATOR											
310												
311			Band 3 Volume Discount Factor									
312				Band 3 Volume Discount	24.55%	%						
313				Forecast Period Flag	-	flag	8	-		-	1	1
314				Band 3 Volume Discount Factor		factor				1.0000	0.7545	0.7545
315												

BALANCE ALLOCATOR

The Balance Allocator collects a balance value that is non-time dependent and allocates it to a flagged period on the timeline within a balance corkscrew.

The syntax in L328 of Figure 77 is:

= IF(L323 = 1, $F322, L325)

FIGURE 77: BALANCE ALLOCATOR EXAMPLE

	A	B	C	D	E	F	G	H	I	J	K	L	M
318										31-Aug-06	28-Feb-07	31-Aug-07	29-Feb-08
319	BALANCE ALLOCATOR												
320													
321			Trade Debtors Balance										
322				Last Closing Trade Debtors Balance	200	nom £k							
323				Last Closing Balance Flag	-	flag	1	-		-	-	1	-
324													
325			Trade Debtors Balance BEG			nom £k					-	-	200
326													
327													
328			Trade Debtors Balance		BS	nom £k				-	-	200	200
329													

Subsequently additions to the balance can be coded in row 326 and deductions to the balance in row 327. When this happens the formula in L328 (and indeed the whole row) can be amended to:

= IF(L323 = 1, $F322, L325 + L326 – L327)

13. IRRs & cover ratios

The IRR is the internal rate of return of a stream of investment and return cash flows, and can be calculated using two Excel functions, IRR and XIRR. IRR assumes the cash flows are annual, whereas XIRR requires a stream of dates as an additional input variable.

IRR OVER SEMI-ANNUAL CASH FLOWS

The IRR function in Excel works fine. The XIRR function requires a leading negative cash flow to seed the calculation, otherwise it returns zero, as shown in Figure 79 in J411.

FIGURE 78: CALCULATING THE INTERNAL RATE OF RETURN USING THE IRR FUNCTION

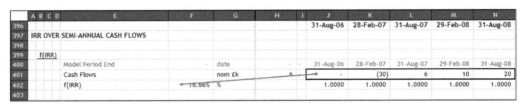

The syntax of the IRR formula in cell F402 of Figure 78 is:

$$= ((1 + IRR(J401:N401)) ^ (2)) - 1$$

This is a de-compounding function of IRR in order to take account of the semi-annual cash flows.

Now consider Figure 79 which shows the use of the XIRR function to calculate the same rate of return. The syntax of the XIRR formula in F412 is:

$$= XIRR(J411:N411, J410:N410)$$

FIGURE 79: CALCULATING THE INTERNAL RATE OF RETURN USING THE XIRR FUNCTION

	A B C D	E	F	G	H	I	J	K	L	M	N
406							31-Aug-06	28-Feb-07	31-Aug-07	29-Feb-08	31-Aug-08
407	IRR OVER SEMI-ANNUAL CASH FLOWS										
408											
409	XIRR										
410		Model Period End		date			31-Aug-06	28-Feb-07	31-Aug-07	29-Feb-08	31-Aug-08
411		Cash Flows		nom £k		6	(0.0001)	(30)	6	10	20
412		XIRR	16.58%	%							
413											

Note that the XIRR function calculates a slightly lower figure.

IRR OVER QUARTERLY CASH FLOWS

To calculate an internal rate of return over quarterly cash flows the XIRR function works in the same way as for the semi-annual cash flows. This is due to the fact that the XIRR function uses the dateline as one of its parameters. However, the IRR function needs to change as it expects annual cash flows.

For quarterly cash flows the syntax of the IRR formula in cell F402 of Figure 78 would then be:

= ((1 + IRR(M401:Q401)) ^ (4)) –1

Similarly with any periodicity that is not annual, the power to which (1 + IRR) is taken is equal to the number of periods in a year; so two for semi-annual, four for quarterly and twelve for monthly.

DOUBLE-DECKER IRR

The double-decker IRR calculation is used when there are a series of historical cash flows that extend back into time periods not covered by the model. Both the IRR and XIRR functions can be used for this purpose.

The cash flows need to be arranged in two rows with the historical cash flows above. For the XIRR function the dates need to be arranged in similar fashion, as shown in Figure 80.

Referring to Figure 80, the syntax for the IRR formula in cell F424 is:

= ((1 + IRR(J422:N423)) ^ (4)) –1

Where the cash flows are in two rows.

Similarly, again referring to Figure 80, the syntax for the XIRR double-decker formula in cell F425 is:

= XIRR(J422:N423, J420:N421)

FIGURE 80: INTERNAL RATE OF RETURN FOR DOUBLE-DECKER QUARTERLY CASH FLOWS

	E	F	G	H	I	J	K	L	M	N
416						31-Dec-08	31-Mar-09	30-Jun-09	30-Sep-09	31-Dec-09
417	IRR AS DOUBLE DECKER									
418										
419	Double Decker IRR & XIRR									
420	Historic Model Period End	-	date	- -	30-Sep-07	31-Dec-07	31-Mar-08	30-Jun-08	30-Sep-08
421	Model Period End	-	date	-	31-Dec-08	31-Mar-09	30-Jun-09	30-Sep-09	31-Dec-09
422	Historic Cash Flows		nom £k	(28) -	(0.0001)	(10)	(26)	2	6
423	Cash Flows		nom £k	36 -	8	12	7	4	5
424	f(IRR)	20.46%	%						
425	XIRR	20.44%	%						
426										

COVER RATIO

Cover ratios are fairly simple to calculate, involving only simple Excel functions. However, in order to graph ratios and calculate average ratios it is necessary to exclude ratios that fall outside of the calculation periods. Combining an IF statement and "n/a" as text achieves this objective.

Referring to Figure 81, the syntax for the cover ratio formula in K438 is:

= IF(K437 = 1, K435 / K436, "n/a")

The syntax of the average formula in cell F439 is:

= AVERAGE(J438:N438)

Where the "n/a" text in cell N438 is included but leaves the averaging calculation unaltered.

FIGURE 81: COVER RATIO CALCULATION INCLUDING AVERAGE

		E	F	G	H	I	J	K	L	M	N
431							31-Dec-08	31-Dec-09	31-Dec-10	31-Dec-11	31-Dec-12
432	COVER RATIOS										
433											
434		Simple Annual Debt Service Cover Ratio									
435		Cash Flow Available For Debt Service (CFADS)	nom £k				2,000	2,100	2,200	2,300	2,400
436		Debt Service POS	nom £k				1,680	1,710	1,590	1,625	-
437		Cover Ratio Flag	flag				1	1	1	1	-
438		Annual Debt Service Cover Ratio (ADSCR)	ratio				1.1905	1.2281	1.3836	1.4154	n/a
439		Average ADSCR	1.3044	ratio							
440											

14. Track, checks & error-trapping

THE CHECK BUILDING BLOCK

The Check building block can be added after any logic that requires a check, as in Figure 82. In this case the Trade Creditors balance is being checked in the period just after the last period in the concession to see if there is a zero balance.

The check building block is made up of four rows:

- Row 459 collects the values from row 456 and is the balance to be checked in this case

- Row 460 collects a flag from the Time sheet to provide the check with a time period definition

- F461 carries out a calculation to see if the balance is actually zero in the first period after the end of the concession, with the syntax of the formula in F461:

= SUMPRODUCT(J459:N459, J460:N460)

- F462 then makes sure that the value returned by F461 is zero, and reports either a 1 if false or a 0 if true. The syntax of the formula in F462 is:

= IF(ABS(F461) > 0.01, 1, 0)

Note the use of the ABS function to calculate the absolute (positive) value of the difference from zero. Note also the tolerance given to the check calculation of 0.01. This level of tolerance can be centralised as a named range from the Inputs sheet if required.

FIGURE 82: THE CHECK BUILDING BLOCK

		E	F	G	H	I	J	K	L	M	N
447							31-Aug-06	28-Feb-07	31-Aug-07	29-Feb-08	31-Aug-08
448											
449	Trade Creditors Balance										
450		Closing Trade Creditors Balance	1,104	nom £k	-	-					
451		Last Closing Balance Flag	-	flag	-		-	-	-	-	-
452											
453		Trade Creditors Balance BEG		nom £k			250	271	293	217	-
454	Plus:	Operating Costs POS		nom £k			2,169	2,342	1,734	-	
455	Less:	Operating Costs Paid POS		nom £k			2,148	2,320	1,810	217	
456		Trade Creditors Balance	BS	nom £k			271	293	217	-	-
457											
458	Check										
459		Trade Creditors Balance	BS	nom £k	-		271	293	217	-	-
460		Post Last Forecast Period Flag		flag	1		-	-	-	1	-
461		Post Last Forecast Period Balance		nom £k							
462		PLFP Balance Check		check							
463											

Once calculated the whole of row 462 is then referenced on the Check sheet, and then reported on every sheet in the Check sum in the sheet header.

THE TRACK & CHECK HEADER BUILDING BLOCK

On each sheet we report the results of four quality control (QC) checks that are calculated on the Track and Check sheets.

These QC results are conditionally formatted to show green when there are either no errors or alerts of differences, and red when there are, as in Figure 83 and Figure 84.

FIGURE 83: TRACK & CHECK HEADER WITH NO TRACK CHANGES OR CHECK ERRORS

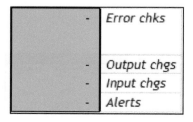

FIGURE 84: TRACK & CHECK WITH ONE CHECK ERRORS AND TRACK CHANGES

1	*Error chks*
1	*Output chgs*
1	*Input chgs*
1	*Alerts*

On every sheet in the model the Track & Check header is reported, as in Figure 85.

FIGURE 85: TRACK & CHECK HEADER

Operations

Model Period Start		·	Error chks
Model Period End		·	Output chgs
Actual vs Forecast		·	Input chgs
Year # for Current Period's Financial Year End		·	Alerts

ERROR TRAPPING BUILDING BLOCK

If there is a risk of a calculation resulting in an error then a possible solution is to wrap the calculation in a further error-trapping calculation. This is standard procedure in programming code and can be very useful in a financial model.

Using Figure 86 as a reference, row 269 contains a formula that yields numeric results in columns L to N, but returns a #N/A error in columns J and K. To this effect the F269 has been labelled with the text 'W / ERROR' and the values of row 269 are not used in the model. Row 270 performs the error-trapping function. J270 has the following error-trapping syntax:

```
= IF( ISNA(J269 ), 0, J269 )
```

In this case the generic Excel function ISNA has been used. Other similar functions are ISERROR and ISREF, although they will only trap singular types of error rather than all errors.

FIGURE 86: ERROR TRAPPING EXAMPLE

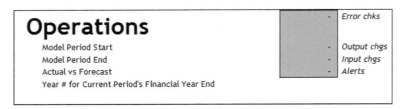

	A	B	C	D	E	F	G	H	I	J	K	L	M	N
264										31-Aug-06	28-Feb-07	31-Aug-07	29-Feb-08	31-Aug-08
265		VLOOKUP COLLECTOR - CALCULATIONS AND ERROR TRAPPING												
266														
267		Insurance Prepayment												
268				Model Period End		-	date	-	-	31-Aug-06	28-Feb-07	31-Aug-07	29-Feb-08	31-Aug-08
269				Insurance		W / ERROR	unesc £k	-		#N/A	#N/A	-	102	-
270				Insurance			unesc £k	508		-	-	-	102	-
271														

15. Text manipulation & truncation

THREE-WAY TEXT ALLOCATION

There are occasions when text must be allocated to a cell dependant on some outside condition. A two-way allocation is straightforward with the IF statement, but a three-way allocation is a little more complex, although also solved by the use of IF statements.

For instance, suppose we wish to allocate the words Actuals, Budget or Forecast to a cell dependant on the numbers 1 for Actuals, 2 for Budget and 3 for Forecast.

Figure 87, cell L3 shows the syntax for a three-way text allocation using two embedded IF statements:

= IF(L2 = 1, "Actuals", IF(L2 = 2, "Budget", "Forecast"))

FIGURE 87: THREE-WAY TEXT ALLOCATION

	E	F	I	J	K	L	T	U	V	W	X
2	Actual Budget & Forecast Flag	flag				1	1	1	2	3	3
3	Actual Budget & Forecast Text	text				Actuals	Actuals	Actuals	Budget	Forecast	Forecast

STANDARDISED WORD TRUNCATION

It is often the case that some text at the far right of a label has to be truncated to form the new label. This is true of any line item that has the letters POS, BEG or NEG added as a further descriptor.

Figure 88 shows the text 'Operating Cost POS' in cell E477 being truncated to 'Operating Cost' in cell E478. The syntax in cell E478 works for all four space or letter truncation:

= LEFT(E477, LEN(E477) - 4)

FIGURE 88: TEXT TRUNCATION EXAMPLE

	A	B	C	D	E
475					
476			Text Truncation		
477					Operating Cost POS
478					Operating Cost
479					

BUILDING BLOCK INDEX BY MODEL FLOW

Inputs sheet	Index and match for scenario choice	page 90
	Data validation (local)	page 93
	Conditional formatting as shown in The Check building block	page 104
	The Check building block	page 104
	Lookup to get last closing balance as shown in LOOKUP Collector for balances to annual periodicity	page 95
	VLOOKUP vertical data as shown in VLOOKUP collector to flip vertical inputs	page 92
Actuals	6. Dateline	page 83
Time	6. Dateline	page 83
	Model period end	page 84
	Model period start	page 85
	5. Flags	page 80
	7. Indexation	page 85
Operations	VLOOKUP to gather vertical inputs as shown in VLOOKUP collector to flip vertical inputs	page 92
	Real to nominal simple indexation as shown in Simple indexation	page 88
	Simple sum	page 76
	Complex sum	page 76
	Balance corkscrew	page 79
	The Check building block	page 104
	8. Uplift	page 88
	2. Division & sign-flip	page 77
Accounting	Simple sum	page 76
	Complex sum	page 76
	Balance corkscrew	page 79
	Percentage multiplication	page 79
Finance	Senior debt interest calculation as shown in Percentage multiplication	page 79
	Balance corkscrew	page 79
	Simple sum	page 76
	Complex sum	page 76
	VLOOKUP vertical data as shown in VLOOKUP collector to flip vertical inputsz	page 92
Tax	Capital allowances calculation as in Percentage multiplication	page 79
	Complex sum	page 76
	2. Division & sign-flip	page 77
Financial statements	Conditional formatting as shown in The Check building block	page 104
Analysis	13. IRRs & cover ratios	page 102
Track	14. Track, checks & error-trapping	page 104
Checks	14. Track, checks & error-trapping	page 104

THE FAST + 2 MODELLING ADAPTATION

The FAST + 2 adaptations are an idea borrowed from the drive to greater classification in the natural sciences.

To enable FAST + 2, two more columns are added to the standard FAST structure, as shown in Figure 89 and described in Table 3. These columns are for additional information.

The additional information is a text comment in column G and a code in column H. The text comment is usefully inserted at-source and is exported around the model through the use of live labelling and whole row referencing. The code is a technical code value that is part of a classification routine that will be useful for error-checking and change log functionality.

TABLE 3: FAST + 2 COLUMN STRUCTURE

Column	Designation
A, B, C	3 levels of heading
D	For use of 'Less:', 'Add:' 'Addbk:'
E	Line-item name
F	Value if non time-dependent
G	Comment
H	Auto_code*
I	Units
J	Totals, min or max as applicable
K	Empty
L	Values start here if time-dependent

FIGURE 89: FAST + 2 SHEET AND COLUMN STRUCTURE

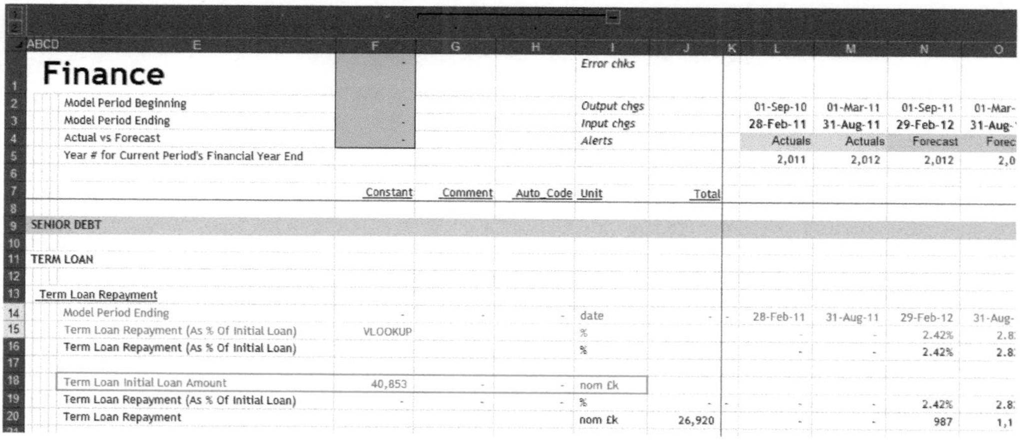

THE BENEFITS OF USING FAST

The true big benefits to using a common language will only accrue as adoption increases beyond a critical mass, and FAST is still somewhat short of that point. However, there are some clear instant benefits of using a language like FAST:

- increased transparency
- increased clarity
- increased speed
- increased accuracy and therefore decreased risk.

Increased transparency

The FAST standard introduces rules to coding in Excel, where there was ambiguity before. Standardisation is an important step because it defines a common language, just as Excel did before it. A common language increases transparency, allowing more users into the model.

Although it is not certain that FAST will become the definitive standard in Excel coding since not everyone uses it, it is probably the most widespread at the time of writing.

Increased clarity

FAST reinforces the formal approach to modelling through the rules. From this formality the users of the model can derive a clearer picture of the project/company finances.

Increased speed

By cutting down on the possible choices available to the modeller, the coding work can greatly speed up.

Increased accuracy

Working in a structured and transparent way increases accuracy.

CHAPTER 4
EXCEL THEORY

This chapter on Excel theory is split into six areas:

1. Setup

2. Formulae

3. Keyboard shortcuts

4. Navigation

5. Automation

6. Known Excel issues.

1. SETUP

Basic Excel setup

Run 'All of Excel from computer', including all VBA options. This will give you all the functionality you may ever require.

This is achieved when loading Excel and Microsoft Office on to the computer and choosing 'Run all of Excel from computer' at the start of the setup process.

Excel options

Press Alt + T + O to access the Excel options as in Figure 90.

FIGURE 90: EXCEL OPTIONS, ACCESSED BY PRESSING ALT + T + O

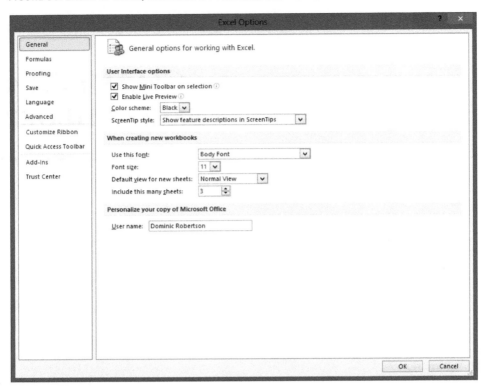

Freeze frame

Freeze frame is a good way to allow important information to remain visible while scrolling along or down. There is an optimal place to have freeze frames as in Figure 91. The position is cell K8, as it allows for the total to remain visible while also retaining the first 8 rows with the dates and periodicity.

FIGURE 91: FREEZE FRAME OPTIMAL POSITIONING

	Constant	Unit	Total			L	M	
Finance		Error chks						
Model Period Beginning	-	Output chgs				01-Sep-10	01-Mar-11	01
Model Period Ending	-	Input chgs				28-Feb-11	31-Aug-11	29-
Actual vs Forecast	-	Alerts				Actuals	Actuals	
Year # for Current Period's Financial Year End						2,011	2,012	
	Constant	Unit		Total				
SENIOR DEBT								
TERM LOAN								
Term Loan Repayment								
Model Period Ending	-	date		-	-	28-Feb-11	31-Aug-11	29
Term Loan Repayment (As % Of Initial Loan)	VLOOKUP	%				-	-	
Term Loan Repayment (As % Of Initial Loan)		%				-	-	
Term Loan Initial Loan Amount	40,853	nom £k						
Term Loan Repayment (As % Of Initial Loan)	-	%		-	-	-	-	
Term Loan Repayment		nom £k		26,920		-	-	

Font size, type and view settings

I like a font size of 10 and Trebuchet, which is a good screen font. However, Arial is also a good screen font and behaves slightly differently to Trebuchet.

This depends somewhat on personal preference and screen resolution. With a screen resolution of 1900 x 1200 font size 10 at a view of 100% is good. With a screen resolution of 1600 x 900 a font size of 8 looks better.

VBA and automation

VBA can be used to automate simple tasks but is not part of the scope of this book.

Excel add-ins and dashboards

Add-ins can be used to supplement the base Excel functionality, although they are not essential. Refer to Appendix 1 (page 245) for a list of useful third-party and Microsoft add-ins that can be downloaded from the internet.

Gridlines

Many modellers like to see the gridlines, but it is a question of personal preference. I like to hide the gridlines as I feel they impede the view of the numbers.

Negative number and zero format

FAST prescribes a money format in comma style. This allows for no decimals and puts brackets around negative numbers, as well as differentiating between an absolute zero, with a dash, and a near-zero as a 0.

Decimal places

FAST prescribes a factor format to four decimal places, which is sufficient in most cases.

Calculation mode and circular references

Personally I prefer Excel to be setup with calculations set to automatic and iteration turned off, as in Figure 92. This way, if a circular reference or a change in results occurs I know about it immediately. Some modellers prefer to have calculations set to manual and then press F9 to calculate.

CIRCULAR REFERENCES

A circular reference is when a formula either directly references itself or indirectly references other cells that reference it. Unless 'enable iterative calculation' is checked in Calculation Options in Excel Options as shown in Figure 92, then the Excel file will not calculate and will show a circular reference warning as in Figure 93.

FIGURE 92: ITERATIVE CALCULATIONS IN CALCULATION OPTIONS IN EXCEL OPTIONS

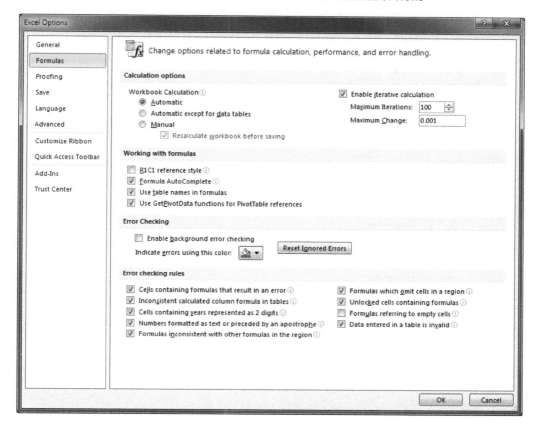

FIGURE 93: EXCEL CIRCULAR REFERENCE WARNING

There are four solutions to a circular reference of this type:

1. Allow the circular reference and turn 'iterative calculations' on in Calculation options within Excel Options (see Figure 94) – this is an exact solution.

2. Carry out a modelling approximation to avoid the circular reference by calculating off the previous period value or balance – this is an approximate solution.

3. Rearrange the formula – this is an exact solution.

4. Use macros to break the circular reference – this is an exact solution.

FIGURE 94: EXCEL CALCULATION OPTIONS UNDER THE FORMULAS TAB

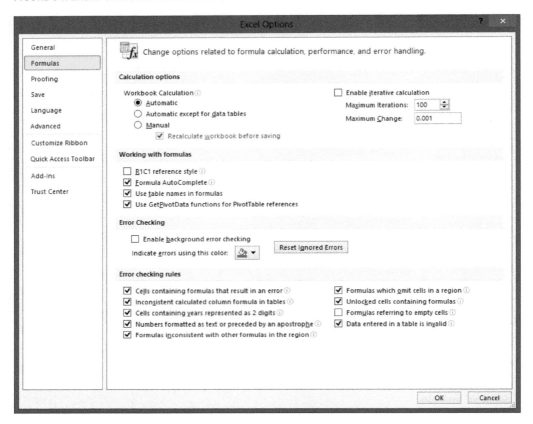

EXAMPLE CIRCULAR REFERENCE PROBLEM

Consider the interest on cash example in Figure 95, where the interest on cash is part of the Cash carried forward calculation that is itself part of the interest on cash calculation. The blue auditing arrows show that row 8 is a function of row 9, that itself also uses row 8, hence giving a circular reference.

The elements of this example are denoted thus:

R = Revenues

C = Costs

I = Interest on Cash

Cash Bal BEG = Brought forward cash balance

Cash Bal = Carried forward cash balance

Ir = Interest rate on cash balances

FIGURE 95: CIRCULAR REFERENCE EXAMPLE PROBLEM

	B	C	D	E	F	G
	Problem					
	Circular reference example					
			Total	Mar-11	Jun-11	Sep-11
	Revenues	R	600	100	200	300
	Costs	C	(225)	(50)	(75)	(100)
	Interest on Cash	I	-	-		
	Cash flow		375	50	125	200
	Cash b/f	Cash Bal BEG		-	50	175
	Cash flow		375	50	125	200
	Cash c/f	Cash Bal		50	175	375
	Interest on Cash c/f balance = CIRCULAR					
	Cash c/f	Cash Bal		50	175	375
	Interest Rate	Ir	5.00%			
	Interest on Cash	I	30	3	9	19

Solution 1: Allow iterative calculations in Excel

The solution is to turn iterative calculations on in Excel Options. See Figure 94.

The benefit of this method is that it is exact, but the drawback is that it has to allow circularities in the model and that could be bad. Circular references could be simple and harmless but one circular reference may hide many others and that can be dangerous in a large model.

Furthermore, if the model is a probabilistic type then iterations cannot be allowed. Generally, modellers do not allow iterative calculations. In fact, circular references are mostly avoided.

Solution 2: Calculate off the previous balance

An approximate solution is to calculate off the previous balance and thus side-step the circular reference issue altogether.

This is not an exact solution but does come very close and in most cases is adequate. The benefit of this solution is that it is simple, and in a big, complex model that can be very important. The drawback is that it requires the calculations to extend for one more period to allow the calculation to catch up, as in Figure 96.

FIGURE 96: SOLUTION 2 USING THE BROUGHT FORWARD BALANCE TO AVOID THE CIRCULAR REFERENCE

			Total	Mar-11	Jun-11	Sep-11	Dec-11
Solution 2							
Modelling approximation on Cash b/f balance							
			Total	Mar-11	Jun-11	Sep-11	Dec-11
Revenues		*R*	600	100	200	300	
Costs		*C*	(225)	(50)	(75)	(100)	
Interest on Cash		*I*	11	-	3	9	19
Cash flow			386	50	128	209	19
Cash b/f	*Cash Balance BEG*			-	50	178	386
Cash flow			386	50	128	209	19
Cash c/f	*Cash Balance*			50	178	386	406
Interest on Cash b/f balance							
Cash b/f	*Cash Balance*			-	50	178	386
Interest Rate	*Ir*		5.00%				
Interest on Cash	*I*		30.6938	-	2.5000	8.8750	19.3188

Solution 3: Rearrange the formula

Rearranging the formula is a mathematical method for solving formulae where the subject of the formula, on the left-hand side, also occurs in the right-hand side. In our example, the interest is on both sides of the formula.

In Excel, the solution looks like Figure 97.

FIGURE 97: SOLUTION 3 REARRANGING THE FORMULA TO AVOID THE CIRCULAR REFERENCE

			Total	Mar-11	Jun-11	Sep-11
Solution 3						
Re-arranging the formula						
			Total	Mar-11	Jun-11	Sep-11
Revenues	R		600	100	200	300
Costs	C		(225)	(50)	(75)	(100)
Interest on Cash	I		32	3	9	20
Cash flow			407	53	134	220
Cash b/f	Cash Balance BEG			-	53	187
Cash flow			407	53	134	220
Cash c/f	Cash Balance			53	187	407
Rearranged formula calculation						
Cash b/f	Cash Balance BEG		-	-	53	187
Revenues	R		600	100	200	300
Costs	C		(225)	(50)	(75)	(100)
Interest Rate	Ir		5.00%			
1-Interest Rate			95.00%			
Interest on Cash	I		32	3	9	20

The formula in E22 is:

= $D$20 * (E18 + E19 + E17) / $D$21

Which corresponds to the mathematical solution given here:

$$I = I_r \times Cash\ Balance$$

$$I = I_r \times (Cash\ Balance\ BEG + R + C + I)$$

$$I = I_r\ Cash\ Balance\ BEG + I_r\ R + I_r\ C + I_r\ I$$

Therefore:

$$I - I_r\ I = I_r\ Cash\ Balance\ BEG + I_r\ R + I_r\ C$$

$$I(1 - I_r) = I_r\ Cash\ Balance\ BEG + I_r\ R + I_r\ C$$

It follows that:

$$I(1 - I_r) = I_r\ Cash\ Balance\ BEG + I_r\ R + I_r\ C$$

Therefore, the rearranged formula for the interest calculation is:

$$I = \frac{I_r \times (Cash\ Balance\ BEG + R + C)}{(1 - I_r)}$$

Effectively this means that the interest is calculated on the rate times the elements of the cash flow waterfall excluding the interest. Then it is inflated by dividing by 1 minus the rate.

Solution 4: Use macros to break the circularity

Figure 98 shows how to break the circularity to prevent the need for iterations, and instead carry out the iterations by a copy and paste macro.

Notice the following points:

- named ranges in E19:G19 and E20:G20 as cInterestOnCash and dInterestOnCash respectively
- Row 19 is the calculated field that if referenced in row 8 would cause a circular reference; hence row 8 references row 20 which is the input field
- macro should be run until row 19 and row 20 show no differences.

FIGURE 98: SOLUTION 4 USING A MACRO TO BREAK THE CIRCULARITY

	A	B	C	D	E	F	G	H
1								
2		**Solution 4**						
3		Macro						
4								Named Ranges
5				Total	Mar-11	Jun-11	Sep-11	
6		Revenues	*R*	600	100	200	300	
7		Costs	*C*	(225)	(50)	(75)	(100)	
8		Interest on Cash (Input)	*I ... input*	32	3	9	20	
9		Cash flow		407	53	134	220	
10								
11		Cash b/f	*Cash Balance BEG*		-	53	187	
12		Cash flow		407	53	134	220	
13		Cash c/f	*Cash Balance*		53	187	407	
14								
15								
16		Macro & breaking circular reference						
17		Cash c/f			53	187	407	
18		Interest Rate	*Ir*	5.00%				
19		Interest on Cash (Calculation)	*I ... calc*	32	3	9	20	= cInterestOnCash
20		Interest on Cash (Input)	*I ... input*	32	3	9	20	= dInterestOnCash
21								
22		Converge						
23								

The macro code activated by the 'Converge' button is shown in Figure 99.

FIGURE 99: SOLUTION 4 VBA MACRO CODE FOR COPY AND PASTE

```
Sub converge_circularity()

"declare variables
Dim i, j As Integer

"stop the application calculating
Application.Calculation = xlCalculationManual

With ActiveWorkbook

   "do copy & paste 8 times
   For i = 1 To 8
     "Copy/paste
     For j = 1 To 3
       .Names("dInterestOnCash").RefersToRange.Cells(1, j).Value = .Names("cInterestOnCash").RefersToRange.Cells(1, j).Value
     Next j
     "calculate the application before next iteration
     Application.Calculate
   Next i

End With

"set application calculation mode to automatic
Application.Calculation = xlCalculationAutomatic

End Sub
```

Editing directly in cell

To 'Allow editing directly in cells' allows the modeller to change a formula in the cell rather than in the formula bar. This is less efficient as it means the brain has to get used to two locations for editing: the formula bar and the cell. Also, double-clicking on a reference will not take the modeller to the source reference.

Use Excel options to uncheck 'Allow editing directly in cells' functionality and actually gain more functionality, as in Figure 100.

FIGURE 100: EXCEL ADVANCED OPTIONS 'ALLOW EDITING DIRECTLY IN CELLS'

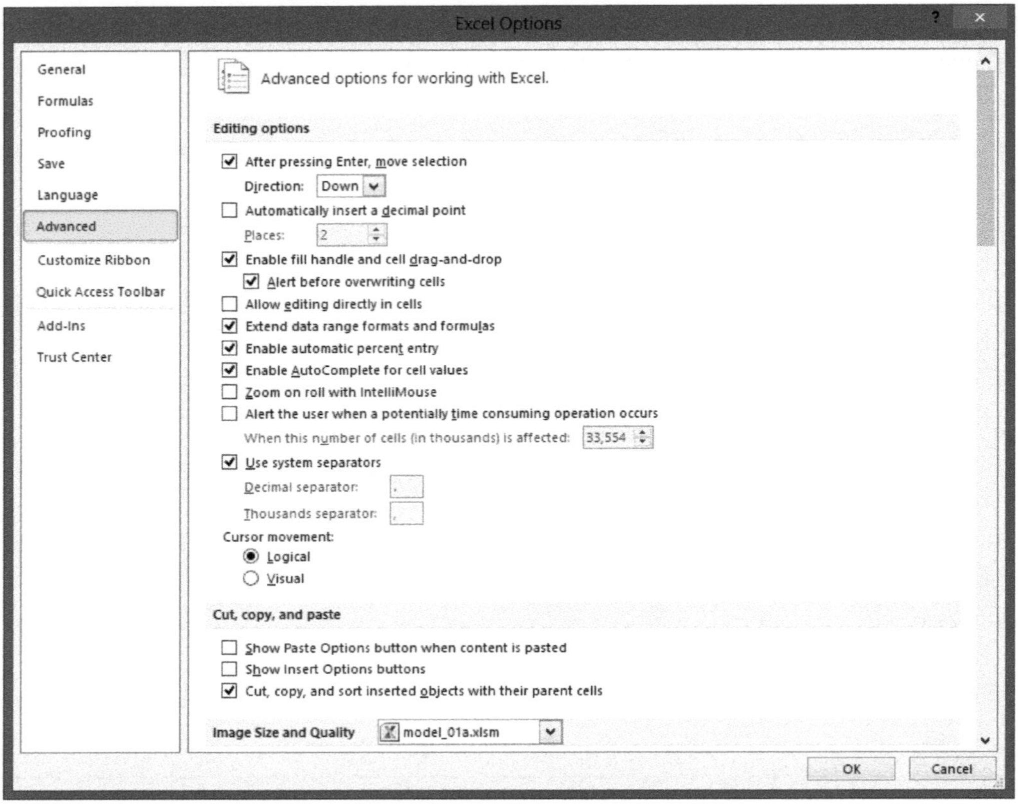

Excel 2003, Excel 2009 and Excel 2010

Excel 2003 was the perfect software for modellers. Then Excel 2009 came along and introduced the ribbon which caused havoc to the shortcuts and did away with the simple menu that everyone had got used to, so modellers did not upgrade unless they had to. Excel 2010 has given modellers the possibility of greater customisation and also the possibility of using the 64-bit version to allow for much larger spreadsheets.

64-bit operating systems and Excel

Computers are increasingly being shipped with 64-bit operating systems such as Windows 7 and Windows 8 64-bit which allow for increased use of RAM and multi-tasking. While the general computer setup is better for this it seems that Excel can perform perfectly well while still set up as a 32-bit software.

Personally, 64-bit Excel is better for me as I have some very large models that only perform well in 64-bit Excel. For some dramatic improvements in performance try choosing the 64-bit Excel when loading Excel 2010.

Date format

Date format is better viewed with dashes between the numbers and letters, as in '23-Jun-13'.

To make this global setting go to the Region and Language control panel in Windows and choose Additional settings. Then go to the third tab called Date and write 'dd-MM-yyyy' in the Short date in the date formats section, as in Figure 101. You can write over the contents of this box, but don't forget to press 'Apply' before pressing OK to leave.

FIGURE 101: DATE FORMAT IN REGION AND LANGUAGE CONTROL PANEL

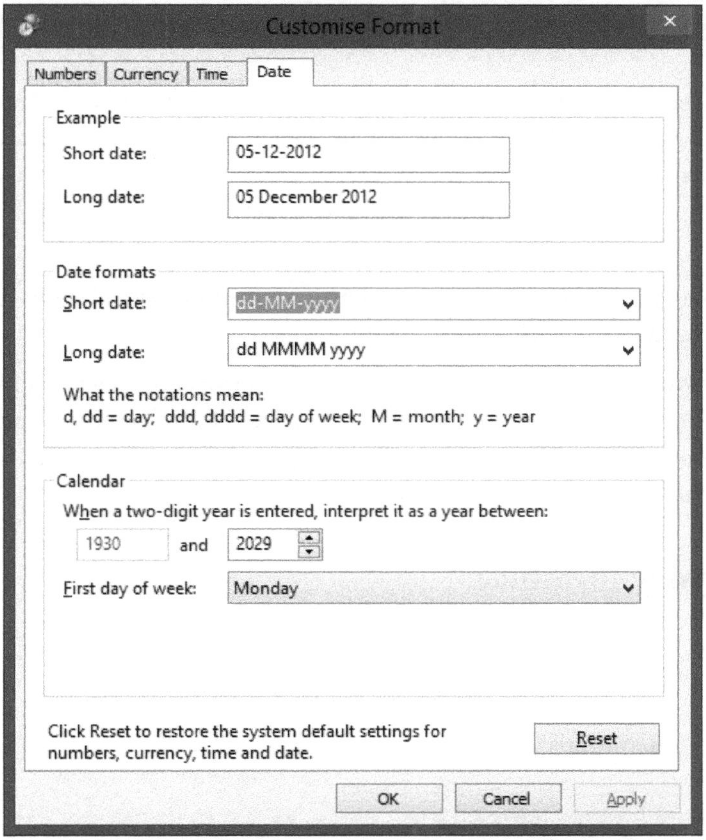

The FAST Excel date will then look like Figure 102.

FIGURE 102: DATE FORMAT IN EXCEL

| 31-Aug-06 |

2. FORMULAE

I like to keep the formulae simple. Primarily this is because the more complex the formulae the harder maintenance of the model will be later.

Another good reason to keep the formulae simple is to avoid un-auditable logic. This type of logic prohibits easy tracking through to source. OFFSET is a perfect example of a formula that prohibits simple tracking – this is because of the offsetting functionality within OFFSET.

Every formula sits within a local context and the efficiency of the formula should be judged within the local context. For example, VLOOKUP can be used sparingly to flip vertical inputs to horizontal strips across time. However, if VLOOKUP is used to look across whole sheets in search of similar types across multiple logical blocks then it becomes memory-intensive and dangerous.

INDEX is another example of a formula that can be used on a multi-dimensional input or track sheet but which is dangerous on a calculation sheet.

The first list of formulae below will provide you with simple, straightforward functionality without any fear of excessive complexity. The second list contains Excel formulae you should use sparingly, while considering the local implications, including auditability. The third list contains formulae that I avoid if I can.

List of simple everyday formulae

- +/-
- *
- SUM
- MAX
- MIN
- IF
- AND
- OR

- IFERROR
- ISNA
- ABS
- AVERAGE
- EOMONTH
- ROUND
- LEFT
- LEN

List of more complex formulae to use sparingly

- / - division can create the error #DIV/0! But this can be either avoided by wrapping in an IF function or by error trapping in a subsequent line of code
- INDEX
- MATCH
- VLOOKUP
- HLOOKUP
- LOOKUP
- SUMIF
- SUMPRODUCT

List of formulae to avoid

- OFFSET

3. KEYBOARD SHORTCUTS

Keyboard shortcuts are an essential part of computer efficiency; they greatly enhance accuracy as well as speed. In fact both PCs and Macs can be entirely accessed using keyboard shortcuts. There are four fundamental shortcuts to know:

1. All menus in any application in Windows can be accessed by pressing the Alt key, followed by a series of letters that take the user to all menu sub-items.

2. Application focus can be switched using the Alt + Tab keys.

3. Focus within an application can be toggled within multiple documents by using the Tab key on its own.

4. Use SHIFT + F10 to access the shortcut (or context) menu for any item – without having to right mouse click.

In summary:

Windows menus	Alt
Application focus	Alt + Tab
Focus within an application	Tab
Context menu	Shift + F10

The keyboard shortcuts in Appendix 3 are an ample set that can form the core shortcuts for modelling and computer use.

4. NAVIGATION

Navigating around an Excel model is an important part of modelling. Speed and ease of navigation can be improved through the use of simple formulae and knowledge of some techniques.

Navigation between sheets is fast when references from one sheet to another are one-to-one. One-to-one references are formulae that reference another cell in the simplest possible way in Excel.

If references are one-to-one then navigation can be performed in one of two ways:

1. Double-clicking
2. Using the keyboard.

'Allow editing directly in cells' in Tools Options needs to be unchecked to be able to double-click. To use the keyboard simply press Ctrl + [to go to the precedent and then F5 + Enter to come back. You can explore and go wherever you like before returning to the original cell as Excel remembers where you initially came from.

5. AUTOMATION

Beware of automation as it can add unnecessary complexity and risk. Generally it is preferable to allow errors to pop up and have to solve these rather than litter the model with complex formulae for every conceivable possibility. However, there is some simple automation that works well in an Excel model.

Data validation

Data validation is simple to set up and use and does not introduce any formulae. Figure 103 shows how cell J6 has been set as a yellow input, but also uses data validation on a list that references $O$6:$AH$6 in order to pick the comparison column name. Once picked it behaves like an input.

FIGURE 103: DATA VALIDATION

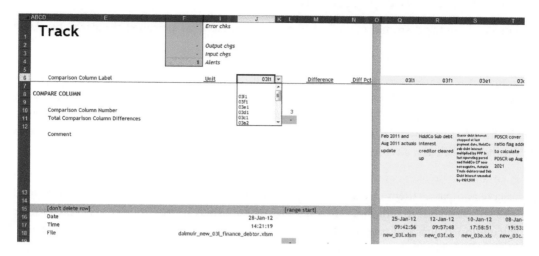

To set up data validation in this way using a list:

- click in the cell where you would like to introduce data validation
- on the Data tab on the ribbon or the Data menu choose Data Validation and then allow List from under Allow: on the Settings tab
- choose the source reference array under Source
- press OK.

FIGURE 104: DATA VALIDATION SETUP

VBA macros and project finance

Financial models do sometimes use macros to automate what are called circularity breakers.

An example best explains a circularity breaker.

Consider a cash reserve account to cover any future breaches of the cover ratio set by the bank. This type of cash reserve needs to know future cash flows in order to put cash away for any future breaches. This look-forward behaviour causes a problem in the model since the future cash flows are also a function of the cash reserve in the past. In mathematics this problem is called a circularity.

A circularity breaker collects the amounts calculated as needing to be deposited in the cash reserve and pastes them into a row where these same values are inputs and do get deposited into the cash reserve. That way the values being deposited are an input rather than a future calculation. The act of pasting these values creates a different future and the process has to be repeated. This is done until stability has been reached and the future no longer changes.

The copy and paste action to avoid the circularity can be carried out manually or automated with the use of a macro. Macros are not part of the scope of this book and will be addressed in a future eBook.

Goal seek

Goal seeking to find results is a useful Excel technique. Without going into too much detail, which can be found on the internet and within Excel, I propose a fast keyboard shortcut to using the goal seek technique in Excel.

First, what is goal seek used for? A simple example best explains the technique.

Consider that *revenue = price per unit x number of units sold in any given period*. If you know the revenue and the price per unit then you can work out the number of units sold by dividing revenue by the price per unit. This is a classic goal seek problem where you can ask Excel to work out what number of units sold will give you the correct revenue.

In general, goal seek allows the computer to work out an input if you already know the result. To use goal seek:

- click on a result cell
- press Alt + T + G
- press Tab (to move to the 'To value' box)
- write the value of the result you know to be correct
- press Tab (to move to the 'By changing cell' box)

- click on the input cell that you wish to find to satisfy the result you know to be correct (it must be an input with a value not a formula as Excel can only change inputs)
- press Enter and wait for the result.

For more help on this function use the Excel help files and the internet.

Conditional formatting

Conditional formatting, if used sparingly, is very useful. The idea is that a cell property such as fill colour can change if the value of the cell changes. This is particularly useful for errors and tracking the number of changes to a set of model results.

I will use the Error example to explain a simple use of conditional formatting. In this example a value of 0 denotes no errors, as in Figure 105, and a value of 1 denotes an error, as in Figure 106. No other values are allowed by the formula.

FIGURE 105: NO ERROR SIGNAL WITH CONDITIONAL FORMATTING

Term Loan Balance Check   -   check

FIGURE 106: ERROR SIGNAL WITH CONDITIONAL FORMATTING

Term Loan Balance Check   1   check

In this example we need to add two layers of conditional formatting to the base fill colour, which is green. So a value of 1 will trigger the fill colour red, as will any value other than 0, and just in case we make a mistake and delete the formula we need to trigger a red in the event there is nothing in the cell.

So to achieve this do the following:

- colour the cell fill colour fluorescent green
- open the Conditional Formatting Rules Manager
- create two new rules as shown in Figure 107 for any value <>0 and a non-value of "", which implies there is nothing in the cell.

FIGURE 107: CONDITIONAL FORMATTING RULES MANAGER

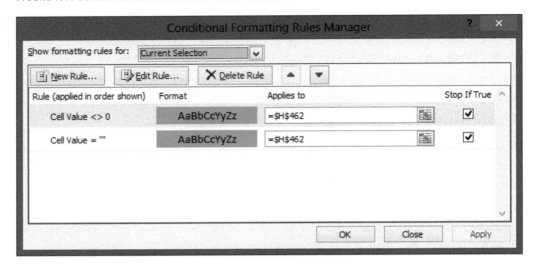

5. KNOWN EXCEL ISSUES

There are some known issues with Excel that modellers need to be aware of.

In general, Excel is known not to be very good at charts but up to the time of writing there do not seem to be any credible charting tools that can be used with Excel.

Charting tips

Here are some charting tips in Excel:

- To write text around the chart just write into the cells behind the chart either as text or as simple formulae linking to a title rather than use the chart functionality for this.

- Similarly for values in charts, just link to a cell with the correct value you wish to show.

- Use pastel colours within the same base colour if you can.

- Use *Economist*-style charts as a template – see a good set of examples on the *Economist* website (**www.economist.com/blogs/graphicdetail**).

Inter-sheet links

Inter-sheet links can cause abnormal behaviour in Excel so keep these to a minimum and as simple as possible. VLOOKUP to the Inputs sheet is an exception and not the rule.

File corruption and saving

Saving and renaming your files frequently is good practice. The ways of avoiding a corrupt or lost file are:

- save the model file every time you do something that you are sure is correct
- change the name of the file to a newer version every time you change a section of logic – regular name changes can protect you against a corrupt file
- try not to use Save As but rather save the model, go to Explorer and copy and paste the file, and then rename the copied file to a newer name.

Formatting (including conditional formatting)

Excessive formatting can sometimes cause the complete loss of a file. All the formatting in this book should keep you comfortably within any limit imposed by Excel. However, beware, as formatting appears to be a strange fish in Excel. Rumour has it that any supplemental formatting added to a file just adds on to all the previous formatting already in the file, so that the old formatting is not deleted. The solution to this is to keep your formatting in check, and this includes conditional formatting.

CHAPTER 5
COMPUTER THEORY

Using the computer is central to being a good modeller and is at the heart of the holistic solution to the modelling problem. Here I discuss:

1. Body posture and eyes while modelling
2. Using PDFs to distribute model reports
3. Using WinZip prior to model distribution
4. File naming convention and file control
5. Backing up and secure file distribution
6. How Skype is useful for modellers
7. VBA Editor
8. Event Driven Analysis for efficient folder naming and organisation.

1. BODY POSTURE AND EYES

It is very important to start with a good body posture when working at the computer for long periods of time. Visit the US government website for a detailed discussion of good working positions (**www.osha.gov/SLTC/etools/computerworkstations/positions.html**).

For the eyes, I have adopted a simple remedy for having to stare at the screen and this is to regularly find a faraway object or architectural detail out of the window and make sure the eyes are able to focus and see all the detail. This ensures that the muscles in the eye are still being properly tested.

2. PDFS

Reduce PDF file size in Acrobat Professional

PDFs can be used as a way of distributing the results of the model. However, PDFs can become huge. A simple trick to keep the file size down is to try Document > Reduce File

Size in Adobe Acrobat Professional. Unfortunately this does not work in Adobe Acrobat Reader, the free version.

3. WINZIP

WinZip is useful for sending files by email or on server exchange systems. The benefits are that file sizes are smaller and the zipped file can be password protected for greater security. In order to use it more efficiently try the following tips.

WinZip quick-fire setup

- Open WinZip
- Go to Options > Configuration and choose the Explorer Enhancements tab
- In the Context Menu Commands area on the right, check only those items shown in Figure 108.

FIGURE 108: WINZIP CONFIGURATION

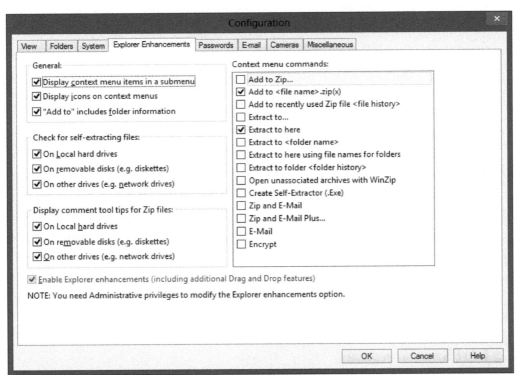

WinZip quick fire-usage

- Once you have this setup in WinZip, using it in Windows Explorer becomes that much easier:
  - To zip a file, select the file and press SHIFT + F10, then Z, then A
  - To unzip a file to the same location, select the zipped file and press SHIFT + F10, then Z, then X

4. FILE NAMING CONVENTION AND FILE CONTROL

A file-naming convention is essential to avoid chaos and add to your computer productivity. F1F9 (**www.f1f9.com**) have devised a simple file naming convention that is well worth adopting.

File-naming convention

Let's use an example to demonstrate how the file-naming convention works. Start with a project code-named project Mercury where we will produce Excel files for our analysis. The first file we will call 'mercury_01a.xls' and as we make a change to this file we will save it as 'mercury_01b.xls'. In this way, we have a multitude of file names at our disposal, changing to 02a after we reach 01z.

mercury_01a.xls

mercury_01b.xls

…

mercury_01z.xls

mercury_02a.xls

…

In this file naming convention I like to use short file names as much as possible otherwise there is a tendency to add descriptive tags to the filename creating unwieldy filenames that easily defy a proper convention.

The benefits of a file-naming convention are apparent when we try to find the latest file in a series in Windows Explorer. They are also apparent when we email a file to someone and they risk saving over the preceding file if the file names are the same. This brings us to file control.

File control

With a file-naming convention goes a file control routine. Due to the international nature of a modelling operation knowing who has file control is key. It is essential that no two people are working on the same file at the same time, as this will lead to unnecessary work or lost work. So, file control is passed between collaborators as the work is done. The strict file-naming convention comes into its own at this point as it is very clear which is the latest file.

5. BACKING UP AND SECURE FILE DISTRIBUTION

Backing up used to be a software or manual process involving an external drive. Now simple online solutions exist of which the simplest is probably Dropbox. Visit **www.dropbox.com** for more information.

You can also use Dropbox to exchange files without the need to send bulky emails. Just follow the instructions on the Dropbox website to invite others to share folders with you.

6. SKYPE

Skype is a wonderful tool that allows users to communicate for free. I use Skype regularly to discuss modelling issues while communicating with voice and Skype chat. The chat can be used to pass formulae, references and comments back and forth, and can also be searched back in time. Furthermore, a dedicated chat can be set up for each project, and conference calls can also be arranged.

What is Skype?

Skype is a way to make calls over the internet rather than over traditional telephone lines. Conference calls are easy and it has an inbuilt internet chat that allows users to chat in real-time, and then search past chat. Communications between Skype users are free, while calls to local, national and international phones and mobiles are very cheap. Skype also allows the user to send low-cost SMS messages by typing through the computer.

Why use Skype?

For each client and project group I create a dedicated and private chat group which enables quick messaging as the work progresses. Furthermore, all calls using Skype are free and this is a substantial cost saving.

What do you need to use Skype?

You need Skype software installed on your computer, a good internet connection and a headset with a microphone. To get the Skype software, download from **www.skype.com**.

What is internet chat?

Internet chat is a little window into short or long messages are typed that can then be seen by all members of the chat in real-time. Chats can be started between individuals or created to include wider groups for specific projects. These chats are useful repositories for ideas, thoughts or specific project-related discussions and they can be searched at any time by any member.

How much does it cost?

Calling and chatting through Skype to another person on Skype is free. Skype also allows for low-cost calls to mobiles and landlines anywhere in the world.

What happens when I have Skype up and running?

A little green icon appears in the system tray at the bottom right of the computer showing that I am online. If I leave the computer for a while the icon turns yellow to show I am away, and if I haven't logged into Skype the icon is white with a green outline to show I am offline. Other users of Skype can see these icons and thereby know of your availability.

How to avoid unwanted promotional messages that come through Skype

To avoid unwanted promotions, go to Tools -> Options -> Notifications -> Alerts & Messages and then uncheck the Promotions box.

7. VBA EDITOR

If you use VBA to solve your Excel problems then you should customise the VBA Editor interface to make it easier to view. The first step is to change the colour scheme that comes as default.

Changing the colour scheme in the VBA Editor

To change the colour scheme in the VBA Editor:

- open Excel
- press ALT + F11 to enter the VBA Editor
- press ALT + T, then O to get to the Options panel, and select the Editor Format tab.

FIGURE 109: VBA EDITOR OPTIONS

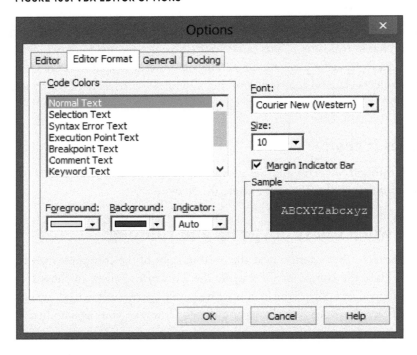

- starting with Normal Text, select the three colours for the Foreground, Background and Indicator to match those in Figure 110, VBA Editor Format.

FIGURE 110: VBA EDITOR OPTIONS

Code colours	Foreground	Background	Indicator
Normal Text	Yellow	Blue	Auto
Selection Text	Auto	Auto	Auto
Syntax Error Text	Red	Auto	Auto
Execution Point Text	Auto	Yellow	Yellow
Breakpoint Text	White	Brown	Brown
Comment Text	Light Grey	Blue	Auto
Keyword Text	Pink	Blue	Auto
Identifier Text	Fluorescent green	Blue	Auto
Bookmark Text	Auto	Auto	Fluorescent blue
Call Return Text	Auto	Auto	Fluorescent green

- press OK
- the VBA Editor will now show the programming code in a rich dark blue background and various colours that make the whole much easier to look at.

8. EVENT DRIVEN ANALYSIS

Event Driven Analysis is a way of naming your folders for your client and other work. It is based around the concept of numbering and naming folders in the order in which events occur. Events dictate our business lives and when looking back into a folder system the events will again come back into memory if they are numbered in the order in which they occurred.

Here are the rules:

- use a numbering system for folders whenever possible
- add some text which reasonably describes the work that you did
- use an underscore between the number and the text.

The idea here is to number your folders for easy recognition. It is amazing how much easier it is to recognise the location of something if you have both a number and letters. For example, I call a folder '5_Update project in Jan 09' and then when the next project comes in I call it '6_Next project'. Notice the use of the underscore; again this makes it easier to read and find.

The numbers serve to keep the event-driven order even though folders have a differing alphabetical order.

When you have to insert folders in between others, adopt a number and letter, for example 6a_ and then 6b_.

See Figure 111 for an example of a starting folder system for a client project along the lines described by Event Driven Analysis.

FIGURE 111: SUGGESTED MODEL FOLDER SYSTEM FOR MODEL BUILD

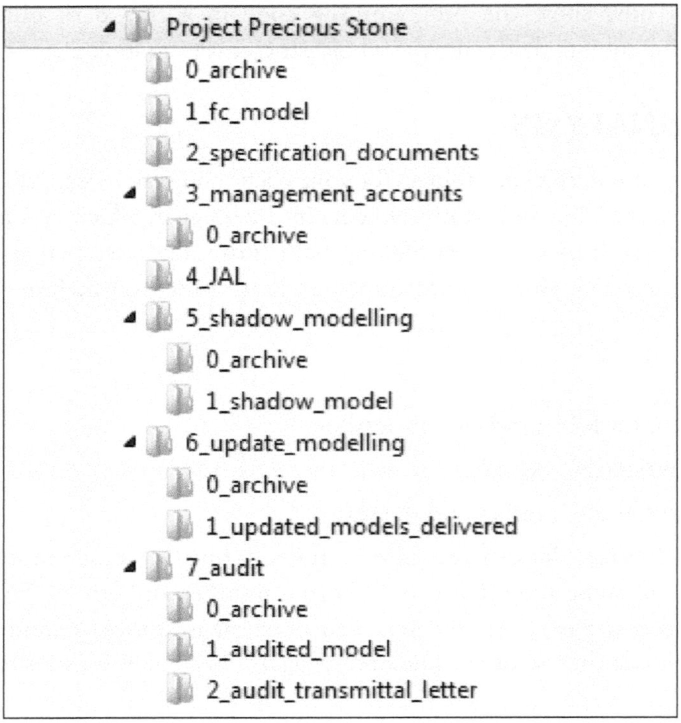

PART 2
PRACTICE

This book is not just about the theory of modelling, but also a prescriptive instruction manual enabling you, the reader, to actually build a model. This section of the book has the objective of giving you a practical, step-by-step set of instructions to build a model, tips-and-tricks for modelling and guidelines to making sure the modelling investment is maintained over time.

Part 2 is accordingly split into three chapters:

1. Building the model
2. Practical modelling techniques
3. Maintaining the investment.

CHAPTER 6
BUILDING THE MODEL

HOW TO USE THIS CHAPTER

To build the model, follow the section in this chapter entitled 'Steps'. This methodology consists of a series of around 60 steps, with each requiring you to perform various tasks in a particular order.

While some steps are very short, for the more involved steps I have introduced the following subdivision to make it clearer to follow:

- Overview
- Specification (or inputs)
- Design
- Build (build sequence and build order)
- Results.

Most of the tasks are described within the step. However, within some of the steps you will also find references to test and deliver tasks. These can be found in the sections titled 'Testing the model' and 'Delivering the model' further on in this chapter.

OVERVIEW
How is a model built?

A model is built by carrying out a series of tasks. Some tasks require understanding the problem, other tasks require designing and building the appropriate solution. Other tasks include testing the solution and delivering the solution to the end user.

These modelling tasks fall into five main categories:

1. Specification
2. Design
3. Build
4. Test
5. Deliver.

Classically these phases occur in this order. However, rapid application development (RAD) concepts, adopted from hard-core software development, have begun to feed into modelling. RAD concepts propose iterating through the tasks within each phase in quick succession, building up only the bare essentials in each phase, and arriving at a delivered model in less time. An illustration of the RAD process is shown in Figure 112.

FIGURE 112: RAPID APPLICATION DEVELOPMENT PHASES AND PROCESS

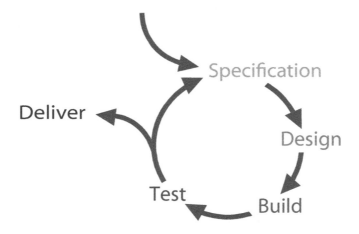

With an eye on the lessons learnt from RAD, I developed the series of steps outlined in this chapter to greatly speed up the process of building a financial model. The steps will take you through the development of a financial model from conception to delivery.

At the core of the series of steps are processes that prescribe specification, design, build, test and deliver tasks to perform. An illustration of the elements of a step in the model-building process is given in Figure 113.

FIGURE 113: BREAKDOWN OF A MODEL-BUILDING STEP

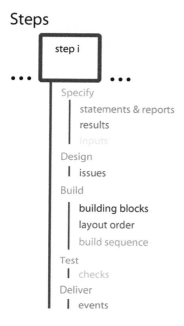

The language of the model-building process

The model-building process uses words that are common in life and business. The important terms are:

- steps
- tasks
- statements & reports
- results
- inputs
- issues
- building blocks
- layout order
- build sequence
- checks
- events.

Let's look at what each of these terms mean in turn.

STEPS

Collections of sensible and balanced tasks from specification, design, build, test or deliver.

Each step contains a collection of tasks from the five modelling phases of specification, design, build, test or deliver. Each step has to be fully completed before progressing to the next step.

Steps are created as:

- sensible collections of tasks
- sets of results that can be compiled within the financial statements and reports without causing problems such as errors and imbalances.

TASKS

Actions from any of specify, design, build, test or deliver.

Tasks are the verbs of the methodology; the do part of the process.

STATEMENTS & REPORTS

Sums and compilations of results in the form of financial statements or reports.

- Statements and reports are the outputs of the model
- Statements and reports are the reason for building the model
- Statements and reports are compilations of results.

Examples of statements and reports are:

- Profit and loss statement
- Cash flow statement
- Balance sheet statement
- Taxation calculation statement
- Investor return report
- Banking covenants report.

RESULTS

The output values of a building block that achieve the specified result.

- Results are the last line of the last building block within a step
- Results are values or streams of calculated values
- Results are the line-items that populate the statements and reports
- Results can be time dependent or non-time dependent.

Examples of results are:

- Operating Revenues Accrued
- Project IRR
- Trade Debtors Balance
- Annual Debt Service Cover Ratios (ADSCR).

INPUTS

Values used to feed a calculation.

- Inputs can be data or calculations
- Inputs can be groups of data or groups of calculations
- Inputs can be time dependent or non-time dependent
- Inputs are always values
- Inputs can be one value or a stream of values over time
- Inputs have various properties, namely:
  - value or stream of values
  - time-dependent or non-time dependent
  - real or nominal or neither
  - data or calculation
  - text description of data or calculation.

Examples of inputs are:

- RPI index
- Concession flag
- Last closing balance period flag
- Interest rate on term loan
- Last closing balance sheet date.

ISSUES

Practical considerations in the structure, content and organisation of the elements of a model.

Designing the structure, content and organisation of a model will throw up a multitude of problems to solve. I call these issues, abbreviated from design issues.

BUILDING BLOCKS

An individual, self-sustaining and contiguous set of Excel calculations fed by values and producing values.

- Building blocks are Excel constructs that perform specific tasks
- Building blocks use the values of inputs to create further calculated values
- Building blocks are reusable
- Building blocks have inputs and create specific outputs
- Building blocks are calculations, however simple.

Examples of building blocks:

- Balance corkscrew
- Flag
- Simple allocator
- IRR over semi-annual cash flows
- Actual + Forecast indexation.

LAYOUT ORDER

The order in which the building blocks are best placed on the sheet, from top to bottom.

The order in which the building blocks are assembled on the sheet has much to do with the availability of information at each stage of the build process. This becomes easier with time and experience.

BUILD SEQUENCE

The order in which the build process is carried out.

The order in which the building blocks are built sometimes requires a partial build of a building block such as a balance corkscrew in order to feed a counter flow. At the end of the build sequence the partially built building block can be completed.

CHECKS

Tests carried out to ensure logical and arithmetic accuracy.

The model builder should carry out a variety of checks on all parts of the model to ensure logical and arithmetic accuracy. There are tests during the build process, prior to delivery of the model and to understand possible errors.

EVENTS

Actions resulting in the delivery of a model.

Events are the abbreviated form for delivery events when a model is handed over to the end user.

Shorthand key for the model-building process

The process also uses a shorthand key to give you more information in less space. This shorthand is found in the steps.

For example, 'Operating Cost ... PL_5, +/-, flow':

- PL_5 means Profit and Loss line-item 5, as defined in Figure 121 (page 162)
- +/- means that the calculations are carried out treating the items as positives and then flipped to negative only in preparation for the financial statements
- flow means that this result is a flow rather than a balance – see 'Flows & balances' on page 45.

Other keys are:

- CF_1: Cash Flow line item 1
- BS_10: Balance sheet line item 10
- +/+: calculated as a positive and compiled in the financial statements as a positive value – as a revenue for example
- Balance: means the result is a balance rather than a flow – see 'Flows & balances' on page 45.

STEPS

The steps to build a PFI model

There are 59 steps to build a PFI/PPP project finance model, and each step must be completed before embarking on the next step. There are not separate steps included for testing, which as described on page 27 is an ongoing process. The issue of these ongoing tests will be covered in detail in a future eBook.

Finance directors and modellers outside of project finance, and those dealing with more general financial modelling problems within enterprises other than PFI, should consider that the core steps here are the same for any modelling project. Core steps are denoted with the label CORE.

1. Create the model folder system on your computer (CORE)
2. Define the timeline and periodicity of the new model (CORE)
3. Create the base Excel file for the new model (CORE)
4. Build the Time sheet (CORE)
5. Build the Inputs sheet (CORE)
6. Build the Track and Check sheets and the track/check header (CORE)
7. Build the Template sheet (CORE)
8. Create Operations, Accounting, Finance, Tax and Financial Statements sheets (CORE)
9. Build the place-holding line-items into the financial statements (CORE)

10. Define the profit & loss statement (CORE)
11. Define the cash flow waterfall (CORE)
12. Define the balance sheet (CORE)
13. Define the tax statement (CORE)
14. Build nine important flags as place-holders in the Time sheet (CORE)
15. Build place-holder indexation in the Time sheet (CORE)
16. Build the Actuals sheet (CORE)
17. Add the financial statement sheet values from the FC model in the actual periods of the new Actuals sheet (CORE)
18. Build the Inputs_C sheet and populate it with the last closing balance sheet from the Actuals sheet (CORE)
19. Build retained earnings balance and retained cash balance in the Finance sheet (CORE)
20. Create FS_Ref and FS_Diff sheets and populate the FS_Ref sheet with the values from the FC model (CORE)
21. Specify, design and build the operating revenues (CORE)
22. Specify, design and build the operating revenues received (CORE)
23. Paint the revenues into the statements (CORE)
24. Specify, design and build the operating costs (CORE)
25. Specify, design and build the operating costs paid (CORE)
26. Specify, design and build the capital expenditure (CORE)
27. Specify, design and build the life cycle expenditure (CORE)
28. Specify, design and build the maintenance reserve account (CORE)
29. Specify, design and build insurance prepayments (CORE)
30. Specify, design and build VAT (CORE)
31. Specify, design and build capitalised interest and fees amortisation (CORE)
32. Specify, design and build development costs amortisation
33. Specify, design and build issue costs amortisation
34. Specify, design and build the term loan repayment (CORE)
35. Specify, design and build the term loan interest and balance (CORE)
36. Specify, design and build the debt service reserve account (DSRA) (CORE)
37. Specify, design and build the subordinated debt (part 1)
38. Specify, design and build the tax depreciation or writing down allowances (CORE)
39. Specify, design and build corporation tax (CORE)
40. Specify, design and build the tax reserve account

41. Specify, design and build interest on cash balances (CORE)
42. Specify, design and build deferred tax (CORE)
43. Specify, design and build share capital repayment
44. Specify, design and build the subordinated debt (part 2)
45. Specify, design and build dividends (CORE)
46. Build the actuals into the financial statements (CORE)
47. Deliver the shadow model to the end user (CORE)
48. Update the Actuals sheet in the model (CORE)
49. Create the Analysis sheet (CORE)
50. Specify, design and build the cover ratios (CORE)
51. Specify, design and build the project return on the investment
52. Specify, design and build the investor return on the investment (CORE)
53. Complete the build of all the flags in the Time sheet (CORE)
54. Complete indexation build (CORE)
55. Specify, design and build further reports (CORE)
56. Specify, design and build the Quick Start sheet (CORE)
57. Deliver the updated model to end user (CORE)
58. Add further final updates to the model (CORE)
59. Deliver the final model to the end user (CORE).

1. Create the model folder system on your computer (CORE)

OBJECTIVE

To create a folder system on your computer suited to the process of building a model that is fast and easy to use.

SPECIFICATION AND BUILD

You will need a sensible folder system to house all the files relating to your new model build. These files include:

- financial close model
- management accounting data
- specification material and documents
- shadow modelling work
- update modelling work.

I suggest you use the concepts of Event Driven Analysis (see '8. Event Driven Analysis' on page 139) and create the folder system that was previously shown in Figure 111.

2. Define the timeline and periodicity of the new model (CORE)

OBJECTIVE

Define the model timeframe and periodicity. By this I mean start dates, end dates, reporting dates, size of the time intervals and very importantly the last actual balance sheet date.

SPECIFICATION & BUILD

To help make these important timeframe decisions, create a simple spreadsheet called 'modelling_timeframe_01a.xlsx' with the information shown in Figure 114.

FIGURE 114: MODEL TIMEFRAME SPECIFICATION GRID

	PFI / PPP / PF project
Concession start date	01-Jan-09
Concession end date	31-Dec-35
Duration of concession	1 yr cstr + 25 years ops
Financial close date	31-Dec-08
Construction Start Date	01-Jan-09
Construction End Date	31-Dec-09
Operations Start Date	01-Jan-10
Operations End Date	31-Dec-35
Banking ratio calculation dates	30 jun & 31 dec
Debt repayment dates	30 jun & 31 dec
Management accounting reporting dates	31 mar, 30 jun, 30 sep, 31 dec

	Financial close model	New operating mocel
Periodicity	monthly cstr + semi-annual ops	quarterly
Period start dates	1 jan, 1 jul	1 jan, 1 apr, 1 jul, 1 oct
Period end dates	30 jun, 31 dec	31 mar, 30 jun, 30 sep, 31 dec
Banking ratio calculation dates	30 jun & 31 dec	30 jun & 31 dec
Debt repayment dates	30 jun & 31 dec	30 jun & 31 dec
Management accounting reporting dates	n/a	31 mar, 30 jun, 30 sep, 31 dec
First model column/period end date	01-Jan-08	01-Jan-09
Last model column/period end date	31-Dec-36	31-Dec-37
Last actual closing balance sheet date	n/a	31-Dec-2011
First model forecast period end date	n/a	31-Mar-2012

The periodicity of a model is the size of the time intervals. For example, these time intervals could be monthly, quarterly, semi-annual or even annual. Normally the periodicity of an operating model is defined by the reporting cycles of the company being modelled, and the reporting cycles are either semi-annual or quarterly.

Reporting cycles of a PFI/PPP company comprise both the management accounting reporting and the investor/lender reporting. These may coincide but can sometimes be different. If they are different then the investor/lender reporting cycle normally takes preference over the management accounting reporting cycle.

Once the periodicity of the new model is defined each period requires definition. Each period has a start date and an end date, as in Figure 115. It is best to assume that each period includes both the start date and the end date.

FIGURE 115: MODEL PERIODICITY AS DEFINED IN EACH SHEET HEADER

01-Jan-09	01-Jul-09	01-Jan-10	01-Jul-10	01-Jan-11	01-Jul-11	01-Jan-12	01-Jul-12	01-Jan-13	01-Jul-13	01-Jan-14
30-Jun-09	31-Dec-09	30-Jun-10	31-Dec-10	30-Jun-11	31-Dec-11	30-Jun-12	31-Dec-12	30-Jun-13	31-Dec-13	30-Jun-14
Actuals	Actuals	Actuals	Actuals	Forecast	Forecast	Forecast	Forecast	Forecast	Forecast	Forecast
2,009	2,009	2,010	2,010	2,011	2,011	2,012	2,012	2,013	2,013	2,014

Define a modelling timeframe starting six months before the start of the concession and finishing two years after the close of the concession. For example, the 'Last model column / period end date' would be defined as a date two years after the end of the concession.

Figure 116 shows the start of the built header rows in the Time sheet. All time-dependent sheets in the model should have identical header rows.

FIGURE 116: TIME SHEET HEADER ROWS

ABCD	E	F	G	H	I	J	K	U	V	W	X	Y
Time					Error chks							
Model Period Beginning					Output chgs		01-Sep-10	01-Mar-11	01-Sep-11	01-Mar-12	01-Sep-12	01-/
Model Period Ending					Input chgs		28-Feb-11	31-Aug-11	29-Feb-12	31-Aug-12	28-Feb-13	31-/
Actual vs Forecast					Alerts		Actuals	Actuals	Forecast	Forecast	Forecast	F
Year # for Current Period's Financial Year End							2,011	2,012	2,012	2,013	2,013	

3. Create the base Excel file for the new model (CORE)

OBJECTIVE

Create a new Excel file for the model.

SPECIFICATION & BUILD

Here you will create the first base file for the model and call it 'model_name_01a.xlsx'. To do this:

1. Open Excel
2. Make sure Excel is set up for modelling – refer to 'Basic Excel setup' on page 111
3. Open the file called 'base_template_01a.xlsx'
4. Familiarise yourself with the contents – refer to 'Chapter 3: Base model template in Excel'
5. Use 'Save As …' to save this file with the name of your choice and in the folder location of your choice – refer to '4. File naming convention and file control' on page 135 and '8. Event driven analysis' on page 139 respectively.

4. Build the Time sheet (CORE)

OBJECTIVE

Use the information from '2. Define the timeline and periodicity of the new model' on page 152 to create the model Time sheet which will produce the header information for the rest of the model.

SPECIFICATION

Use the time specification (from Figure 114) to specify the following inputs:

- *start period end date* – the end date of the first column in the model timeline
- *end period end date* – the end date of the last column in the model timeline
- *periodicity in months* – how many months between column end dates
- *last actuals period end date* – the end date of the last actuals period
- *first forecast period end date* – the end date of the first forecast period
- *last forecast date as end date* – the end date of the last forecast period.

DESIGN

The simplest design is to leave all the time calculations for period end date, beginning period end date, 'actual vs forecast' label and year number in the Time sheet. From the Time sheet each other sheet in the model references these export rows in row 2 to row 5.

BUILD

Use both Figure 117 and Figure 118 as visual templates to build the timeline header:

1. Calculate the Period End Date for each period in the model, as in row 3 of Figure 117

2. Calculate the Period Beginning Date for each period in the model, as in row 2 of Figure 117

3. For each period calculate whether it is an actuals period or a forecast period, as in row 4 of Figure 117

4. Calculate the year number for each period in the model, as in row 5 of Figure 117

FIGURE 117: TIMELINE HEADER AT THE START OF THE CONCESSION

Time		Error chks							
Model Period Start		Output chgs	01-Jan-09	01-Jul-09	01-Jan-10	01-Jul-10	01-Jan-11	01-Jul-11
Model Period End		Input chgs	30-Jun-09	31-Dec-09	30-Jun-10	31-Dec-10	30-Jun-11	31-Dec-11
Actual vs Forecast		Alerts	Actuals	Actuals	Actuals	Actuals	Forecast	Forecast
Year # for Current Period's Financial Year End			2,009	2,009	2,010	2,010	2,011	2,011

FIGURE 118: TIMELINE HEADER AT THE END OF THE CONCESSION

S	AT	AU	AV	AW	AX	AY	AZ	BA	BB	BC	BD
ep-22	01-Mar-23	01-Sep-23	01-Mar-24	01-Sep-24	01-Mar-25	01-Sep-25	01-Mar-26	01-Sep-26	01-Mar-27	01-Sep-27	01-Mar-28
eb-23	31-Aug-23	29-Feb-24	31-Aug-24	28-Feb-25	31-Aug-25	28-Feb-26	31-Aug-26	28-Feb-27	31-Aug-27	29-Feb-28	31-Aug-28
orecast	Forecast	Forecast	Forecast	Forecast	Forecast	Forecast	Forecast	Post-Frcst	Post-Frcst	Post-Frcst	Post-Frcst
2,023	2,024	2,024	2,025	2,025	2,026	2,026	2,027	2,027	2,028	2,028	2,029

5. Allow for two years of post-forecast after the end of the concession and highlight the columns beyond this point and first delete the contents and then hide the contents.

6. Use conditional formatting to format row 4 under the timeline in three colours depending on whether the period is an 'Actual', a 'Forecast' or Post-Frcst' period – see 'Conditional formatting' on page 129.

5. Build the Inputs sheet (CORE)

OBJECTIVE

Create a column input sheet that can be expanded as required.

SPECIFICATION

The Inputs sheet looks like Figure 119. The properties of this sheet are:

- The Inputs sheet has a standard format from columns A to I, so that the inputs can be referenced in the rest of the model.

- For a detailed explanation of time-dependent inputs in column format see 'VLOOKUP Collector' on page 92 and 'Inputs' on pages 68 and 90.

- The input sets are in column format between columns M and P.

- Column F uses an INDEX function to gather the data from the designated column by referring to cell L10.

- Cells F6 and F7 define the data set that is run through the model.

- Notice the pairs of grey fill in rows 16 and 36 and columns M and P – formulae referencing these areas also include the grey fills, thus ensuring that all rows or columns remain referenced as the areas are stretched.

FIGURE 119: INPUTS SHEET

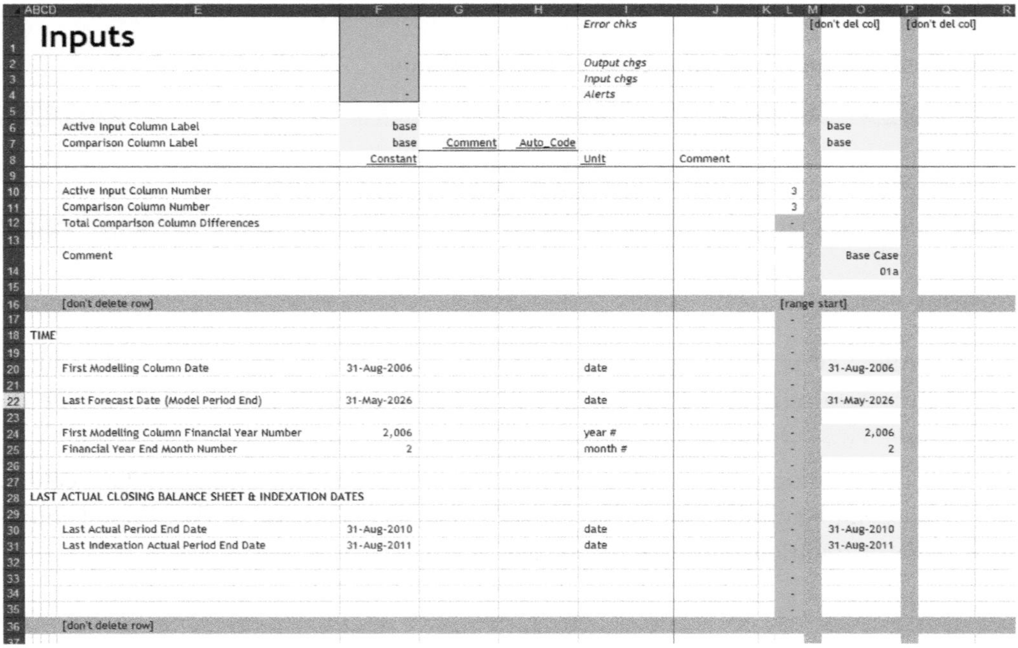

DESIGN

Rows are added before row 36 to add more inputs. Refer back to Figure 9 (page 21) for the column format time-dependent values, which are in the same format as Figure 119.

BUILD

Carry out this build sequence:

1. Create a new sheet with the same structure as described in the specification
2. Referring to Figure 119 the formulae are:
   - in L10 = MATCH(F6, M6:P6, FALSE)
   - in L11 = MATCH(F7, M7:P7, FALSE)
   - in F20 = INDEX(M20:P20, $L$10)
   - in L12 = SUM(L16:L36)
   - in L20 = IF(F20 = INDEX(M20:P20, $L$11), 0, 1)
3. Colour the sheet tab with yellow for input
4. Place the Inputs sheet at the front of the model

RESULTS

The result is an Input sheet awaiting the forecast inputs as they are created.

6. Build the Track and Check sheets and the track/check header (CORE)

OBJECTIVE

Create the Track and Check sheets and then build the track/check header.

SPECIFICATION

Both the Track and Check sheets have their own sheet structure. The Track sheet was shown in Figure 34 (page 70) and the Check sheet (page 71) was shown in Figure 35.

Both sheets produce summary values that are used in the Track and Check header shown in Figure 120.

FIGURE 120: TRACK AND CHECK HEADER

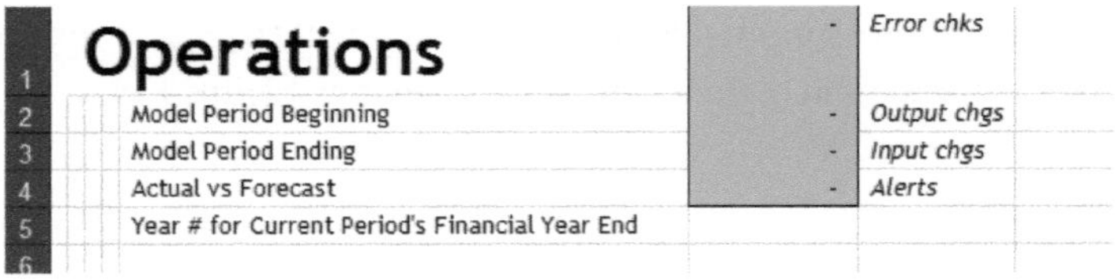

The specification items are:

- Track sheet structure
- Check sheet structure

DESIGN

The design of both sheets is simple although there are some important formulae to use.

BUILD

Carry out the following build sequence:

1. Use a copy of the Inputs sheet shown in Figure 33 (page 69) as a starting template for the Track sheet and add/change the following formulae:

   - Use data validation in cell J6 with reference to the range O6:AC6
   - Use = MATCH($J$6, O6:AC6, 0) in cell L10
   - Use = SUM(L15:L326) in cell L11 – this range should include the grey row at the foot of the Track sheet
   - Use = TODAY() in J16
   - Use = NOW() in J17
   - Use = MID(CELL("filename",$A$1), SEARCH("[", CELL("filename",$A$1)) + 1, SEARCH("]", CELL("filename",$A$1)) - SEARCH("[", CELL("filename",$A$1)) - 1) in cell J18 – this formula is a true monster but does collect the filename
   - Use = IF(ABS(M26) > 0.001, 1, 0) in L26 and down the sheet
   - Use = IF(ISTEXT(J26), 0, J26 - INDEX(O26:AC26, $L$10)) in M26 and down the sheet
   - Use = IF(OR(INDEX(O26:AC26, $L$10) = 0, ISTEXT(INDEX(O26:AC26, $L$10))), 0, J26 / INDEX(O26:AC26, $L$10) - 1) in N26 and down the sheet

2. The formula in cell L11 summarises all the track changes in the same column and is the ultimate value from this sheet

3. Add the formula = Track!$L$11 to cell F2 and conditionally format it as defined in 'Conditional formatting' on page 129

4. Use a copy of the Track sheet as the initial template for the Check sheet and delete the content from column J onwards

5. Format the Check sheet as shown in Figure 35 (page 71)

6. Add the following formulae:
   - = SUM(F12:F49) in cell F10, this is the summary of all checks

7. Add the formula = Check!$F$10 to cell F1 and conditionally format it as defined in 'Conditional formatting' on page 129

8. Create a new section below the Checks on the Check sheet called Alerts and then take the summary alerts value to cell F4 on the Check sheet with the formula = Check!$F$54 (or referencing the cell that contains the summary alerts)

9. Make sure that cell F3 on the Checks sheet contains the formula = Inputs!$L$12

10. Add the Track/Check header to all sheets in the model – the cells to copy are F1:I4 for FAST + 2 and F1:G4 for FAST.

RESULTS

Track and Check sheets with the Track/Check header awaiting compilation.

7. Build the Template sheet (CORE)

OBJECTIVE

Create a template sheet that can be re-used to create other calculation and result sheets in the model.

SPECIFICATION & BUILD

1. Copy the Time sheet and rename it as 'Template'

2. Re-link the time strip across the top of the Template sheet to the Time sheet

3. Delete all the calculations that came with the Time sheet and below the six header rows at the top of the sheet

4. Add the Track/Check header created in the previous step at the top of the Check and Track sheets – the cells to copy are F1:I4.

This Template sheet now forms the basis of any new sheet in the model. Place the template sheet down at the far right, beyond the Check sheet. You will need it later on.

8. Create Operations, Accounting, Finance, Tax and Financial Statements sheets (CORE)

OBJECTIVE

Create the Operations, Accounting, Finance, Financial Statements and Tax sheets.

SPECIFICATION & BUILD

Copy the Template sheet three times to a position after the Time sheet and before the Financial Statements sheet and name these new sheets according to and in the order of the list below:

- Operations
- Accounting
- Finance
- Tax
- Financial Statements.

9. Build the place-holding line-items into the financial statements (CORE)

OBJECTIVE

Create financial statements in structural form with line-item names in expectation of the linking process.

SPECIFICATION & BUILD

As a guide, place-holding financial statements have the following properties:

- Line-item names of results in column E
- Sums in the appropriate rows from column L onwards
- Sums of whole row in column J
- Basic formatting
- PL, CF then BS in this order
- PL, CF and BS checks in a section at the bottom of the sheet.

Further important points:

- The financial statements should be built according to the specification for statements in the next three steps.

- The two links between the financial statements are the retained profit balance and the retained cash balance. The Retained Profit Balance appears at the bottom of the P&L and in the Balance Sheet. The Retained Cash Balance appears at the bottom of the P&L and in the Balance Sheet. To make sure that these balances have the same value they are calculated separately at the bottom of the Finance sheet, as discussed in step 10.

Carry out the following:

1. Copy the Template sheet to before the Track sheet and after the Finance sheet and call it Financial Statements.

2. Consult with your work on the specification for the FS in steps 3, 4 and 5 and build the structure and basic summation formulae for the financial statements in this new sheet.

10. Define the profit & loss statement (CORE)

OBJECTIVE

Precisely define the line-items in the profit & loss statement of the project model, and write this list in column E of the Financial Statements sheet.

SPECIFICATION & BUILD

The financial statements need to be defined line-by-line. Use the original FC model as a guide. The FC model is the model that existed at the time of financial close, and normally serves as the base for the operational model.

All new line-items in the Op model, with respect to the FC model, will cause difficulties in the build process, so beware of adding extra line-items. However, adding extra line-items may be necessary. Consider making additions or exclusions during the subsequent Update phase of the model build instead.

All excluded line-items in the Op model, with respect to the FC model, will cause difficulties in the build process, so similarly to the additional line-items consider adding these during the Update part of the process.

An illustration of a profit & loss is given in Figure 121.

FIGURE 121: PROFIT & LOSS STATEMENT EXAMPLE

		Formula
PL_1	Operating Revenues	... from Operations sheet
PL_2	**Total Revenue**	= SUM(PL_1)
PL_3	Operating Costs	... from Operations sheet
PL_4	Directors Fees	... from Operations sheet
PL_5	Life Cycle Expenditure (Expensed Portion)	... from Operations sheet
PL_6	**Total Operating Costs Accrued**	= SUM(PL_3:PL_5)
PL_7	Depreciation Of Fixed Assets 25 Years & Over	... from Operations sheet
PL_8	Depreciation Of Fixed Assets 10 To 25 Years	... from Operations sheet
PL_9	Depreciation Of Fixed Assets Up To 10 Years	... from Operations sheet
PL_10	**Total Depreciation**	= SUM(PL_7:PL_9)
PL_11	Capitalised Interest & Fees Amortisation	... from Accounting sheet
PL_12	Capitalised Development Costs Amortisation	... from Accounting sheet
PL_13	Capitalised Issue Costs Amortisation	... from Accounting sheet
PL_14	**Total Amortisation**	= SUM(PL_11:PL_13)
PL_15	**Operating Profit / (Loss)**	= PL_2 + PL_6 + PL_10 + PL_14
PL_16	Term Loan Interest	... from Finance sheet
PL_17	Sub Debt Interest	... from Finance sheet
PL_18	Interest Earnings Received	... from Finance sheet
PL_19	Overdraft Interest Paid	... from Finance sheet
PL_20	**Profit / (Loss) Before Tax**	= SUM(PL_15:PL_19)
PL_21	Corporation Tax	... from Tax sheet
PL_22	Deferred Tax Credit / (Charge)	... from Tax sheet
PL_23	**Profit / (Loss) After Tax**	= SUM(PL_20:PL_22)
PL_24	Dividends	... from Finance sheet
PL_25	**Retained Profit / (Loss) In Period**	= SUM(PL_23:PL_24)
PL_26	Retained Earnings Balance BEG	... from Finance sheet
PL_27	Retained Profit / (Loss) In Period	= PL_25
PL_28	**Retained Earnings Balance**	= SUM(PL_26:PL_27)

11. Define the cash flow waterfall (CORE)

OBJECTIVE

Precisely define the line-items in the cash flow statement of the project model, and write this list in column E of the Financial Statements sheet, under the profit & loss statement from the previous step.

SPECIFICATION & BUILD

An illustration of a cash flow statement is given in Figure 122.

It may be that the FC model included a cash flow rather than a cash flow waterfall. It does not take much reorganisation to turn a cash flow into a cash flow waterfall, but it is well worth it. Refer to 'Deferred tax' on page 49 for the theory.

You will possibly need to convince the client that a cash flow waterfall is necessary. Here is some ammunition for that discussion:

- The cash flow waterfall is a very important tool and central location for all 'cash available' calculations.

- The CFW normally exists in a model, except it is spread all over the model and is not explicit, so building one as a key result is transparent, explicit and pragmatic.

- As in the previous point, the CFW is a practical solution to the creation of necessary counter flows for the 'cash available' for a variety of crucial calculations in the model. These include:

  - Profit before tax for the calculation of corporation tax

  - Cash Available For Debt Service (known as CFADS) for the calculation of the cover ratios

  - Cash Available For Mezzanine Interest for the calculation/allocation of cash to the payment of mezzanine interest

  - Similarly for the repayment of mezzanine, sub debt interest, sub debt repayments and dividends.

FIGURE 122: CASH FLOW STATEMENT EXAMPLE

		Formula
CF_1	Operating Revenues Received	... from Operations sheet
CF_2	**Operating Revenue Received**	= SUM(CF_1)
CF_3	Operating Costs Paid	... from Operations sheet
CF_4	Directors Fees Paid	... from Operations sheet
CF_5	**Operating Costs Paid**	= SUM(CF_3:CF_4)
CF_6	Capital Expenditure Paid	... from Operations sheet
CF_7	Equity Drawn	... from Finance sheet
CF_8	Sub Debt Drawn	... from Finance sheet
CF_9	Life Cycle Expenditure (Expensed Portion) Paid	... from Operations sheet
CF_10	Life Cycle Expenditure (Capitalised Portion) Paid	... from Operations sheet
CF_11	**Operating Cash Flow**	= CF_2 + CF_5 + SUM(CF_6:CF_10)
CF_12	VAT Reclaimed / (Paid)	... from Tax sheet
CF_13	Interest Earnings Received	... from Finance sheet
CF_14	Overdraft Interest Paid	... from Finance sheet
CF_15	Corporation Tax Paid	... from Tax sheet
CF_16	**Cash Flow Available For DSRA**	= SUM(CF_11:CF_15)
CF_17	DSRA Deposits	... from Finance sheet
CF_18	DSRA Withdrawals	... from Finance sheet
CF_19	**Cash Flow Available For Debt Service**	= SUM(CF_16:CF_18)
CF_20	Term Loan Drawdown	... from Finance sheet
CF_21	Term Loan Interest Paid	... from Finance sheet
CF_22	Term Loan Repayment	... from Finance sheet
CF_23	**Cash Flow Available For MRA**	= SUM(CF_19:CF_22)
CF_24	MRA Deposits	... from Operations sheet
CF_25	MRA Withdrawals	... from Operations sheet
CF_26	**Cash Flow Available For TRA**	= SUM(CF_23:CF_25)
CF_27	TRA Deposits	... from Tax sheet
CF_28	TRA Withdrawals	... from Tax sheet
CF_29	**Cash Flow Available For Sub Debt**	= SUM(CF_26:CF_28)
CF_30	Sub Debt Interest Paid	... from Finance sheet
CF_31	Sub Debt Repayment	... from Finance sheet
CF_32	**Cash Flow Available For Share Capita Repayment**	= SUM(CF_29:CF_31)
CF_33	Share Capital Repayment	... from Finance sheet
CF_34	**Cash Flow Available For Dividends**	= SUM(CF_32:CF_33)
CF_35	Dividends Paid	... from Finance sheet
CF_36	**Net Cash Flow In Period**	= SUM(CF_34:CF_35)
CF_37	Retained Cash Balance BEG	... from Finance sheet
CF_38	Net Cash Flow In Period	= CF_36
CF_39	**Retained Cash Balance**	= SUM(CF_37:CF_38)

12. Define the balance sheet (CORE)

OBJECTIVE

Precisely define the line-items in the balance sheet statement of the project model, and write this list in column E of the Financial Statements sheet, after the cash flow statement from the previous step.

SPECIFICATION & BUILD

Figure 123 shows an illustrative balance sheet statement.

FIGURE 123: BALANCE SHEET STATEMENT EXAMPLE

		Formula
BS_1	Fixed Assets (1) - 25 Years & Over NBV Balance	... from Operations sheet
BS_2	Fixed Assets (2) - 10 To 25 Years NBV Balance	... from Operations sheet
BS_3	Fixed Assets (3) - Up To 10 Years NBV Balance	... from Operations sheet
BS_4	**Net Fixed Assets**	= SUM(BS_1:BS_3)
BS_5	Capitalised Interest & Fees Balance	... from Accounting sheet
BS_6	Capitalised Development Costs Balance	... from Accounting sheet
BS_7	Capitalised Issue Costs Balance	... from Accounting sheet
BS_8	**Total Fixed Assets**	= SUM(BS_4:BS_7)
BS_9	Trade Debtors Balance	... from Operations sheet
BS_10	VAT Balance	... from Tax sheet
BS_11	DSRA Balance	... from Finance sheet
BS_12	MRA Balance	... from Operations sheet
BS_13	TRA Balance	... from Tax sheet
BS_14	Retained Cash Balance	... from Finance sheet
BS_15	Insurance Prepayments Balance	... from Operations sheet
BS_16	**Total Current Assets**	= SUM(BS_9:BS_15)
BS_17	Trade Creditors Balance	... from Operations sheet
BS_18	Term Loan Interest Payable Balance	... from Finance sheet
BS_19	Su Debt Interest Payable Balance	... from Finance sheet
BS_20	Corporation Tax Payable Balance	... from Tax sheet
BS_21	Dividend Payable Balance	... from Finance sheet
BS_22	Deferred Tax Liability/(Asset) Balance	... from Tax sheet
BS_23	**Total Current Liabilities**	= SUM(BS_17:BS_22)
BS_24	**Net Current Assets / (Liabilities)**	= BS_16 + BS_23
BS_25	Term Loan Balance	... from Finance sheet
BS_26	Sub Debt Balance	... from Finance sheet
BS_27	**Net Assets**	= SUM(BS_24:BS_26)
BS_28	Share Capital Balance	... from Finance sheet
BS_29	Retained Earnings Balance	... from Finance sheet
BS_30	**Total Shareholders' Funds**	= SUM(BS_28:BS_29)

13. Define the tax statement (CORE)

OBJECTIVE

Precisely define the line-items in the tax statement of the project model, and write this list in column E of the Tax sheet under the heading 'Corporation Tax'.

SPECIFICATION & BUILD

Figure 124 shows an illustrative tax statement.

FIGURE 124: TAX STATEMENT EXAMPLE

		Formula
TC_1	Profit Before Tax	... from Financial Statements sheet
TC_2	Depreciation Of Fixed Assets 25 Years & Over POS	... from Operations sheet
TC_3	Depreciation Of Fixed Assets 10 To 25 Years POS	... from Operations sheet
TC_4	Depreciation Of Fixed Assets Up To 10 Years POS	... from Operations sheet
TC_5	Long Life Assets Tax Depreciation	... from Operations sheet
TC_6	Short Life Assets Tax Depreciation	... from Operations sheet
TC_7	Industrial Buildings Assets Tax Depreciation	... from Operations sheet
TC_8	**Taxable Profit Or Loss Before Losses Utilised (1)**	$= SUM(\ TC\_1{:}TC\_7\ )$
TC_9	Interest Earnings Accrued & Received NEG	... from Finance sheet
TC_10	Overdraft Interest Accrued & Paid NEG	... from Finance sheet
TC_11	**Taxable Profit Or Loss Before Losses Utilised (2)**	$= SUM(\ TC\_8{:}TC\_10\ )$
TC_12	Losses Utilised	... from Tax sheet
TC_13	**Taxable Profit Or Loss After Losses Utilised**	$= SUM(\ TC\_11{:}TC\_12\ )$
TC_14	Interest Earnings Accrued & Received	... from Finance sheet
TC_15	Overdraft Interest Accrued & Paid	... from Finance sheet
TC_16	**Taxable Profit Or Loss**	$= SUM(\ TC\_13{:}TC\_15\ )$
TC_17	Corporation Tax Due	... from Tax sheet

14. Build nine important flags as place-holders in the Time sheet (CORE)

OBJECTIVE

Specify and build nine base flags required to build the model.

SPECIFICATION & BUILD

Build all essential flags in temporary status in the Time sheet in the top half of the sheet under the main heading 'Flags'.

In summary, a temporary flag is built by creating a line-item with the properties in Table 4.

TABLE 4: PROPERTIES OF AN EXAMPLE CONCESSION FLAG

Name	Units	Totals	Time-dependent values	Non-time dependent values
Concession Flag	flag	Yes, insert sum of row	0 = off, 1 = on	n/a

Each flag will require an understanding of the dates in which it is active (i.e. has a value of 1) and the periods in which it is not active (i.e. will have a value of 0). Use the dates for the project specified in Step 1.

The fully-complete flag will be built by using the building block called **Time Flag** – see the FAST theory on Flags on pages 80 to 83.

Each Flag will have:

- one row
- flag name in column E
- units set as 'flag' in column I
- sum of the whole row in column J
- the values (1 or 0) on a yellow background in column L onwards.

Create these flags now:

- *Concession Flag* – set this at 1 for any period that is in the concession and 0 for all periods not in the concession
- *Actuals Flag* – set this at 1 for all actuals periods for which management accounts exist, 0 thereafter
- *Forecast Flag* – this is the reverse of the Actuals Flag, with 0 for the actuals periods and 1 for all remaining periods of the concession
- *First Forecast Period Flag* – set this flag at 1 for the first forecast period, 0 elsewhere

- *Last Actuals Period Flag* – set this at 1 for the last actuals period, 0 elsewhere
- *Term Loan Flag* – set this at 1 for all periods where the term loan is active, 0 elsewhere
- *Sub Debt Flag* – set this at 1 for all forecast periods of the concession
- *Amortisation Flag* – set this at 1 for all forecast periods of the concession
- *Tax Calculation Flag* – set this at 1 for all forecast periods of the concession.

15. Build place-holder indexation in the Time sheet (CORE)

OBJECTIVE

To create a time-dependent macro-economic indexation factor based on values taken from the FC model. This strip will be populated by place-holder inputs at this stage.

SPECIFICATION

Indexation needs to be ready to use before the construction of the operating calculations as it is an integral component of the build process. However, at this stage a place-holding strip of input values is sufficient. This step only requires the creation of dummy indices made up purely from inputs drawn from the FC model.

I consider only one index, the Retail Price Index. Some projects may use more complex indices made up of a basket of published indices so the specification here can serve as the basis for those calculations.

For the theory in this section see 'The Macro-Economy' on page 44 and 'Intersection and exclusion event flag' on page 81.

DESIGN

For this step the design is very simple. Each index should be a single row on the Time sheet.

BUILD

Create a single row for each index with the same values as used in the FC model. Prepare each for use throughout the model by colour-coding the indices as an export in red font.

RESULTS

Indices, each on a single row on the Time sheet.

16. Build the Actuals sheet (CORE)

OBJECTIVE

To create a new Actuals inputs sheet in an identical structure to the Financial Statements sheet.

SPECIFICATION

- Last Closing Balance Sheet Date
- Profit & loss and Cash Flow structure from the Financial Statements sheet
- Last closing balance sheet structure from the Financial Statements sheet.

DESIGN

No design issues.

BUILD

Carry out this build sequence:

1. Create a new sheet with the same structure as the financial statements sheet – to do this copy the sheet.
2. Colour the sheet yellow and place this sheet before the Time sheet and after the Inputs sheet.
3. Ignore the P&L and the CFW for the moment.
4. Using the timeline specification from '2. Define the timeline and periodicity of the new model' on page 152 create an input on the Inputs sheet with this name and date and call it 'Last Closing Balance Date'.
5. On the BS and excluding the sums of balances formulae, colour all the rows under the timeline a background yellow fill and compile the last closing balance sheet from the FC model.

RESULTS

A new Actuals sheet with the same structure as the Financial Statements sheet but with no values as yet.

17. Add the financial statement sheet values from the FC model in the actual periods of the new Actuals sheet (CORE)

OBJECTIVE

To add the actuals period financial statements, as values, from the FC model to the new operating model in the Actuals sheet.

For generic financial modellers, the historic financial statements referred to here can be interpreted as the historic financial statements of the enterprise/entity being modelled.

SPECIFICATION

This step requires adding the profit & loss, cash flow waterfall and the last closing balance sheet from the FC model to the Actuals sheet.

Since the overall objective is to first re-perform the FC model, the values in the financial statements that fall into the actuals period as defined in 'Define the timeline and periodicity of the new model' on page 152 should be copied into the Actuals sheet.

This step may take some time, but is absolutely vital.

So, the specification elements are:

- Last Closing Balance Date
- Historical P&L and CF financial statements from FC model
- Last Actual Closing Balance Sheet from the FC model.

DESIGN

No design issues.

BUILD

Carry out this build sequence:

1. Using the existing Actuals sheet as a format, collect the financial statement values from the FC model and compile the Actuals sheet actuals periods with these values

2. Make sure that the statements that are added to the Actuals sheet have basic internal integrity – i.e. they balance and the retained cash and retained profit values are consistent across statements.

RESULTS

The Actuals sheet with the FC model financial statements as actual inputs. In particular, the Actuals sheet will now contain the last closing balance sheet as well as the historical profit & loss and historical cash flow.

18. Build the Inputs_C sheet and populate it with the last closing balance sheet from the Actuals sheet (CORE)

OBJECTIVE

To create a new Inputs_C sheet with the last closing balance sheet in column input format and dependent on the Last Closing Balance Sheet Date input from the Inputs sheet.

For generic financial modellers, the last closing balance sheet referred to here can be interpreted as the last closing balance sheet of the enterprise/entity being modelled.

SPECIFICATION

- Actuals sheet
- Last Closing Balance Sheet Date.

DESIGN

The main design feature here is to create a sheet called Inputs_C which is to contain an identical column structure to the Inputs sheet except that it is to contain calculated inputs. There are two sets of calculated inputs: the last closing balance sheet that drives all balances in the model: and the technical inputs that tend to stay fixed.

So in design terms the Inputs_C sheet is identical in structure to the Inputs sheet but is static. It serves only to channel the last closing balance sheet from the Actuals sheet and to the rest of the model.

BUILD

Carry out this build sequence:

1. Create a new sheet with the same structure as the Inputs sheet by copying the Inputs sheet and renaming it Inputs_C

2. Clear out all inputs that came from the copy of the Inputs sheets

3. Import the Last Closing Balance Sheet date from the inputs sheet

4. As in Figure 125, in row 21 use a simple formula in the O21 to reference the date in F21 – the formula should be = F21

5. Create a space for the last closing balance sheet as in Figure 125

6. In column O from row 24 down write a formula and shade the cell grey, as in Figure 125

7. The formula in the grey shaded cells in O24 down should be = LOOKUP(O$21, Actuals!$L$3:$BD$3, Actuals!$L107:$BD107)

8. The last formula is in F24 down, which should reference the values in the O column.

FIGURE 125: INPUTS_C LAST CLOSING BALANCE SHEET STRUCTURE

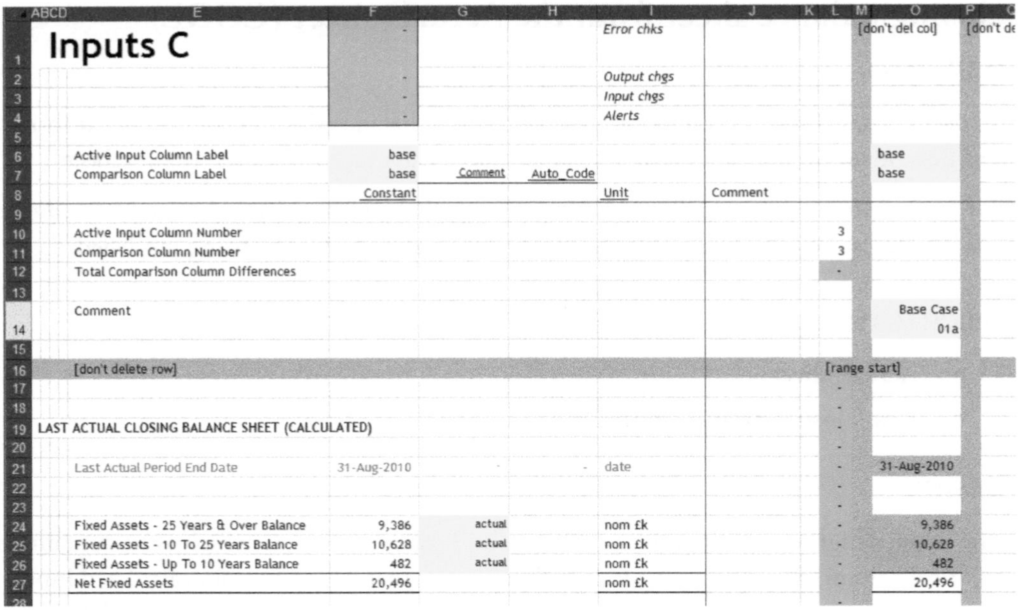

RESULTS

The result is the 'Inputs_C' sheet with the last closing balance sheet values in column F ready as quasi-inputs to be imported throughout the model as required.

19. Build retained earnings balance and retained cash balance in the Finance sheet (CORE)

OBJECTIVE

To create two balance corkscrews for the retained earnings brought forward and carried forward balance and the retained cash brought forward and carried forward balance, and paint these results into the financial statements sheet.

SPECIFICATION

At the bottom of the P&L and CF are the brought forward and carried forward balances for retained earnings and retained cash respectively. Each of these four items requires knowledge of the last closing balance and this requires some space, so they are best calculated at the bottom of the Finance sheet.

Specify the following inputs:

- Retained Earnings Last Closing Balance
- Net Profit In Period
- Retained Cash Last Closing Balance
- Net Cash In Period
- Forecast periods, Last actual period, First forecast period.

DESIGN

The design should incorporate a balance corkscrew and the usual colour-coding.

BUILD

Each of these corkscrews will have an opening balance in the first row of the corkscrew. These should not be linked for the moment but highlighted in yellow for future linking.

RESULTS

The following items are painted into the Financial Statements sheet:

- Retained Earnings Balance BEG in the Profit & Loss ... PL_26
- Retained Earnings Balance in the Profit & Loss ... PL_28
- Retained Earnings Balance in the Balance Sheet ... BS_29
- Retained Cash Balance BEG in the Cash Flow ... CF_37
- Retained Cash Balance in the Cash Flow ... CF_39
- Retained Cash Balance in the Balance Sheet ... BS_14

20. Create FS_Ref and FS_Diff sheets and populate the FS_Ref sheet with the values from the FC model (CORE)

OBJECTIVE

The immediate objective is to understand the line-by-line and period-by-period differences between the FC results and the results that we are building in the shadow operational model. In the longer term the objective is to have a detailed change analysis tool for the modeller.

For non-project finance financial modellers, the Ref and Diff sheets are invaluable tools for the financial analyst and should be built in any case, although not populated at this stage.

SPECIFICATION

The elements of this specification are the FC model financial statements in the format of the new model.

DESIGN

The two new sheets should be placed after the FS sheet.

BUILD

1. Copy the FS sheet to its right and call it FS_Ref.
2. Copy the FS sheet to the right of the FS_Ref sheet and call it FS_Diff.
3. Select all content below line 9 in the FS_Ref sheet and copy and then paste values in order to leave no formulae. Colour this whole selected area a light shade of blue to signify hard-coded input.
4. Select the first sum formula in column J of the FS_Diff sheet and create a formula that should reference the same cell in the FS sheet and take away the same cell in the FS_Ref sheet. Now select the cell J9 where this formula was written and copy it. Now select all cells from J9 along the whole row and all the way down to the last line of the balance sheet and copy the formula to all the selection using the ALT + E, S, F. The formatting will not change and all the formulae should give a result of zero.

RESULTS

Use the values from the Actuals sheet to populate the FS_Ref sheet. The objective is to populate the FS_Ref sheet so that the FS_Diff sheet will show the difference between the original FC model and this new model.

As the new model is built the modeller will be able to see the differences on a period-by-period and line-by-line basis and use this knowledge to hone the calculations in the new model.

21. Specify, design and build the operating revenues (CORE)

OBJECTIVE

Build the nominal operating revenues for the profit & loss of the project as per the FC model.

For non-project finance financial modellers, depending on the business being modelled, the operating revenues may be far more complex. However, the expected result is the same; operating revenues for the profit & loss.

SPECIFICATION

Multiply the real revenues by the appropriate index and flag in order to create the nominal revenues in the concession periods. There could also be other inputs particular to the industry in question to consider. The example in Figure 126 considers water flows as the volume element.

Figure 126 shows the formula syntax for operating revenues within one building block.

FIGURE 126: OPERATING REVENUES FORMULA SYNTAX

		Constant	Comment	Auto_Code	Unit	Total							
	Band 1 Indexed Operating Revenue	F	G	H	I	J	K	L	M	N	O	P
11	Band 1 Volume for the period ending June 2006	86,000,000	-		m3 p.a.								
12	Operating Revenue Index		-	-	index	-	-	1.0000	1.0000	1.0000	1.0250	1.0250
13	Band 1 Price	-			p / m3	-	-	-	-	-	11.12	11.56
14	Forecast Period Flag	-	-		flag	42	-	-	-	-	1	1
15	Band 1 Indexed Operating Revenue	-			nom £k	786,015		-		-	7,751	8,061

Notes on the syntax:

- The formula in cell O15 is = IF(O14 = 1, $F11 * O13 * O12, 0) / (100 * 1000)
- The units are 'p / m3' and 'm3 pa' and the periodicity is annual so the result must be converted to £ and then £k by dividing by 100 and then dividing by 1,000
- The IF statement makes sure the result is only active in the forecast periods of the model
- The $F10 makes sure that the reference for the non-time dependent annual water flow remains absolute as the formula is dragged across the row.

The operating revenues can sometimes be defined in two parts: the indexed portion and the un-indexed portion. At their simplest both can be a strip of real numbers defined by contract, with a defined index for the indexed portion. At the more complicated end the revenues can be defined as a product of volume multiplied by price. In this case the price is a tariff and will be either indexed or un-indexed.

In summary, the formulae would be:

indexed revenues = volume * tariff * index * flag

un-indexed revenues = volume * tariff * flag

The ingredients required for this step are:

- Volume, units of volume
- Tariff, units of tariff
- Index
- Forecast period flag (the active period).

DESIGN

There are no specific design issues.

BUILD

Carry out this build process:

1. Create a new section entitled Operating revenues on the Operations sheet
2. Collect the ingredients for the operating revenues as per the specification
3. Calculate the operating revenues as per the specification.

RESULTS

- Operating Revenues ... PL_1, +/+, flow

22. Specify, design and build the operating revenues received (CORE)

OBJECTIVE

Build the operating revenues received for the cash flow waterfall of the project as per the FC model.

For non-project finance financial modellers, to calculate the cash revenues medium to long-term strategic models will require a similar treatment as described here. Short-term operating models tend to deal with working capital issues in a much more detailed fashion. The extreme situation that deals only with working capital should do exactly and only that, and probably across a monthly or even weekly timeline.

SPECIFICATION

Operating Revenues Received is a function of the Indexed and un-indexed Operating Revenues defined previously. The Operating Revenues Received is delayed by the time it takes between the invoicing and the cash receipt.

The Trade Debtors Balance shows the amount of revenues that are accrued but not yet received in cash. The Operating Revenues increases this balance and the Operating Revenues Received decreases this balance. Furthermore, a standard calculation to deal with the trade debtors last closing balance is to assume that they are received in the first forecast period.

Figure 127 shows the blocks of calculations required to calculate a simple trade debtors balance based upon operating revenues and operating revenues received.

FIGURE 127: OPERATING REVENUES RECEIVED AND TRADE DEBTORS BALANCE

Operations		Error chks		01-Jan-09	01-Jul-09	01-Jan-10	01-Jul-10	01-Jan-11	01-Jul-11	01-Jan-12	01-Jul-12
Model Period Start		Output chgs		30-Jun-09	31-Dec-09	30-Jun-10	31-Dec-10	30-Jun-11	31-Dec-11	30-Jun-12	31-Dec-12
Model Period End		Input chgs		Actuals	Actuals	Actuals	Actuals	Forecast	Forecast	Forecast	Forecast
Actual vs Forecast		Alerts		2,009	2,009	2,010	2,010	2,011	2,011	2,012	2,012
Year # for Current Period's Financial Year End											
	Constant	Unit	Total								
OPERATING REVENUE RECEIVED & TRADE DEBTORS BALANCE											
Operating Revenue Received											
Current Period Operating Revenues Received	4	months									
Months per Model Period	6	months									
Previous Period Operating Revenues Received	2	months									
Forecast Period Flag	-	flag	27	-	-	-	-	1	1	1	1
Operating Revenue	PL	nom £k	444,981	-	-	-	-	9,178	9,436	9,699	9,970
Current Period Operating Revenues Received		nom £k	228,124	-	-	-	-	6,119	6,290	6,466	6,646
Previous Period Operating Revenues Received	1 PD LK BK	nom £k	108,667	-	-	-	-	-	3,059	3,145	3,233
Trade Debtors Balance BEG		nom £k		-	-	-	-	2,956	3,059	3,145	3,233
First Forecast Period Flag	-	flag	1	-	-	-	-	1			
Trade Debtors Balance BEG Received in First Forecast Period		nom £k	2,956	-	-	-	-	2,956			
Trade Debtors Balance BEG Received in First Forecast Period	-	nom £k	2,956	-	-	-	-	2,956	-	-	-
Current Period Operating Revenues Received	-	nom £k	228,124	-	-	-	-	6,119	6,290	6,466	6,646
Previous Period Operating Revenues Received	1 PD LK BK	nom £k	108,667	-	-	-	-	-	3,059	3,145	3,233
Operating Revenue Received	CF	nom £k	339,747	-	-	-	-	9,075	9,350	9,611	9,880
Trade Debtors Balance											
Closing Trade Debtors Balance	2,956	nom £k									
Last Closing Balance Flag	-		-	-	-	-	1	-	-	-	-
Trade Debtors Balance BEG		nom £k		-	-	-	-	2,956	3,059	3,145	3,233
Plus: Operating Revenue	PL	nom £k	444,981	-	-	-	-	9,178	9,436	9,699	9,970
Less: Operating Revenue Received	CF	nom £k	339,747	-	-	-	-	9,075	9,350	9,611	9,880
Trade Debtors Balance	BS	nom £k		-	-	-	2,956	3,059	3,145	3,233	3,323

Specify the following inputs:

- Indexed Operating Revenues

- Un-indexed Operating Revenues

- Percentage (sometimes expressed as 'months/model periodicity in months') of Operating Revenues received in current period (called p0)

- Percentage of Operating Revenues received in next period (called p1) – (also calculated as 100% - % received in p0)

- Trade Debtors Opening Balance

- Trade Debtors Opening Balance Date

- Forecast periods, Last actual period, First forecast period.

ISSUES

For a PFI project company, operating revenues are received in cash not long after they are logged in the profit and loss. It is normally a matter of days. However, for other types of company the lag between the profit and loss operating revenues and the cash receipt of these can be substantial. The modeller has to decide how to deal with this working capital issue and the solution may be the introduction of Percentage of 'Operating Revenues received in p2', or for periods further out.

DESIGN

The design has largely been achieved as shown in Figure 127, although this can be expanded for more revenue lines.

BUILD

Consider these points first:

- For simplicity consider the un-indexed and indexed revenues added together as one.
- This build process is very useful for many other similar situations so it is well worth understanding properly.
- The build sequence requires that the balance corkscrew be partially built before the calculation to pay the opening debtors balance in the first forecast period.
- The last step is to populate the trade debtors balance corkscrew with the revenues and the received revenues.
- The revenues increase the balance and the received revenues decrease the balance.
- The build sequence is therefore different from the layout sequence.

Carry out this build sequence, and refer to the section 'The modelling sheets' on page 75 for help on the building blocks:

1. Create a new section entitled Operating Revenues Received in the Operating revenues section on the Operations sheet.
2. Use the building block called Factor Allocator to calculate the value of the current period accrued paid in the current period, including the amount of the brought forward trade debtors balance that is also paid in the current period.
3. Use the building block called Factor Allocator to calculate the value of the current period accrued paid in the subsequent period.
4. Use the building block called Balance Corkscrew to calculate the amount of the forecast trade debtors balance.
5. Use the building block called Balance Allocator to calculate the value of the trade debtors balance paid in the current period.
6. Use the building block called Simple Sum to add together the three paid amounts.
7. Compile the total from the simple sum into the trade debtors balance in the 'Less' line so that the values deduct from the balance.

RESULTS

See the next step to compile these results into the financial statements. In summary, the results in this step are:

- Operating Revenues ... PL_1, +/+, flow
- Operating Revenues Received ... CF_1, +/+, flow
- Trade Debtors Balance ... BS_ , +/+, balance.

23. Paint the revenues into the statements (CORE)

OBJECTIVE

The objective is to take a set of results to the financial statements while making sure that the balance sheet still balances after completing the task.

SPECIFICATION

The modeller will have to suspend judgement while performing the three separate links as the checks will show red during the process and only show green at the end.

This is the first stage of this very important process – it is vital to understand it, as it will be repeated many times over. The three results (in red font EXPORT format) to paint in the financial statements are:

1. Operating Revenues ... PL_1, +/+, flow
2. Operating Revenues Received ... CF_1, +/+, flow
3. Trade Debtors Balance ... BS_9 , +/+, balance.

DESIGN

There are no design issues for this step.

BUILD

Build the three results into the financial statements:

1. Paint the Operating Revenues into the PL
2. Paint the Operating Revenues Received in the CF
3. Paint the Trade Debtors Balance in the BS.

This allows the BS to show the balance of Operating Revenues in the retained earnings balance and the balance of the Operating Revenues Received in the retained cash balance, while reporting the unpaid revenues in the Trade Debtors Balance.

1. Start in the PL_1 and PL_2 and start in column E by calling up the two Operating Revenues from the Operation sheet, also in column E. Proceed to do the same for the Operating Revenues Received and the Trade Debtors Balance.

2. There is no particular order to respect as long as all three references are carried out.

For further details on *painting* in general terms see '19. Paint the exports into the financial statements' on page 232.

RESULTS

The result of this step is balanced financial statements with Operating Revenues, Operating Revenues Received and Trade Debtors Balance compiled in the financial statements.

24. Specify, design and build the operating costs (CORE)

OBJECTIVE

To define and build the nominal operating costs of the project as per the FC model.

SPECIFICATION

Operating Costs can include various categories of cost. I deal with two here: operating costs and director's fees due. Other costs can be dealt with in the same way.

These costs should be relatively simple to define as they will divide into two categories: those that require indexation and those that don't. The indexed costs will be calculated as a real component multiplied by an index.

The specification items are:

- Operating cost in real terms
- Director's fees in real terms
- Index for operating costs
- Index for director's fees
- Active periods flag.

DESIGN

Each of the costs should follow a very simple design. The ordered elements in the design are:

- Cost in real terms as a positive value
- Index
- Cost in nominal terms as a positive value
- Cost in nominal terms as a negative value for the financial statements

BUILD

For each cost carry out the following build sequence:

1. Create a new section in the Operations sheet called Operating Costs
2. Collect all the specified ingredients
3. Carry out the calculation in the row beneath the ingredients.

RESULTS

- Operating Cost ... PL_3, +/-, flow
- Director's Fees Due ... PL_4, +/-, flow.

25. Specify, design and build the operating costs paid (CORE)

OBJECTIVE

To build the operating costs paid as per the FC model.

SPECIFICATION

Operating Costs Paid is a function of the Indexed and un-indexed Operating Costs defined previously. The Operating Costs Paid is delayed by the time it takes from the invoicing to the payment of the invoice.

This balance shows the amount of accrued but as yet unpaid costs. The Operating Costs increases this balance and the Operating Costs Paid decreases this balance.

The specification elements are:

- Indexed and un-indexed Operating Costs
- Percentage of Operating Costs paid in current period (called p0)
- Percentage of Operating Costs paid in next period (called p1)
- Percentage of Operating Costs paid in period after next period (called p2)
- Last closing Trade Debtors Balance
- Last Closing Balance Sheet Date and Flag
- As a note on the above, the percentages should add up to 100% otherwise some Operating Costs will never be paid
- Active periods
- Calculated as a positive number(s), used in FS as a negative number(s).

ISSUES

For most companies, operating costs are paid in cash according to their type and the underlying contract. There are two possible solutions to dealing with this working capital issue, although in this step I only deal with the simple version of the first solution.

Solution 1 is to introduce as many 'Percentage of Operating Costs paid in period pi' as necessary to effectively delay the payment of operating costs to reflect reality. This is similar to the solution suggested for the working capital issue of operating revenues.

Solution 2 is to introduce an ongoing creditor balance. This will be based upon the period in question and the deeper understanding of the timing of the payment of the operating costs. For example, the project company could expect to have a creditor balance (unpaid operating costs) of a certain level in a February period end and a different balance in an August period end, and then expect these balances in a cyclical pattern thereafter. This solution is balance-driven. This means the modeller must set an input balance strip for the whole timeline of the project and calculate the cash from the balance and the profit and loss operating costs. The input balance must also reflect the fact that it is likely to increase over time due to the indexation effect.

DESIGN

The design should be simple. For each of the costs the ordered elements are:

- Cost in nominal terms as a positive value
- Paid cost in nominal terms as a positive value
- Paid cost in nominal terms as a negative value for the financial statements
- Trade creditors balance.

BUILD

Carry out this build sequence:

1. Create a new section within Operating Costs on the Operations sheet and call it Operating Costs Paid
2. Assemble the ingredients:
   - Costs
   - Percentage of Operating Costs paid in current period (called p0)
   - Percentage of Operating Costs paid in next period (called p1)
   - Percentage of Operating Costs paid in period after next period (called p2)
3. Calculate the costs paid in current period, next period and the period after that
4. Create the trade creditors balance standard 7-line balance corkscrew

5. Add some lines beneath the costs paid calculations and use the trade creditors opening balance as a counter flow to calculate the opening costs balance paid

6. Add together the four costs paid lines to create one single costs paid line as a positive value

7. Create the costs paid as a negative value for the financial statements

8. Add operating costs and operating costs paid to the balance corkscrew to calculate the trade creditors balance.

RESULTS

- Operating Cost Paid ... CF_3, +/-, flow
- Directors Fees Paid ... CF _4, +/-, flow
- Trade Creditors Balance ... BS_17, +/+, balance.

26. Specify, design and build the capital expenditure (CORE)

Capital Expenditure is normally defined as the capital costs during construction and as such should be present as actuals in the Cash Flow statement relating to the construction period. For capital costs during the operational phase of the project see Life Cycle Expenditure in the next section.

This will already have been done in the FC model. You will need to emulate the allocation of the capital expenditure to the three fixed asset classes for both accounting and tax purposes.

27. Specify, design and build the life cycle expenditure (CORE)

OBJECTIVE

To define and build the nominal life cycle expenditure as per the FC model and paint the results into the financial statements.

SPECIFICATION

Life Cycle Expenditure is the ongoing capital maintenance costs incurred during the operational phase of the project. The life cycle costs are defined as a real time-dependent strip over the life of the project and are indexed to nominal values for the cash flow. Since they are a form of capital cost they are collected in a balance corkscrew and depreciated over the life of the project.

There is sometimes a distinction between Life Cycle Expenditure that can be treated as a straight operating cost and that which is treated as a capital cost as described above. The expensed portion behaves like any operating costs shown as accrued on the PL and in cash on the CF. The capital portion is instead treated as a capital cost with the associated depreciation on the PL, the cash on the CF and the accounting net book value reported on the BS.

The specification elements are:

- Life Cycle Expenditure (Expensed Portion) real profile
- Life Cycle Expenditure (Capital Portion) real profile
- Life Cycle Expenditure (Capital Portion) [nominal value] allocation to Fixed Assets (1), (2) or (3)
- Index
- Active periods
- Calculated as a positive number, used in FS as a negative number.

DESIGN

Set the information out in a simple, clear and progressive way.

BUILD

Carry out the following build sequence:

1. Create a new section called Life Cycle Expenditure on the Operations sheet for the build-up to nominal life cycle expenditure

2. Create a new section called Fixed Assets on the Accounting sheet for the accounting depreciation and net book value calculations

3. Allocate the real life cycle expenditure values to be expensed and capitalised

4. Prepare the expensed portion of LCE for the financial statements by flipping its sign

5. Allocate the capitalised portion of the LCE to the three fixed asset groups

6. For each asset group create an asset balance corkscrew on the Fixed Assets section on the Accounting sheet

7. For each asset group calculate the accounting depreciation and reference this line into the asset balance corkscrew

8. For both portions of the life cycle expenditure calculate the life cycle expenditure paid (which may be the same) and take both the expenditure and the expenditure paid to the Trade Creditors Balance on the Operations sheet in the same way as in Step 24 on page 180.

9. Paint the results into the financial statements.

RESULTS

- Life Cycle Expenditure (Expensed Portion) ... PL_5, +/-, flow
- Life Cycle Expenditure (Expensed Portion) Paid ... CF_9, +/-, flow
- Life Cycle Expenditure (Capital Portion) Paid ... CF_10, +/-, flow
- Fixed Assets (1) – 25 Years & Over Balance ... BS_1, +/+, balance
- Fixed Assets (2) – 10 To 25 Years Balance ... BS_2, +/+, balance
- Fixed Assets (3) – Up To 10 Years Balance ... BS_3, +/+, balance
- Depreciation Of Fixed Assets (1) – 25 Years & Over ... PL_7, +/-, flow
- Depreciation Of Fixed Assets (2) – 10 To 25 Years ... PL_8, +/-, flow
- Depreciation Of Fixed Assets (3) – Up To 10 Years ... PL_9, +/-, flow.

OTHER MATTERS

Sub-results, accounting and working capital effect

- Fixed Assets (1) – 25 Years & Over Basis Balance
- Fixed Assets (2) – 10 To 25 Years Basis Balance
- Fixed Assets (3) – Up To 10 Years Basis Balance.

Accounting effect

- Life Cycle Expenditure (Capital Portion) Paid increases the Fixed Assets Balance reported on the balance sheet
- Depreciation of the Fixed Assets Basis Balances (1), (2) and (3) reduces the Fixed Assets Balances (1), (2) and (3)
- Depreciation of the Fixed Assets Basis Balances (1), (2) and (3) is charged (as a cost) to the PL.

Working capital effect

- Difference between Life Cycle Expenditure (Expensed Portion) and Life Cycle Expenditure (Expensed Portion) Paid requires calculation, although often the accounting value is assumed to equal the paid value.
- Trade Creditors Balance will carry the accrued expenses that are yet to be paid, if any.

28. Specify, design and build the maintenance reserve account (CORE)

OBJECTIVE

To define and build the maintenance reserve account as per the FC model and paint the results into the financial statements.

SPECIFICATION

Otherwise known as the Life Cycle Reserve Account this normally works using the target balance method combined with a look-forward calculation.

The flow in question is the Life Cycle Expenditure Paid in its entirety over time. The target balance for the reserve is calculated in y_0 by taking the sum of a fixed %y_i multiplied by the Life Cycle Expenditure Paid in y_i for each of the defined years. The defined years are normally four, so i=1 to 4. The result is that the target balance starts to increase in the years prior to expenditure and decrease in the years immediately after expenditure. However, it fulfils the need to have a cash reserve put aside for this expenditure.

The deposits into the MRA are defined as the difference between the opening MRA balance and the target MRA balance.

The withdrawals from the MRA are defined to be equal to the Life Cycle expenditure.

The specification elements are:

- Target MRA definition in terms of future Life Cycle Expenditure Paid
- Life Cycle Expenditure Paid in p1, p2, p3, p4, p5, p6, p7, p8, p9, p10
- Last closing MRA Balance
- Last Closing Balance Sheet Date and Flag
- MRA Balance BEG
- Active periods.

DESIGN

Arrange the logic so that the balance corkscrew and check are the last pieces of logic. The target balance calculation should be the first, followed by the deposits and withdrawals calculations that use counter flow opening balances from the final piece of logic, the balance.

BUILD

Carry out the following build sequence:

1. Create a new section called Maintenance Reserve Account at the bottom of the Operations sheet
2. Collect the ingredients as specified

3. Create sub-sections called:
   - Target MRA balance
   - MRA Deposits
   - MRA Withdrawals
   - MRA Balance
4. Collect the ingredients for the target MRA balance calculations and carry out these calculations
5. Create the MRA balance corkscrew
6. Collect the target MRA balance and the MRA Balance BEG and calculate whether a deposit or a withdrawal is required
7. Add the deposits and withdrawals into the MRA Balance corkscrew
8. Paint the results into the financial statements.

RESULTS

- MRA Deposits ... CF_24, +/-, flow
- MRA Withdrawals ... CF_25, +/+, flow
- MRA Balance ... BS_12, +/+, balance.

29. Specify, design and build insurance prepayments (CORE)

OBJECTIVE

To define and build the insurance prepayments as per the FC model and paint the results into the financial statements.

SPECIFICATION

Most insurance contracts require annual payments in advance that will accrue over the subsequent year.

Insurance prepayments are one example of cash payments that precede the receipt of the service, in this case insurance. The result is that the payments made in advance of the accounting effect are held accounted for as an asset on the balance sheet.

The specification elements are:

- Insurance prepayment schedule
- Insurance prepayment period
- Last closing Insurance Prepayments Balance
- Last Closing Balance Sheet Date and Flag
- Active periods.

DESIGN

There is nothing unusual in the design of insurance prepayments. The components for this are the nominal insurance prepayments, the insurance cost and finally the balance corkscrew that takes account of the timing difference.

BUILD

1. Create a new section called Insurance Prepayments within the Operating Costs section on the Operations sheet.
2. Calculate the nominal prepayments as a POS and add to Operating Costs Paid.
3. Calculate the nominal insurance cost as a POS and add to Operating Costs.
4. Create a classic 7-line balance corkscrew and add the insurance prepayments POS and deduct the insurance cost POS.
5. Paint the result into the financial statements.

RESULTS

- Insurance Prepayments … CF_3, as part of Operating Costs Paid, +/-, flow
- Insurance Cost … PL_3 as part of Operating Costs , +/-, flow
- Insurance Prepayments Balance … BS_20, +/+, balance.

30. Specify, design and build VAT (CORE)

OBJECTIVE

Calculate VAT on chargeable items such as operating revenues and operating costs as per the FC model, and paint the two resulting VAT line-items into the financial statements.

SPECIFICATION

The cash flow waterfall will be affected by the cash effect of having to pay and receive VAT on behalf of the government. A company is VAT neutral – i.e. all VAT paid by companies is refunded and all VAT collected by companies is passed on to the government. Since companies can recover the VAT they spend they effectively are not paying it. This means they are acting as a collection service for the government and the overall effect of VAT on a company is of the timing of cash.

VAT is calculated as a fixed percentage of a base of income subject to VAT and another base of expenditure subject to VAT.

VAT is currently 20% on VAT-rated sales. This means that income is subject to VAT, as is expenditure. Only insurance and staff costs are exempt from VAT. PFI revenues are normally VAT-exempt.

The standard way to model VAT is to assume to affect the cash flow waterfall with only the VAT net effect as an independent calculation, rather than associate VAT with every cash flow.

In the UK, HMRC require quarterly VAT returns that are lagged by a little over one month. This means that all VAT flows for July, August and September are considered in the VAT return at the end of October, effectively meaning that the October VAT flows will be considered in the subsequent VAT return. For the model this means that the VAT balance will always have the current month of flows sitting on it, whether the model is quarterly or semi-annual.

The specification elements are:

- List of revenues subject to VAT
- List of expenditure subject to VAT
- Days Of Previous Period VAT Reclaimed
- Days In Model Period On A 365.25 Days Basis (182.625 for a semi-annual model and 91.3125 for a quarterly model)
- Last closing VAT (To Reclaim) Balance
- Last Closing Balance Sheet Date and Flag
- VAT Rate (%)
- Active periods.

DESIGN

As in most model design situations the first steps are to collect multi-line groups of ingredients and distil them to single-line effects. The multi-line groups are the revenues and then the costs that are subject to VAT. Following all the flow calculations the balance corkscrew is at the bottom of the VAT section on the Tax sheet.

Considering revenues for most PFI projects are not subject to VAT, the VAT balance in question is the VAT to reclaim balance driven entirely by the VAT paid on the operating costs.

BUILD

1. Create a section called VAT at the top of the Tax sheet
2. Calculate the VAT received from the revenues received that are subject to VAT
3. Calculate the VAT paid from the operating costs paid that are subject to VAT
4. Calculate the Net VAT (Received) / Paid On Revenues And Costs in the period by taking the VAT received on revenues away from the VAT paid (as a POS) on the costs

5. Calculate the Current Period VAT Reclaimed / (Paid) by multiplying Net VAT Reclaimed/(Paid) in the current period by { 1 - Days Of Previous Period VAT Reclaimed/ Days In Model Period On A 365.25 Days Basis }. This is = 1 - 31 / 182.265 for a semi-annual model and = 1 - 31 / 91.3125 for a quarterly model

6. Calculate the Previous Period VAT Reclaimed / (Paid) by multiplying Net VAT Reclaimed/(Paid) in the previous period by { Days Of Previous Period VAT Reclaimed/ Days In Model Period On A 365.25 Days Basis }. This is = 31 / 182.265 for a semi-annual model and = 31 / 91.3125 for a quarterly model

7. Create the VAT balance corkscrew and allow for three sandwiched items

8. Calculate the VAT Reclaimed (Paid), above the VAT balance corkscrew, in the last forecast period by using the last forecast period flag and the VAT (To Reclaim) Balance BEG as a counter flow

9. Add some more rows above the VAT balance corkscrew to VAT Reclaimed / (Paid) which is the sum of:
   - Current Period VAT Reclaimed / (Paid)
   - Previous Period VAT Reclaimed / (Paid)
   - VAT Reclaimed (Paid) in the last forecast period

10. Calculate Net VAT Reclaimed / (Paid) (this is one of the two results of this section) as:
    - VAT Reclaimed (Paid)
    - Less: Net VAT (Received) / Paid On Revenues And Costs

11. Now compile the three rows in the VAT balance corkscrew to complete the balance calculation:
    - Plus: VAT Paid On Costs POS
    - Less: VAT Received On Revenues
    - Less: VAT Reclaimed / (Paid)

12. The suggested order of the components is:
    - VAT Received On Revenues
    - VAT Paid On Costs
    - Net VAT (Received) / Paid On Revenues And Costs
    - Current Period VAT Reclaimed / (Paid)
    - Previous Period VAT Reclaimed / (Paid)
    - Last Forecast Period VAT Reclaimed / (Paid)
    - VAT Reclaimed / (Paid)
    - Net VAT Reclaimed / (Paid)
    - VAT To Reclaim Balance (called VAT Balance)

13. Paint the results into the financial statements.

RESULTS

- Net VAT Reclaimed / (Paid) … CF_12, +/-, flow
- VAT Balance … BS_10, +/+, balance

31. Specify, design and build capitalised interest and fees amortisation (CORE)

OBJECTIVE

For purely accounting purposes, to define and build the amortisation of the balance of capitalised interest and fees as per the FC model, and paint the results into the financial statements.

SPECIFICATION

The amortisation charge is not tax-deductible as the interest and fees will also have been included in the long-term and short-term assets for which the tax depreciation is allowed for tax purposes.

If the capitalised interest and fees are mostly funded by the term loan then the project company will amortise these fees over the life of the term loan.

The specification elements are:

- Amortisation life, in years
- Last closing Capitalised Interest & Fees Balance
- Last Closing Balance Sheet Date and Flag
- Active periods
- Calculated as a positive number, used in FS as a positive number.

DESIGN

Amortisation construct with opening balance counter flow followed by the balance corkscrew.

BUILD

1. Create the Capitalised Interest & Fees Balance section on the Accounting sheet
2. Add some rows above the balance corkscrew and use the opening balance as a counter flow to calculate the amortisation of the balance in line with the life of the term loan
3. Paint the results into the financial statements.

RESULTS

- Capitalised Interest & Fees Amortisation ... PL_11, +/-, flow
- Capitalised Interest & Fees Balance ... BS_5, +/+, balance

32. Specify, design and build development costs amortisation

OBJECTIVE

For purely accounting purposes, to define and build the amortisation of the balance of capitalised development costs as per the FC model, and paint the results into the financial statements.

SPECIFICATION

In fact the amortisation charge is not tax-deductible as the interest and fees will have also been included in the long-term and short-term assets for which the tax depreciation is allowed for tax purposes.

If the capitalised development costs are mostly funded by term loan then the project company will amortise these costs over the life of the term loan.

The specification elements are:

- Amortisation life, in years
- Last closing Capitalised Development Costs Balance
- Last Closing Balance Sheet Date and Flag
- Active periods
- Calculated as a positive number, used in FS as a positive number.

DESIGN

Amortisation construct with opening balance counter flow followed by the balance corkscrew.

BUILD

1. Create the Capitalised Development Costs Balance section on the Accounting sheet
2. Add some rows above the balance corkscrew and use the opening balance as a counter flow to calculate the amortisation of the balance in line with the life of the term loan
3. Paint the results into the financial statements.

RESULTS

- Capitalised Development Costs Amortisation ... PL_12, +/-, flow
- Capitalised Development Costs Balance ... BS_6, +/+, balance

33. Specify, design and build issue costs amortisation

OBJECTIVE

For purely accounting purposes, to define and build the amortisation of the balance of capitalised issue costs as per the FC model, and paint the results into the financial statements.

SPECIFICATION

In fact the amortisation charge is not tax-deductible as the interest and fees will have also been included in the long-term and short-term assets for which the tax depreciation is allowed for tax purposes.

The specification elements are:

- Amortisation life, in years
- Capitalised Interest & Fees Balance @ Last Closing Balance Sheet Date
- Last Closing Balance Sheet Flag
- Active periods
- Calculated as a positive number, used in FS as a positive number.

DESIGN

Amortisation construct with opening balance counter flow followed by the balance corkscrew.

BUILD

1. Create the Capitalised Issue Costs Balance section on the Accounting sheet
2. Add some rows above the balance corkscrew and use the opening balance as a counter flow to calculate the amortisation of the balance in line with the life of the term loan
3. Paint the results into the financial statements.

RESULTS

- Capitalised Issue Costs Amortisation ... PL_13, +/-, flow
- Capitalised Issue Costs Balance ... BS_7, +/+, balance

34. Specify, design and build the term loan repayment (CORE)

OBJECTIVE

To calculate the Term Loan Repayment amount for the cash flow waterfall as per the FC model and paint the results into the financial statements.

SPECIFICATION

Term Loan Repayment is a fixed set of repayment amounts on the Term Loan set by contract. Each future repayment is deducted from the Term Loan Balance BEG to give the Term Loan Balance for each period.

The specification elements are:

- Term Loan Repayment time-dependent nominal profile
- Last closing Term Loan Balance
- Date of last closing balance sheet
- Active periods.

DESIGN

Two chunks of logic with the balance corkscrew in second place.

BUILD

1. Create a section called Term Loan Repayment within the Senior debt section on the Finance sheet
2. Calculate the term loan repayments in both positive and negative
3. Create the Term Loan Balance corkscrew section and deduct the positive repayments
4. Paint the results into the financial statements.

RESULTS

- Term Loan Repayment ... CF_22, +/-, flow
- Term Loan Balance ... BS_25, +/+, balance

35. Specify, design and build the term loan interest and balance (CORE)

OBJECTIVE

To calculate the Term Loan Interest amount and the Term Loan Interest Payable Balance, as per the FC model, and paint the results into the financial statements.

SPECIFICATION

Term Loan Interest is defined as the all-in interest rate percentage per period multiplied by the Term Loan Balance outstanding in that period.

The all-in interest rate in any one period is defined as the sum of the interest rate components made up of the margin, the base rate (whether swapped or not) and the MLAs.

The balance outstanding in any period is most often assumed to be the opening balance in that period.

The Term Loan Interest Paid is again defined by contract and can be delayed with respect to the Term Loan Interest. In this case the timing difference creates the need for a reported Term Loan Interest Payable Balance on the balance sheet.

This depends on the periodicity of the model. In the example of a semi-annual model it may be assumed that the accounting interest is equal to the paid interest, therefore creating a zero payable balance.

The specification elements are:

- Term Loan Margin Interest Rate (%pa)
- Term Loan Base Interest Rate (%pa)
- Term Loan Swapped Interest Rate (%pa)
- Term Loan MLAs (%pa)
- Term Loan Balance BEG
- Term Loan Interest Payable Balance @ Last Closing Balance Sheet Date
- Last Closing Balance Sheet Flag
- Active periods.

DESIGN

- Generally the interest on a loan balance is calculated after or below the calculations for the balance (as described in the previous step) so as to avoid unnecessary counter flows.
- Generally the accounting interest is set to be equal to the interest paid.

BUILD

1. Create a section called Term Loan Interest within the senior debt section on the Finance sheet.

2. Calculate the all-in-interest rate per period of calculation first from its component ingredients.

3. Calculate the interest on the brought forward loan balance for each period.

4. Calculate the interest paid as the sum of the brought forward balance and the interest accrued in each period – this will/could mean the first forecast period has proportionately more interest being paid than other forecast periods.

5. Using a balance corkscrew calculate the interest payable balance from the opening payable balance, the addition of the interest and the deduction of the interest paid (although this may be zero for the whole forecast period).

6. Paint the results into the financial statements.

RESULTS

- Term Loan Interest ... PL_16, +/-, flow
- Term Loan Interest Paid ... CF_21, +/-, flow
- Term Loan Interest Payable Balance ... BS_18, +/+, balance.

36. Specify, design and build the debt service reserve account (DSRA) (CORE)

OBJECTIVE

To calculate the Debt Service Reserve Account balance, inclusive of deposits and withdrawals as per the FC model, and paint the results into the financial statements.

SPECIFICATION

The DSRA is normally calculated using the target balance method. The DSRA target balance is normally defined as the value of the next six months of debt service (interest + repayments) on the term loan as calculated by the model.

DSRA deposits and withdrawals are defined by comparing the opening DSRA balance and the calculated target balance. If the opening DSRA balance is lower the difference is the DSRA deposit and this replenishes the DSRA balance and is taken out of the Cash Flow. However, if the opening DSRA balance contains more than the target balance then the difference is withdrawn from the DSRA reserve and becomes a positive flow in the Cash Flow.

The calculation means that there is either a deposit or a withdrawal, but not both together, in any one period.

The specification elements are:

- Target DSRA Balance definition in terms of future Debt Service
- Debt Service = Term Loan Interest Paid + Term Loan Repayment
- Debt Service in periods p1, p2, p3 and p4

- Last closing DSRA Balance
- Date of last closing balance sheet
- DSRA Balance BEG
- Active periods.

DESIGN

- Set the calculation blocks out in this order: target balance, target deposit/withdrawal, deposits, withdrawals, balance
- The only counter flow should be the use of the DSRA balance brought forward for the calculation of the target deposit/withdrawal.

BUILD

1. Create a section called DSRA on the Finance sheet, below the Senior debt section.
2. Collect the debt service ingredients and add them together as positives.
3. Calculate the target DSRA balance by looking forward in each period at the debt service.
4. Create the DSRA balance corkscrew with its opening balance in a classic 7-line construct.
5. Calculate the target deposit/withdrawal from the target balance and the DSRA balance BEG.
6. Insert rows above the DSRA balance and add the deposits and withdrawals sections based upon the target calculations.
7. Add the deposits and withdrawals to the DSRA balance corkscrew.
8. Paint the results into the financial statements.

RESULTS

- DSRA Deposits ... CF_17, +/-, flow
- DSRA Withdrawals ... CF_18, +/+, flow
- DSRA Balance ... BS_11, +/+, balance.

37. Specify, design and build the subordinated debt (part 1)

OBJECTIVE

To build the interest calculation on the subordinated debt and the subordinated debt balance but excluding repayment as per the FC model, and paint into the financial statements.

SPECIFICATION

Subordinated Debt Interest is calculated by multiplying the coupon percentage per period by the outstanding balance in the period. The interest is always calculated and if unpaid it is capitalised into a separate balance to be paid when possible. The paid interest is subject to the cash available constraint. The interest is tax deductible.

Subordinated Debt Interest Payable Balance is defined to hold all the interest that is as yet unpaid. Subordinated Debt Interest adds to this balance and Subordinated Debt Interest Paid is deducted from this balance.

In each new forecast period the interest paid is the addition of the new interest and the balance of interest payable, subject to cash available.

The cash available for payment of any subordinated debt interest is the imported counter flow reference from the cash flow waterfall.

The specification elements are:

- Subordinated Debt Coupon (Interest Rate) (%pa)
- Subordinated Debt Balance BEG
- Subordinated Debt Interest Payable Balance @ Last Closing Balance Sheet Date
- Cash Available For Sub Debt
- Last Closing Balance Sheet Flag
- Active periods.

DESIGN

Part 1 of the subordinated debt build is to calculate the interest in order to have this ready for the tax calculation which follows. The repayment of the subordinated debt is a separate exercise and best left until later when the project cash flows available are clearer. So the design premise is to split the subordinated debt build into two sections, before and after the corporation tax build.

Further:

- Generally the interest on a loan balance is calculated after or below the calculations for the balance (as described in the previous step) so as to avoid unnecessary counter flows.
- Generally the accounting interest is set to be equal to the interest paid.

BUILD

1. Create a section called Subordinated Debt on the Finance sheet.
2. Calculate the all-in-interest-rate per period of calculation first from its component ingredients (this may be a single annual coupon rate).

3. Create a balance corkscrew at the foot of the subordinated debt section on the Finance sheet and call in the Subordinated Debt Balance.

4. Calculate the interest on the brought forward loan balance for each period.

5. Calculate the interest paid as the sum of the brought forward balance and the interest in each period – this will/could mean the first forecast period has proportionately more interest being paid than other forecast periods.

6. Using a balance corkscrew calculate the interest payable balance from the opening payable balance, the addition of the accounting interest and the deduction of the interest paid (although this may be zero for the whole forecast period).

7. Paint the results into the financial statements.

RESULTS

- Subordinated Debt Balance ... BS_26, +/+, balance
- Subordinated Debt Interest ... PL_17, +/-, flow
- Subordinated Debt Interest Paid ... CF_30, +/-, flow
- Subordinated Debt Interest Payable Balance ... BS_19, +/+, balance.

38. Specify, design and build the tax depreciation or writing down allowances (CORE)

OBJECTIVE

To build the tax depreciation on the assets allowed for tax purposes as per the FC model.

SPECIFICATION

The tax calculation uses tax depreciation as opposed to accounting depreciation. Tax depreciation is calculated only on the assets that are allowed for tax, which are a subset of the accounting assets.

- Tax depreciation is similar in calculation to accounting depreciation except that the amortisation method differs
- Tax depreciation is calculated on a reducing balance basis in the UK
- Each year the written down value of the asset is further written down by the allowed amount.

The specification elements are:

- Tax Asset Class Writing Down Allowance (Annual Rate) (%pa)
- Tax Asset Class Written Down Balance BEG
- Last Closing Balance Sheet Flag
- Active periods.

DESIGN

The design is similar to that of accounting depreciation in structure with a balance corkscrew and depreciation of that balance. One fundamental difference is that there is no need for both the basis calculation and the balance calculation – only the balance calculation is required for the reducing balance amortisation method.

BUILD

1. Create a section called Tax Depreciation on the Tax sheet.
2. For each asset class calculate the allowed proportion from the brought forward balance and the additions.
3. Take this allowed proportion into a Writing Down Allowance Balance corkscrew for that asset.
4. Calculate the tax depreciation as a percentage of the WDA BEG balance.
5. Deduct the amortisation from the WDA balance.
6. Repeat this process for each of the asset classes.

SUB-RESULTS

- Tax Asset Class Written Down Balance … +/+, balance
- Tax Asset Class Writing Down Allowance … +/+, flow.

39. Specify, design and build corporation tax (CORE)

OBJECTIVE

To calculate all aspects of corporation tax as per the FC model and paint the results into the financial statements.

SPECIFICATION

Corporation Tax is calculated as a percentage of taxable profits of the corporation. The taxable profits of the corporation are derived by first taking the Profit before Tax (PBT) from the P&L and making some adjustments. However, trading and non-trading profits are taxed separately and only trading profits are subject to the adjustments.

The adjustments are divided into two types: those generic to all such calculations and those particular to the corporation in question.

The generic adjustments include taking into account any negative profits, or losses, in the same corporation, previously collected in the Tax Loss Balance. Other generic adjustments include adding back accounting depreciation and then deducting tax depreciation.

Particular adjustments vary from project to project.

The Corporation Tax rate percentage is multiplied by the taxable profit in the period on an annual basis and Corporation Tax Due is calculated.

Corporation Tax Payable is defined so as to hold all Corporation Tax Due but as yet unpaid. Corporation Tax Due increases the Dividends Payable Balance and Corporation Tax Paid decreases the Corporation Tax Payable Balance.

The specification elements are:

- Corporation Tax Rate (%)
- Profit / (Loss) Before Tax
- Depreciation Of Fixed Assets (1) – 25 Years & Over
- Depreciation Of Fixed Assets (2) – 10 To 25 Years
- Depreciation Of Fixed Assets (3) – Up To 10 Years
- Tax Depreciation Of Allowed Fixed Assets (1) – 25 Years & Over
- Tax Depreciation Of Allowed Fixed Assets (2) – 10 To 25 Years
- Tax Depreciation Of Allowed Fixed Assets (3) – Up To 10 Years
- Last closing Tax Loss Balance
- Last closing Corporation Tax Payable Balance
- Last closing balance sheet flag
- Corporation Tax Balance BEG
- Active periods.

DESIGN

The tax calculation follows the standard evolution from taxable profits, through utilised losses to the calculation of the actual accounting corporation tax. However, a good design feature is to include the deduction of any interest on cash income before utilising the losses available if the interest on cash income is included in the Profit before Tax from the P&L.

After utilising the losses the interest on cash income can be added back. The upshot of this is that the resultant taxable profit should tax the non-trading income (in this case the interest on cash income) even though the project may be creating losses on the trading side – this is fairly normal for the initial years of a PFI project.

BUILD

1. Create a section called Corporation Tax below the Tax Depreciation section on the Tax sheet
2. Create two standard 7-line balance corkscrews that will end up being pushed down to the bottom of this section called:

- Corporation Tax Loss Balance
- Corporation Tax Payable Balance

3. Calculate the Taxable Profit / (Loss) before Losses Utilised (1) by adding or deducting the items as listed in Figure 124.

4. Proceed to calculate Taxable Profit / (Loss) before Losses Utilised (2) by deducting any interest received on the cash account (or paid on overdrafts – this is not allowed for a PFI project)

5. Annualise the Taxable Profit / (Loss) before Losses Utilised (2) in the period when the annual tax calculation is to be calculated by looking back at the current year's profits

6. If the resultant annualised value is a loss, add this loss (as a positive value) to the Corporation Tax Loss Balance corkscrew

7. If the resultant annualised value is a profit then deduct the maximum losses (capped by the profits) from this profit available in the corporation tax loss balance and deduct these utilised losses from the corporation tax loss balance

8. Add annualised interest on cash income to these annualised profits

9. If following the utilisation of any of these losses and the subsequent addition of interest on cash income there remains an annual profit, then multiply this profit by the period corporation tax rate to calculate the corporation tax accrued

10. Corporation tax paid can be calculated by dividing the previous years' corporation tax accrued into the number of model periods in a year and paying these amounts the year after

11. The tax paid will play catch up on the tax due throughout the project so calculate that the last year of tax should be paid in the single period just after the end of the concession

12. Add corporation tax due to the corporation tax payable balance and deduct corporation tax paid from this same balance – both should be treated as positive numbers

13. Paint the results into the financial statements

RESULTS

- Corporation Tax Due ... PL_21, +/-, flow
- Corporation Tax Paid ... CF_15, +/+, flow
- Corporation Tax Payable Balance ... BS_20, +/+, balance

SUB-RESULTS

- Corporation Tax Losses ... +/+, flow
- Tax Depreciation ... +/+, flow
- Corporation Tax Losses Utilised ... +/+, flow
- Corporation Tax Loss Balance ... +/+, balance

40. Specify, design and build the tax reserve account

OBJECTIVE

To calculate the tax reserve results as per the FC model and paint the results into the financial statements.

SPECIFICATION

This reserve normally works using the target balance method combined with a look-forward calculation based upon a future corporation tax expenditure forecast at financial close.

The flow in question is Corporation Tax Paid in its entirety over time. The target balance for the reserve is calculated in $year_0$ by taking the sum of a fixed percentage year i multiplied by the Corporation Tax Paid in year i for each of the defined years. The result is that the target balance starts to increase in the years prior to expenditure and decrease in the years immediately after expenditure.

The deposits into the TRA are defined as the difference between the opening TRA balance and the target TRA balance.

The withdrawals from the TRA are defined to be equal to Corporation Tax Paid.

The specification elements are:

- Target TRA definition in terms of future Corporation Tax Paid at financial close
- Corporation Tax Paid in p1, p2, p3, p4, p5, p6, p7, p8, p9, p10 ... pn
- Last closing TRA Balance
- Last closing balance sheet flag
- TRA Balance BEG
- Active periods.

DESIGN

Target balance driven reserves work by first calculating the target balance and then checking in each period that the actual balance is at the level of the target. The upshot of this check is that either a deposit or a withdrawal, or neither, is required to achieve this.

BUILD

1. Create a section called TRA on the Tax sheet, below the Corporation Tax section.
2. Create the Tax Reserve balance standard 7-line corkscrew and allow for all the flow calculations to push this down as required.
3. Calculate the target balance above the tax reserve balance.
4. Calculate the tax reserve surplus/deficit as the difference between the actual balance and the target balance by adding and deducting these items:
   - Actual Tax Reserve balance
   - Less: Target Tax Reserve balance.
5. If the result is positive then the value is called a Tax Reserve Withdrawal and is a positive in the project cash flow and a deduction on the Tax Reserve Balance.
6. If the tax reserve surplus/deficit is negative then this is called a deposit and the positive is added to the tax reserve balance while deducting from the project cash flow as the Tax Reserve Deposit.
7. Paint the results into the financial statements.

RESULTS

- TRA Deposits ... CF_27, +/-, flow
- TRA Withdrawals ... CF_28, +/+, flow
- TRA Balance ... BS_13, +/+, balance

41. Specify, design and build interest on cash balances (CORE)

OBJECTIVE

Create the interest on cash calculations as per the FC model and report these on the financial statements.

SPECIFICATION

Interest On Cash Balances is defined as the product of a period market bank deposit rate and the total of all cash balances held by the project company. This includes cash reserves such as the DSRA, TRA and the MRA.

For simplicity this interest is best assumed to be paid as it is accrued thereby producing a net zero effect on the balance sheet. Also for simplicity, and to avoid unnecessary circularities, the opening cash balances are used rather than more complicated average cash balances.

The specification elements are:

- TRA Balance BEG
- DSRA Balance BEG
- MRA Balance BEG
- Retained Cash Balance BEG
- Last closing balance sheet flag
- Active periods.

DESIGN

For mathematical reasons it is best to assume that the interest on cash is calculated on the brought forward balances in all cases.

BUILD

1. Create a section called Interest On Cash near the bottom of the Finance sheet
2. Collect all the opening cash balances listed in the specification and add them together to create one single balance subject to the interest calculation
3. Calculate the period interest rate
4. Calculate the period interest payable
5. Assume that the interest payable is the same as the interest received
6. Paint the results into the financial statements.

RESULTS

- Interest Earnings Received … PL_18, CF_13, both +/-, both flow

42. Specify, design and build deferred tax (CORE)

OBJECTIVE

To build the deferred tax calculations as in the FC model and paint the results into the financial statements.

SPECIFICATION

Deferred tax is an accounting concept that effectively takes account of future tax assets or liabilities – see 'Deferred tax' on page 49 for more details.

The specification elements are:

- Tax loss balance
- Deferred Tax Liability/(Asset) Balance from last closing balance sheet
- Deferred Tax Liability/(Asset) Balance BEG from last closing balance sheet
- Tax depreciation balance on all assets allowed for tax
- Net book value on all assets allowed for tax
- Finance Debtor Balance on all assets allowed for tax
- Tax Allowable Proportion of Finance Debtor Balance %
- Corporation Tax Rate.

DESIGN

The deferred tax calculations are laid out in a standard way, with the deferred tax asset balance and the deferred tax liability balance at the bottom of the section. Each of the timing differences and the tax loss balance contribute to the charge/credit calculations and reside above the balances.

BUILD

Carry out the following build sequence:

1. Create the Deferred Tax section on the Tax sheet.
2. Create a balance corkscrew called Deferred Tax Liability/(Asset) Balance.
3. Above the balance collect the ingredients required to calculate the deferred tax effect of the difference between the accounting depreciation and the tax depreciation.
4. Create a section called Accounting Versus Tax Deferred Tax Effect.
5. In this section collect the ingredients for the accounting versus tax effect calculations:
   - Net book value on all assets allowed for tax = NBV Of Allowable Assets
   - Finance Debtor Allowed Balance = Finance Debtor Balance * Tax Allowable Proportion of Finance Debtor Balance % if the project uses the finance debtor accounting treatment
   - Tax depreciation balance on all assets allowed for tax.
6. Take the Tax depreciated Balance away from the NBV Of Allowable Assets or Finance Debtor Allowed Balance and multiply the result by the Corporation Tax Rate in the period to obtain the Accounting Versus Tax Deferred Tax Effect.
7. Create a section called Tax Loss Deferred Tax Effect.
8. Collect the ingredients for this calculation:
   - Tax Loss Balance
   - Corporation Tax Rate.

9. Multiply the Tax Loss Balance by the Corporation Tax Rate to obtain the Tax Loss Deferred Tax Effect.

10. Carry out the following calculations:

   - Deferred Tax Liability/(Asset) Target Balance = Accounting Vs Tax Deferred Tax Effect - Tax Loss Deferred Tax Effect

   - Deferred Tax Charge/(Credit) = - 1 * (Deferred Tax Liability/(Asset) Target Balance - Deferred Tax Liability/(Asset) Balance BEG).

11. Further, the results of this section are:

   - Deferred Tax Charge/(Credit), to the profit & loss

   - Deferred Tax Liability/(Asset) Balance = Deferred Tax Liability/(Asset) Target Balance, to the balance sheet.

RESULTS

- Deferred Tax Charge/(Credit) ... PL_22, +/-, flow
- Deferred Tax Liability/(Asset) Balance ... BS_22, +/+, balance

43. Specify, design and build share capital repayment

OBJECTIVE

To build Share Capital Repayment as in the FC model and paint the result into the financial statements.

SPECIFICATION

Share Capital Repayment is particular to a project finance company where at the end of the concession the invested share capital is repaid to the shareholders.

Share Capital Repayment is defined as the repayment of the outstanding share capital balance subject to the availability of cash to pay it.

The cash constraint on the repayment of share capital is the sum of Retained Cash Balance BEG and Cash Available For Share Capital Repayment in the first period following the last forecast period of the model.

The specification elements are:

- Cash Available For Share Capital Repayment
- Retained Cash Balance BEG
- Share Capital Balance @ First Post Last Forecast Period
- Last Closing Balance Sheet Flag
- First Post Last Forecast Period Flag
- Active periods.

DESIGN

No particular design issues.

BUILD

Carry out the following build sequence:

1. Create the Equity section of the Finance sheet for the share capital repayment.

2. Create a Share Capital Balance corkscrew at the foot of this Equity section.

3. Calculate the repayment subject to the cash available for the repayment as a counter flow from the cash flow waterfall.

4. Using the appropriate flag calculate the share capital repayment in the period just after the end of the concession.

5. Paint the results into the financial statements.

RESULTS

- Share Capital Repayment ... CF_33, +/-, flow
- Share Capital Balance ... BS_28, +/+, balance

44. Specify, design and build the subordinated debt (part 2)

OBJECTIVE

To build the Subordinated Debt Repayments as in the FC model and paint this result into the financial statements.

SPECIFICATION

Sub Debt Repayment can be defined in a variety of ways, these depend on the directors of the company.

In order to optimise the tax benefit derived from interest on the sub debt the repayment of the sub debt should be as back-ended as possible. To this end try a profile over time that starts low and ends high following an exponential growth pattern – however decisions on this are entirely the remit of the company directors.

The cash available for payment of any Subordinated Debt Repayment is the imported counter flow reference from the cash flow waterfall with the deduction of the Subordinated Debt Interest Paid POS.

- Subordinated Debt Repayment Profile
- Subordinated Debt Balance @ Last Closing Balance Sheet Date
- Cash Available For Sub Debt

- Subordinated Debt Interest Paid
- Last Closing Balance Sheet Flag
- Active periods.

DESIGN

The design feature of this section is to break the subordinated debt build up into two parts to allow for the debt repayment to be calculated near the end of the model build in order to optimise according to available cash flows.

BUILD

Carry out this build sequence:

1. Create some rows above the Subordinated Debt Balance on the Finance sheet
2. Add some rows above the Subordinated Debt Balance corkscrew on the Finance sheet and use a counter flow from the balance as well as a counter flow from the cash available for sub debt from the cash flow waterfall to calculate the Subordinated Debt Repayment.
3. Add the repayment into the Subordinated Debt Balance and then concurrently paint the same into the financial statements.

RESULTS

- Subordinated Debt Repayment … CF_31, +/-, flow

45. Specify, design and build dividends (CORE)

OBJECTIVE

To calculate the dividends and build them into the financial statements, resulting in an identical profile to the FC model.

SPECIFICATION

The dividends should be paid as quickly as possible subject to the availability of Retained Earnings and Retained Cash. However, there may be a delay between the declaration of dividends and the payment of dividends.

Dividends Payable Balance is defined to hold all dividends declared but as yet unpaid. Dividends Due increases the Dividends Payable Balance and Dividends Paid decreases the Dividends Payable Balance.

The retained earnings constraint on declaring dividends is the sum of Profit/Loss after Tax and The Retained Earnings Balance BEG. The retained cash constraint on declaring dividends is the sum of Cash Flow Available for Dividends and Retained Cash Balance BEG.

The specification items are:

- Dividend Payable Balance @ Last Closing Balance Sheet Date
- Profit/Loss after Tax
- Retained Earnings Balance BEG
- Cash Flow Available for Dividends
- Retained Cash Balance BEG
- Last Closing Balance Sheet Flag
- Dividend Flag
- Active periods.

DESIGN

To calculate dividends it is first necessary to calculate the two constraints on dividends, firstly with distributable profits and secondly from available cash. Therefore the organisational structure of this section necessarily follows this progression from constraints to dividends due to dividends paid. Any unpaid dividends are logged in the Dividends Payable Balance, the balance corkscrew.

Use the 'MAX(0 , MIN(A , B))' formula construct to find the positive value of the minimum value of two numbers.

BUILD

Carry out this build sequence:

1. Create a section called Dividends on the Finance sheet.
2. Use a balance corkscrew to create Dividends Payable Balance and bring in the last actual from the Inputs_C sheet.
3. Above the balance corkscrew create two subsections called Dividends by Profit & Loss and Dividends by Cash Flow.
4. In the Dividends by Profit & Loss, collect the ingredients for the distributable profits constraint calculation:
   - Profit/Loss After Tax as a counter flow from the Financial Statements sheet
   - Retained Earnings Balance BEG as a counter flow from the Financial Statements sheet
   - Dividend Flag.
5. Use this formula to calculate Dividends From Accounting Perspective:
   - = MAX(0, Retained Earnings BEG + Profit/Loss After Tax) * Dividend Flag.

6. In the Dividends by Cash Flow subsection, collect the ingredients:
   - Cash Flow Available For Dividends
   - Retained Cash Balance BEG
   - Dividend Flag.

7. Use this formula to calculate Dividends From Cash Perspective:
   - = MAX(0, Retained Cash BEG + Cash Flow Available For Dividends) * Dividend Flag.

8. Use this formula to calculate the Dividends Due:
   - = MAX(0, MIN(Dividends From Accounting Perspective, Dividends From Cash Perspective)).

9. Define Dividends Paid. It is customary to try to get the dividends paid as soon as they are payable. However, if there is a lag at all, then the Dividends Payable Balance should reflect this. Therefore add Dividends Due to the balance and take away Dividends Paid.

10. Paint the results into the financial statements.

RESULTS

- Dividends Due ... PL_24, +/-, flow
- Dividends Paid ... CF_35, +/-, flow
- Dividends Payable Balance ... BS_21, +/+, balance

46. Build the actuals into the financial statements (CORE)

OBJECTIVE

To add profit & loss, cash flow and balance sheet values from the FC model into the three financial statements. The result is shown in schematic form in Figure 128.

FIGURE 128: ACTUAL + FORECAST FINANCIAL STATEMENTS

	Actuals	Actuals	Actuals	Forecast	Forecast	Forecast	Forecast
Profit & loss	actual	actual	actual	forecast	forecast	forecast	forecast
Cash flow waterfall	actual	actual	actual	forecast	forecast	forecast	forecast
Balance sheet	actual	actual	last actual bs	forecast	forecast	forecast	forecast

SPECIFICATION

At this point, the financial statements contain only forecast numbers, except the balance sheet which contains the last actual closing balance sheet, as in Figure 129. Adding the actuals to the financial statements will not affect the forecast numbers already present in the financial statements.

FIGURE 129: FORECAST STATEMENTS (WITH LAST ACTUAL CLOSING BALANCE SHEET)

	Actuals	Actuals	Actuals	Forecast	Forecast	Forecast	Forecast
Profit & loss				forecast	forecast	forecast	forecast
Cash flow waterfall				forecast	forecast	forecast	forecast
Balance sheet			last actual	forecast	forecast	forecast	forecast

The Actuals sheet should by now contain the balanced actual financial statements from the FC model as inputs, see Step 15 on page 168 and Step 16 on page 169. Also, the Actuals sheet will have the identical structure and line-items to the Financial Statements sheet.

So, the specification elements are:

- Actuals sheet
- Financial Statements sheet.

DESIGN

The design objective is to create a formula in the Financial Statements sheet that brings values from the Actuals sheet if the period is an actuals period, but also brings in the forecast value from wherever in the model if the period is a forecast period.

BUILD

Carry out this build sequence:

1. For the first line-item in the financial statements, starting at the top of the profit & loss, and in the first time period (in an example where the first row is 13 and the first column is L), wrap the existing formula with the following IF statement:

= IF(L$4 = "Actuals", Actuals!L13, <EXISTING FORMULA>)

2. Now copy this formula all along the row, and you should find that the formula references the actuals value from the Actuals sheet during the actuals periods and then references the original forecast calculation in the forecast periods.

Now go to the next row down, in the example this would be row 14, and repeat the process by wrapping the existing formula as in the previous build tasks.

Now repeat for every line-item in the financial statements.

RESULTS

This step may take some time but the results and the effect on the model are very powerful. At the end of this step the model will contain a mixture of actuals and forecast values in the financial statements, which is a long way towards producing an operating model. At this stage the new model should re-perform the exact results of the FC model.

47. Deliver the shadow model to the end user (CORE)

The objectives of the shadow model are to re-perform the results of the FC model and this should now be the case. At this point the shadow model can be delivered to the end user.

The structural difference between the FC model and the new model lies in the make-up of the values in the financial statements sheet. Whereas the FC model was all calculated, the new model will contain inputs in the actual periods and calculations in the forecast periods. See 'Shadow delivery (V1)' on page 35 for more detail.

Subsequent steps specify:

- updating with actuals from management accounts
- investment returns
- cover ratios
- finalising the flags
- finalising the indexation
- adding some further reports
- delivering the final model to the end user.

48. Update the Actuals sheet in the model (CORE)

OBJECTIVE

To update the model with the latest management accounting actuals and produce a new forecast with no errors.

SPECIFICATION

The new model has been built from the FC model results and so re-performs the results of the FC model. Structurally, the new model has a dividing line between input actuals and calculated forecast, and the input actuals come from the FC model. Now it is time to update the input actuals with the latest live actuals and this will necessarily produce a new forecast.

Collect the following information to complete this step:

- All last actuals including:
  - Profit and loss actuals
  - Cash flow actuals
  - Balance sheet actuals
  - Tax loss balance actuals and tax written down value actuals of assets allowed for tax.

49. Create the Analysis sheet (CORE)

OBJECTIVE

Create the Analysis sheet.

SPECIFICATION & BUILD

Copy the Template sheet to after the Financial Statements sheet and call it Analysis.

50. Specify, design and build the cover ratios (CORE)

OBJECTIVE

Build the following banking cover ratios in the Analysis sheet:

1. Annual Debt Service Cover Ratio (ADSCR)
2. Loan Life Cover Ratio (LLCR)
3. Project Life Cover Ratio (PLCR).

SPECIFICATION

The banking cover ratios are the Annual Debt Service Cover Ratio (ADSCR), the Loan Life Cover Ratio (LLCR) and the Project Life Cover Ratio (PLCR).

The ADSCR is calculated using annual figures. It can be forward looking using the next year's figures or backward looking using the current year's figures. The ADSCR has as numerator the Cash Flow Available for Debt Service from the Cash Flow Waterfall and as denominator the Debt Service for the same period. The ADSCR is calculated for every period – actual and forecast – while the term loan is outstanding.

The LLCR is calculated for every period – actual and forecast – while the term loan is outstanding. The LLCR numerator is the sum of all future CFADS over the scheduled life of the loan discounted at the current Term Loan interest rate. The LLCR denominator is the outstanding term loan balance in the period.

The PLCR is a variation on the LLCR. The PLCR is also calculated for every period – actual and forecast – while the term loan is outstanding. The PLCR numerator is the sum of all future CFADS over the life of the concession discounted at the current Term Loan interest rate. The PLCR denominator is the outstanding term loan balance in the period.

All three ratios should be calculated taking values from the financial statements. This ensures the results properly reflect a mix of actuals and forecast.

For each ratio, and over the active life of the ratio, it is useful to calculate an average value, a minimum value, and the date of the minimum value.

Specify the following inputs:

- Annual Debt Service Cover Ratio … ratio, TD
- Average ADSCR … ratio, NTD
- Minimum ADSCR … ratio, NTD
- Date of minimum ADSCR … date, NTD
- Loan Life Cover Ratio … ratio, TD
- Average LLCR … ratio, NTD
- Minimum LLCR … ratio, NTD
- Date of minimum LLCR … date, NTD
- Term Loan Interest Rate
- Term Loan Balance
- Project Life Cover Ratio … ratio, TD
- Average PLCR … ratio, NTD
- Minimum PLCR … ratio, NTD
- Date of minimum PLCR
- Period End Dates
- Periods over which the cover ratio is to be calculated, denoted by a flag
- Periods of the concession, denoted by a flag.

DESIGN

The cover ratio design follows a four-level pattern of first collecting the cash flows, then calculating the cover ratio, then calculating the average cover ratio and lastly calculating the minimum cover ratio.

BUILD

To calculate the ADSCR carry out this build sequence:

1. Create a new section on the Analysis sheet for each of:
   - ADSCR
   - LLCR
   - PLCR.

2. For the ADSCR, collect the following cash flows:
   - Cash Available for Debt Service from the cash flow waterfall as a counter flow
   - Debt Service, including the senior debt repayment and senior debt interest from the cash flow waterfall as a counter flow.

3. Examine the ADSCR specification regarding forward-looking or backward-looking cash flows and according to this specification SUM the appropriate annual cash flows (this will include four quarterly periods) for each of the cash available and the debt service.

4. Collect the CFADS and the Debt Service in two rows followed by the flag defining the periods over which the cover ratio is to be calculated.

5. Use the formula given here to calculate the ADSCR:
   - = IF(FLAG = 1, (CFADS) / (Debt Service), "n/a").

6. Following on from the calculation of the cover ratio, collect the same cover ratio and calculate the average cover ratio by using the AVERAGE function – the 'n/a' will not contribute in any way to the calculation of this average
   - Similarly, use the MIN function to calculate the minimum
   - Using the value of the minimum and the cover ratio use this function to calculate a flag that shows the period in which the minimum is achieved:
      - = IF((Minimum cover ratio = Period End Date), 1, 0).

7. Using the flag calculated and the period end dates use this function to calculate the date of the minimum cover ratio:
   - = flag * date.

To calculate the LLCR carry out this build sequence:

1. For the LLCR, collect the following cash flows from the ADSCR section:
   - Cash Available for Debt Service.

2. Collect the Term Loan Interest rate, CFADS and the cover ratio flag and calculate the present value of the CFADS cash flows discounted at the term loan interest rate with the following formula:
   - = IF(FLAG = 1, (CFADS in current period + PV in next period) / (1 + Term Loan Interest rate in current period), 0).

3. Collect the PV of CFADS and the Term Loan Balance and using the formula given here calculate the LLCR:

  - = IF(FLAG = 1, (PV of CFADS) / (Term Loan Balance), "n/a").

4. Following on from the calculation of the cover ratio, collect the same cover ratio and calculate the average cover ratio by using the AVERAGE function – the 'n/a' will not contribute in any way to the calculation of this average.

5. Similarly, use the MIN function to calculate the minimum.

6. Using the value of the minimum and the cover ratio use this function to calculate a flag that shows the period in which the minimum is achieved:

  - = IF((Minimum cover ratio = Period End Date), 1, 0).

7. Using the flag calculated and the period end dates use this function to calculate the date of the minimum cover ratio:

  - = flag * date.

To calculate the PLCR carry out this build sequence:

1. Carry out the same steps as for the LLCR, except instead of using the cover ratio flag, use the concession period flag in order to include all cash flows until the end of the concession – the PLCR will necessarily be a higher ratio than the LLCR because of the inclusion of the cash flows after the debt has been repaid.

RESULTS

The results in this step are:

- Annual Debt Service Cover Ratio … ratio, TD
- Average ADSCR … ratio, NTD
- Minimum ADSCR … ratio, NTD
- Date of minimum ADSCR … date, NTD
- Loan Life Cover Ratio … ratio, TD
- Average LLCR … ratio, NTD
- Minimum LLCR … ratio, NTD
- Date of minimum LLCR … date, NTD
- Project Life Cover Ratio … ratio, TD
- Average PLCR … ratio, NTD
- Minimum PLCR … ratio, NTD
- Date of minimum PLCR … date, NTD.

51. Specify, design and build the project return on the investment

OBJECTIVE

Build the project return IRR from values in the financial statements.

SPECIFICATION

The common return metric for the operating portion of the project is the pre-tax project return.

Rates of return are commonly calculated using the internal rate of return (IRR) mathematical method.

Refer to 'Project return' on page 55 for the theory on project return calculations.

The pre-tax project IRR is calculated using the XIRR function in Excel which takes into account the dates of the cash flows. For XIRR to work the cash flows must have no lead zeroes but start with a negative number representing the cash investment. This should be followed by zeroes or positive numbers representing the cash return on the investment.

The pre-tax project return is defined as the IRR of the project operational cash flows from financial close to the end of the concession. The project operational cash flows are defined as the addition of the capital expenditure paid to construct the project infrastructure, the operating costs paid, the life cycle expenditure paid and operating revenues received.

The project return is a commonly used metric for the project developers. It describes the unleveraged ability of the project to sustain a return on investment. If the project return is higher than the current market cost of debt in the project industry then there is potential to increase the investor return by adding debt to the finance mix (see Weighted Average Cost of Capital theory).

The specification elements are:

- Operating Revenue Received ... CF_1
- Operating Costs Paid ... CF_3
- Capital Expenditure Paid ... CF_6
- Life Cycle Expenditure (Expensed Portion) Paid ... CF_9
- Life Cycle Expenditure (Capitalised Portion) Paid ... CF_10
- Period End Dates
- Actual + Forecast Period Flag.

DESIGN

This calculation only works if the new operating model contains all data back into the construction period to the start of construction. The design of an IRR calculation is first to collect the cash flows for the calculation and then to carry out the IRR calculation.

BUILD

Carry out the following build sequence:

1. Sum the following over time:
   - Operating Revenue Received ... CF_1
   - Operating Costs Paid ... CF_3
   - Capital Expenditure Paid ... CF_6
   - Life Cycle Expenditure (Expensed Portion) Paid ... CF_9
   - Life Cycle Expenditure (Capitalised Portion) Paid ... CF_10
   - Use the XIRR function in column F to find the IRR of these cash flows.

RESULTS

- Project IRR

52. Specify, design and build the investor return on the investment (CORE)

OBJECTIVE

Build the Equity IRR, Sub Debt IRR and Blended Equity IRR from values in the financial statements.

SPECIFICATION

The common return metrics for the shareholders are the equity return, the sub debt return and the blended equity and sub debt return which takes both equity and sub debt into account.

Rates of return are commonly calculated using the internal rate of return (IRR) mathematical method.

Refer to 'Investor return calculations' on page 57 for the theory on investor return calculations.

All three IRRs are calculated using the XIRR function in Excel which takes into account the dates of the cash flows. For XIRR to work the cash flows must have no lead zeroes but start with a negative number representing the cash investment. This should be followed by zeroes or positive numbers representing the cash return on the investment.

Technically the equity return is defined as the IRR of the equity cash flows. The equity cash flows are the equity invested at the start of the project plus the dividends paid out during the life of the project. The initial equity investment is treated as a negative cash flow and the dividends are treated as positive cash flows, which is the opposite of the way the project company sees these cash flows. The equity cash flows are defined as the addition of the equity invested, the dividends paid and the share capital repayment.

The sub debt return is defined as the IRR of the sub debt cash flows. The sub debt cash flows are the addition of the sub debt invested, the sub debt interest paid and the sub debt repayments.

The blended equity and sub debt return is defined as the IRR of the equity and sub debt blended cash flows. The equity and sub debt blended cash flows are the addition of the equity invested, the dividends paid, the share capital repayment, the sub debt invested, the sub debt interest paid and the sub debt interest repayments.

Specify the following inputs:

- Equity Drawn … CF_7
- Sub Debt Drawn … CF_8
- Dividends Paid … CF_35
- Share Capital Repayment … CF_33
- Sub Debt Interest Paid … CF_30
- Sub Debt Repayments … CF_31
- Period End Dates
- RPI Index.

DESIGN

Similarly to the previous step, the design of an IRR calculation is first to collect the cash flows for the calculation and then to carry out the IRR calculation.

BUILD

Carry out the following build sequence:

1. For the Equity IRR, SUM the following over time:
   - Equity Drawn … CF_7
   - Dividends Paid … CF_35
   - Share Capital Repayment … CF_33

2. Use the XIRR function in column F to find the nominal IRR of these cash flows

3. Divide the cash flows by the RPI Index for each period to create a real set of cash flows

4. Use the XIRR function in column F to find the real IRR of these cash flows

5. For the Sub Debt IRR, SUM the following cash flows:
   - Sub Debt Drawn ... CF_8
   - Sub Debt Interest Paid ... CF_30
   - Sub Debt Repayments ... CF_31

6. Use the XIRR function in column F to find the nominal IRR of these cash flows

7. Divide the cash flows by the RPI Index for each period to create a real set of cash flows

8. Use the XIRR function in column F to find the real IRR of these cash flows

9. For the Blended IRR, SUM the following cash flows:
   - Equity Drawn ... CF_7
   - Sub Debt Drawn ... CF_8
   - Dividends Paid ... CF_35
   - Share Capital Repayment ... CF_33
   - Sub Debt Interest Paid ... CF_30
   - Sub Debt Repayments ... CF_31
   - Period End Dates

10. Use the XIRR function in column F to find the nominal IRR of these cash flows

11. Divide the cash flows by the RPI Index for each period to create a real set of cash flows

12. Use the XIRR function in column F to find the real IRR of these cash flows.

RESULTS

The results in this step are:

- Equity IRR (nominal & real)
- Sub Debt IRR (nominal & real)
- Blended Equity IRR (nominal & real).

53. Complete the build of all the flags in the Time sheet (CORE)

OBJECTIVE

Complete the flag calculations in the Time sheet.

SPECIFICATION, DESIGN & BUILD

Completing the flag calculations is part of the model clean-up. This is necessary before model delivery.

The Time sheet contains two main sections: the Flags section and the Indexation section. So, in terms of good design it is important to keep these sections distinct and well organised.

Carry out the following build sequence for each flag:

1. Collect the ingredients necessary to calculate the flag, such as dates.
2. If the ingredient doesn't exist, create the input on the Inputs sheet and import it into the Time sheet.

Use various FAST building blocks to carry out the calculation, see '1. Sums' on page 75.

RESULTS

Completed flag calculations in the Time sheet.

54. Complete indexation build (CORE)

OBJECTIVE

To create a multiplicative RPI factor based on historic actuals and future forecasts to inflate real numbers and bring them to prices of the day – also known as nominal prices. These factors are called indices.

In Step 16 you created place-holder indexation made of hard-coded values from the FC model on the Time sheet. Now you will create the logic that drives the same index results as the FC model by using the combination of inputs, period-by-period rates of change and logic.

SPECIFICATION

I consider only one index, the Retail Price Index. Some projects may use more complex indices made up of a basket of published indices so the specification here can serve as the basis for those calculations.

TABLE 5: PROPERTIES OF AN EXAMPLE INDEX

Name	Units	Totals	Time-dependent values	Non-time dependent values
RPI Index	Index = multiplicative factor (format: decimal with 4 decimal places)	No, not relevant	1.0000 in the base period, to 1.0250 one year later if RPI is 2.50% per annum	n/a

An index is a multiplicative factor. It is defined as a function of a starting seed index (the index at the base date of the values to be inflated), the latest actual published index and some forecast assumptions of the ongoing rate of change of the index. The index is only used in the forecast periods of the operating model. Refer to Figure 53 which shows the precedents of an index created to inflate operating revenues by RPI.

In summary, model indexation is a function of three elements:

1. The actual historic values of an underlying government published price index.
2. A base date for the start of the indexation.
3. A sensible forecast rate for the government published price index.

Although not directly used, the index in all periods of the model is defined as the published index divided by the index at the base date for the values to be inflated.

In particular, the index in all periods is:

$$index_{all\_periods} = RPI_{act+forecast} / RPI_{base\_index}$$

DESIGN

The simplest design for this step is to use the building block called Actual + Forecast Indexation as shown in Figure 50 (page 86). In particular it is the index on a semi-annual timeline from the Time sheet that should be used, as shown in Figure 51 (page 87). In order to rebase this index to the base date for the model inputs, divide it by the published index at that base date throughout.

For this step the design should be for the use of a few rows of inputs and calculations as in Figure 53. It may be that your design gets more complicated because of the need for a basket of rates. In this more complicated case some prior calculations may be required although the final calculation should have the same inputs.

It is also necessary to create a sheet with an annual timeline to best deal with the indexation calculations.

BUILD

The build objective is to create the dynamic index for the model and exchange the hard-coded version for this new dynamic version without having to re-link all the precedents throughout the model. To do this, carry out this build sequence:

1. Create an annual sheet called 'Index_A' with an appropriate annual timeline and construct the indexation building block called 'Actual + Forecast Indexation' as shown in Figure 50.

2. Collect the ingredients, in particular the chosen index from the Time sheet as shown in Figure 51.

3. Create the index calculation result in the row above the previously created 'input index' (that is linked to the rest of the model).

4. Make sure the new calculated row and the hard-coded row give the same index for all periods.

5. Select the first calculation cell and press F2 to edit, then copy the formula.

6. Select the first cell of the 'input index' in the row below and press F2, select all the existing values and press Ctrl + V to paste.

7. Copy this new formula along the whole row and re-format as an export.

8. Delete the whole row that included the first calculated index, leaving the original 'input index', which is now a calculation but also linked into the model.

RESULTS

There are two results for this step. First, a sheet called Index_A with an annual timeline and the annual indexation calculations, and second, a calculated index called RPI on a single row on the Time sheet, linked into the model.

55. Specify, design and build further reports (CORE)

Further reports will need to be specified, designed and built. These reports will depend on the industry and complexity of the underlying business. Further reports could include:

- annual summaries of the financial statements
- financing summaries
- operational summaries
- debt covenant or cover ratio summaries
- valuation and investor return summaries.

This will be dealt with in full detail in a forthcoming eBook.

56. Specify, design and build the Quick Start sheet (CORE)

The Quick Start sheet should contain a compilation of links to areas of the model that the manager may be interested in. Use the Quick Start sheet picture in Appendix 5 to design and build it.

This will be dealt with in full detail in a forthcoming eBook.

57. Deliver the updated model to end user (CORE)

The objectives of the updated model were to create a new forecast of the model results from a combination of actuals and forecast assumptions. This should now be the case and the updated model can be delivered to the end user. This delivery should also include a detailed introduction to the model for the end user.

See 'Shadow delivery (V1)' on page 35 for more detail.

Subsequent steps specify:

- adding any further updates to the model
- delivering the final model to the end user.

58. Add further final updates to the model (CORE)

There are always some final updates and changes to bring a modelling project to conclusion within the contracted budget and specification. These may include:

- amendments to the actuals
- revisions to cash reserving and accounting amortisations
- last minute contractual changes requiring logic amendments
- re-formatting of model reports
- addition of some new shareholder calculations
- correction of any errors and bugs.

59. Deliver the final model to the end user (CORE)

The objectives of the Final model are to clear up any changes following the delivery of the Updated model. To a certain extent this is up to the goodwill of the modeller and the client, and the relationship between the two, as well as the strength of the initial contract and specification from the outset.

At some point the modeller will reasonably need to stop working on the model – any further work then required will fall into subsequent maintenance as new work.

CHAPTER 7
PRACTICAL MODELLING TECHNIQUES

This chapter looks at a series of practical modelling techniques that are a vital part of the modeller's everyday arsenal. I will look at these in terms of the two model phases: the Shadow phase and the Update phase.

Generic financial modellers should note that the practical techniques described in this chapter are all equally valid for corporate financial modelling. Interpret the distinction between Shadow and Update phases as:

- *Shadow phase* is all modelling prior to the first update of the model with the latest management accounting figures.

- *Update phase* is all modelling from the first update of the model with the latest management accounting figures.

TECHNIQUES FOR THE SHADOW PHASE

1. Tracking the outputs

Use the Track sheet to compile the results of the FC model in order to properly measure the difference between the value of the new calculations and the FC model original calculations.

To create a new tracked output set, refer to Figure 10 and follow these steps:

1. Go to the Track sheet.
2. Create a new column for storing the output set between columns O and Q.
3. Define a new name for this new tracked output set in cell Q6.
4. Write a comment explaining the new tracked output set in cell Q13.
5. Copy the live output set from column J from row 16 to the bottom.
6. Paste the live output set as values into the new column created in 2 (it will be the new Q column) from row 16 down.

7. Point the comparison drop down switch in cell J6 to the new tracked output set or compare this tracked output set to any other by pointing to any other tracked output set.

2. Define the last closing balance sheet from the FC model as at the end of construction

Define the last closing balance sheet from the compiled financial statements of the old model as at the end of the construction period. This usually coincides with the time when the FC model is rebuilt in the form of the operating model discussed by this book.

Defining this balance sheet is an important step in starting work on the new operating model.

3. Driving out the inputs

The modelling process starts by defining the outputs which in turn define the required calculations. The required calculations will need their own input ingredients to work. So the inputs are driven out as work progresses. In general the inputs should not be defined in advance but rather allowed to naturally be created in this way.

4. Create place holder inputs & clean up the inputs

The most efficient way of dealing with the inputs is to build the calculations while generating inputs as required on the fly. At this point the modeller should only format these inputs with a light yellow fill colour directly on the calculation sheet. Once the results have been derived the inputs can be cleaned up and placed on the Inputs or Actuals sheets as required. This allows the modeller to concentrate on the calculation in hand.

Some things to remember:

- Place holders should include the whole row and should be colour-coded in yellow.
- Place holders enable fast coding allowing the modeller to concentrate on the main logic rather than distracting technical sideshows.

5. Collect the ingredients

All ingredients for every new calculation should be re-collected from source, whether an input or a calculated value.

6. Reusing chunks of logic

Chunks of logic can be reused, such as:

- balance corkscrews
- standard indexation
- flag manipulations
- retained earnings
- retained cash flow
- VLOOKUP input flip to horizontal
- double-decker IRR, NPV calculations
- simple IRR, NPV calculations.

7. Reusing single line-items

If line-items are called up and row-anchored (with $ on the row and not in the column) then they can be easily reused. Select the whole row using SHIFT + SPACE BAR, copy and then select the new destination row.

8. Format as you go

All logic requires some number formatting for the correct units, such as %, £0,000 or as flag, as well as colour-formatting for imports, exports or counter flows. The most efficient way of dealing with this is to carry out the formatting as the logic is produced.

Please visit **www.lazulisolutions.com** for formatting macros that you can download for free.

9. The one-off balance sheet imbalance

If we assume the modeller is advancing through the model-building steps and painting the results into the financial statements, then the balance sheet will show a one-off imbalance in the first forecast period. This is caused by the lack of a complete balance sheet picture and is the case until all balance sheet items have been properly painted into the balance sheet – i.e. until completion of the shadow phase.

The temporary solution to this is to allow a changing one-off imbalance at the bottom of the balance sheet. Use a local cell at the bottom of the balance sheet for this purpose and link this to all the forecast balance sheet check calculations. As each batch of results is painted into the financial statements this value will change and so the modeller will have to find the new value. The important check throughout this shadow phase is that there are no other imbalances other than this one-off imbalance.

10. Other balance sheet solutions

A changing imbalance through the forecast periods of the model is a problem at any stage of the model build and needs to be solved before proceeding any further. This is because it will only be harder to find the longer it lingers and one imbalance may hide other imbalances.

Here are some solutions:

- *Large number test* to drive out the source of the imbalance
- *Delete test* to drive out the source of the imbalance
- *Check/Line-by-line opening balance sheet method* for driving out the source of the imbalance. This method uses:
  - *Check sheet temporary logic change* – check that the one-off difference does not change (i.e. a change will cause a check error)
  - *Actuals sheet temporary imbalance logic change* – while the model is being built there may be insufficient logic to deal with all opening balance sheet items. This causes an imbalance in all forecast periods of the model. If the imbalance is the same throughout all the forecast periods, then the temporary solution is to manage this amount. To do this, add an input cell under the value of the first forecast period imbalance, copy the value of the imbalance and hard-code it into this cell.

    Next re-code the formula in the formula cell containing the imbalance by subtracting the absolute value of the hard-coded cell – do this by adding ' - $J$95' to the formula, for example. Then copy this formula all along the row to the right and the imbalance should disappear. You will need to update the value of the hard-coded cell each time you tackle the logic of a new balance sheet item, but this should ensure that you control any 'new' imbalances caused for reasons other than that you have not completed the model. Once the model is complete the imbalance should be zero and you can permanently delete the hard-coded input cell and any references to it.
  - *Line-by-line actuals sheet tests* – investigate each line-item from the actual financial statements through the model logic to make sure each one is behaving appropriately.

11. Build the skeleton financial statements

As specified by the old model and the client – there may be changes to the FS from the old model. Include all sum formulae for totals and subtotals.

12. Add the links between the financial statements

This means connecting the retained cash balance and the retained profit balance to the balance sheet.

Also build the RCB and RPB into the Finance sheet as these balances will need to gather the actuals data as all other balances and this is best done on the calculation sheets and not on the output sheets such as the financial statements.

13. Add the financial statement checks

These are compiled at the bottom of the new FS sheet and the three checks are:

1. Retained Earnings Balance in balance sheet is the same as the Retained Earnings Balance at the bottom of the P&L.
2. Retained Cash Balance in balance sheet is the same as the Retained Cash Balance at the bottom of the Cash Flow.
3. The balance sheet is balanced.

14. Add the last closing balance sheet

1. Create an input version of the financial statements on the Actuals sheet.
2. Add the last closing balance sheet to the Actuals sheet.

15. Add the FS_Ref and FS_Diff sheets

1. Add these sheets with FS_Diff sheet difference functions.
2. Copy and Paste Special as Values the tracked FS sheet from the old model into the FS_Ref sheet in the new model.
3. Glance in the FS_Diff sheet to note that all the differences should be reported for each line-item and across all time periods.

16. Create an input sheet for the actuals

1. Route the actuals through an input sheet called Inputs_C which means calculated inputs using a LOOKUP function.
2. This will need small tweaks but can be part of the modeller collection of sheets as it is not normally altered.

17. Event flags

1. Event Flags should be compiled as inputs in the calculation sheets until such time as you begin to use them very frequently and then cleaned up and properly coded in the Time sheet.
2. Event flags are mostly input date driven although some may be a function of other flags.

18. Build and use a balance corkscrew

To complete the logic to deal with revenues and costs accrued and paid, the debtors and creditors balances need to be built.

19. Paint the exports into the financial statements

Each modelling component has a set of double entries that mean that once compiled on the financial statements they will leave a balanced balance sheet.

For example, adding:

- operating revenues
- revenues received
- debtors balance

ensures that if the balance sheet balanced before adding them then it will also again balance after adding them.

20. Add analysis sheet and calculations

Analysis calculations include cover ratios (ADSCR, LLCR, PLCR), NPVs of cash streams, IRRs for all investors, project returns, real and nominal versions of each return calculation, pre and post-tax versions of all return calculations, and possibly calculations of tax leakage at the holding company level.

21. Add control sheet

Leave as titled blank sheet.

22. Add any charts

Use *Economist* charts as a guideline for the formatting.

23. Rebase the FS_Ref and FS_Diff sheets

Rebase by copying the FS sheet outputs and pasting as values on to the FS_Ref sheet.

FS_Diff sheet should now show zeroes throughout.

TECHNIQUES FOR THE UPDATE PHASE

1. Collecting vertical inputs into horizontal calculation sheets

Vertical input sheets allow for fast sensitivity analysis so the VLOOKUP function and a row of dates can be used as ingredients to collect these vertical inputs and transform them into horizontal values.

2. Summarising financial statements into annual time-buckets

Use the SUMIF function to do this by testing for the correct dates. To avoid unnecessary multi-dimensional memory usage it is important not to also check for the correct line-item. Do this by ensuring that the annual statements have precisely the same line-items as the original statements.

3. Solutions to common modelling problems

ALLOW FOR ERRORS AND USE ERROR-TRAPPING

Consider the case where there is a possibility that a function could yield an error due to the nature of the values it is assessing. In this case it is preferable to allow for the error and add an extra row of code that traps the error for use in the rest of the model.

A good example of the use of error trapping is when the VLOOKUP function yields an error when the fourth parameter is set to FALSE, in which case if there is no exact match the function will yield an error. In this case this is preferable to an approximate solution when the fourth parameter is set as TRUE.

The two-lines of code in cells B2 and B3 could be:

```
= VLOOKUP( B1, Inputs!$E$35:$F$73, 2, FALSE )

= IF( ISNA( B2), 0, B2)
```

AVOID CIRCULARITIES WITH AN IF STATEMENT

In some situations the direct reference of a cell or series of cells will result in a circular reference. In some of these cases there is a possible solution with the use of an IF statement. The IF statement makes sure the cell is only referenced in certain cases, as defined by the IF statement, thus avoiding the circular reference. This solution only works when the referenced cell does not result in a circular reference under the alternative conditions of the IF statement.

AVOID DIV#/0 ERRORS BY FIRST CHECKING THE VALUE OF THE DENOMINATOR WITH AN IF STATEMENT

If the denominator of a fraction is zero, then any non-zero value for the numerator will result in a value of infinity (∞) for the fraction. Excel will return DIV#/0 for the value of infinity, and this can cause errors throughout a model.

A simple IF statement effectively serves to error trap this problem. The first part of the IF statement should test whether the denominator is equal to zero, in which case the IF statement should return zero, otherwise the fraction should be calculated.

In code:

```
= IF( AT11 = 0, 0, AT10 / AT11 )
```

4. Update with new actuals

Test the integrity of the model logic by carrying out a full update for actuals:

- update financial statement actuals
- update other actuals such as tax, indexation and accounting
- change the last actuals closing balance sheet date
- consider the checks and audit and repair any errors.

CHAPTER 8
MAINTAINING THE INVESTMENT

DESIGN, APPLICATION AND MAINTENANCE

There are three phases in the life of a model: design, application and maintenance.

I have used the example of the French Grande Ecole system of top universities in France. Within technical subject matters such as telecommunications the French Grande Ecole system has split study into three schools to deal with the three distinct phases of technical evolution. After the design and build investment, there is the serious consideration of the maintenance and this should neither be underestimated nor ignored.

Responding to the quarterly update and ad-hoc analysis

Proper maintenance requires a well-organised computer. I propose that you use the A system for organising your files and folders so that you can easily find them afterwards

Responding to the need to properly specify new logic/functionality

Use cases is a way to envisage clearly the actual use that people make of software.

To specify a Use Case consider a person, a role, an event, and objective, frequency of use, report and audience.

MODEL CONTROL & MODEL NAMING CONVENTION

A simple model naming convention and clear model control are absolutely necessary for good maintenance of the model.

A model naming convention avoids unnecessary confusion.

Model control is designated to the person making changes to the mother version of the model. It should be formally appointed and known at all times and in all communications. For example, an email that delivers a model should either retain or give over model control.

See '4. File naming convention and file control' on page 135 for a detailed discussion on both these topics.

RUNNING SENSITIVITIES

To run sensitivities using the column-format input sheet, the Track sheet and the FS_Ref and FS_Diff sheets follow these steps:

1. Reference the current outputs from the FS sheet to the FS_Ref sheet and make sure there are no differences showing on the FS_Diff sheet.

2. Make sure the track is set at no differences, i.e. the current output set is the active set on the Track sheet.

3. Create a new column input set in the Inputs sheet and make sure it:
   - has the same values as the previous active set
   - is set as the active set.

4. Change the inputs as required by the sensitivity in question.

5. Use the FS_Diff sheet to analyse the differences to the model results.

6. Use the Track sheet to see the differences in key outputs.

LINKS AND MODEL INTERFACE ISSUES

Generally links are not a good idea, so I prefer creating an interface and an interface process for any data that comes from outside the model.

PART 3
FURTHER LESSONS

CHAPTER 9
LESSONS FROM PFI

LESSONS FROM PFI AND STRUCTURED FINANCE

UK PFI and structured finance has taught the modelling community a lot about better modelling. Here is a list of modelling areas that have benefitted from the UK PFI model:

- the business structure imposed on a model was developed from the project finance entity approach; from legal structure to entity structure in the model.

- project finance is centred on the cash flow waterfall from which the story of the project can be told. All financial models benefit from a robust cash flow waterfall approach to the allocation of cash, particularly if there are tranches of finances to deal with.

- UK PFI introduced us to operational modelling in a big way. The power of the actual plus forecast lesson has now been learnt and adapted across many different industries outside UK PFI.

- UK PFI models are succinct with no duplication of logic. This is vital for all models.

- UK PFI has showed us that succinct and elegant modelling is not beyond us, and this has clarified the strategic view of both the manager and the modeller.

SUCCESSFUL ADAPTATIONS TO OTHER INDUSTRIES

The methodology for building UK PFI project finance strategic operating models has been used successfully in numerous other industries. Recently, strategic operating models have been built for these industries:

- energy (power and gas) distribution and regulated businesses in the UK
- media financing, in particular feature film slate financing in the US and EU
- rail concessions in the UK
- ports and shipping in the EU

The similarities of models for these industries with the UK PFI project finance version are:

- updating for actuals and re-forecast
- running the model from a last closing balance sheet
- core model organisation and technical setup
- core financing structures
- core taxation structures
- core working capital structures
- core accounting methodologies
- core analysis methodologies.

The differences of models for these industries with the UK PFI project finance version are:

- multiple-company legal structures and consolidation of financial statements
- operating revenues and costs
- structure of actuals can include price and volume as well as revenue or cost
- depreciation of historical assets
- disposal and profit on disposal of assets
- further acquisition of assets
- additional financing structures such as revolving credit facilities and specific asset financing
- market indexation assumptions rather than contractual indexation
- banking covenants as opposed to banking cover ratios.

TOPICS FOR FURTHER STUDY

Inevitably some topics of operational modelling have not been covered by this book. However, the intention is to deal with these and other newer items on the Lazuli Solutions website (**www.lazulisolutions.com**) and in future eBooks.

Areas for further study include:

- actual, budget and forecast models
- IFRS reporting issues
- multi-company and consolidation operating models
- actuals other than the standard financial statements actuals – i.e. when actuals are required deeper in the company operations and are not simply management accounting actuals
- short-term monthly operating models
- long-term strategic operating models

- interfaces between short-term operating models and long-term strategic operating models
- operating models for the energy distribution and regulated business
- operating models for the media financing business
- operating models for the rail concession business
- operating models for the ports and shipping business
- using VBA for advanced modelling
- detailed model testing theory and practice.

APPENDICES

APPENDICES

APPENDIX 1
LINKS AND REFERENCES

THE BOOK'S WEBSITE

You will find the dedicated webpage for the book on the Lazuli Solutions website (**www.lazulisolutions.com/book**).

LAZULI SOLUTIONS, INNOVATIVE MODELLING SOLUTIONS FOR BUSINESS DECISION MAKERS

Dominic Robertson is a director of Lazuli Solutions. Find the Lazuli Solutions website at: **www.lazulisolutions.com**

FAST MODELLING STANDARD

FAST website (**www.fast-standard.org**)

OTHER USEFUL LINKS

Here is a list of other useful links for help, information and add-ins related to Excel:

- PUP Utility v7.1 available from **spreadsheetpage.com** offers an array of useful functions that don't exist in Excel. Beware when using some of these functions on big models as they may take a long time to run.
- Excel Savvy mapping software (**www.ExcelSavvy.com**) produce Excel mapping software for the initial step in the professional audit of Excel models. Mapping the Excel sheets is only the first step and subsequent steps involve detailed work by highly skilled professionals.
- Names Manager (**www.jkp-ads.com/OfficeMarketPlaceNM-EN**) is a very useful utility for dealing with named ranges in Excel models.

- There are many Excel add-ins at the Office Automation website (**www.oaltd.co.uk**). These are advanced users of Excel that are recognisable names in the Excel market, and these add-ins cover a multitude of uses. Notice that they are directed at anything up to Excel 2003, as the latest version of Excel has not been accepted within the core Excel users community.

- Excel dashboards and mini charts (**www.exceluser.com**) are very useful for producing one-page reports on the outputs of Excel models. I have used various products from this site and they have all been very good.

- Excel dashboards (**www.excelcharts.com/blog**). Jorge offers dashboard solutions that contain extensive use of pivot tables and VBA (although there is a non-VBA version that I have not tried). The outcome is dynamic dashboards with powerful messages. Try out his demographic dashboard (**www.excelcharts.com/blog/data-visualization-courses/demographic-dashboard-lookup-edition**) for a taster.

- Excel and VBA tips and tricks website at Daily Dose of Excel (**www.dailydoseofexcel.com/dicks-blogroll**) is a particularly useful resource when looking to answer technical Excel or VBA questions. Use the list of links to access a number of Excel focused blogs/pages.

- A very popular Excel add-in used across industry, accountancy firms, banks and other financial institutions is the OAK Analysis Kit (**www.operisanalysiskit.com**). This add-in gives a variety of additional functionality to Excel, most notably the comparison tool for finding and categorising changes in spreadsheets.

APPENDIX 2
DICTIONARY OF TERMINOLOGY, UNITS & ABBREVIATIONS

MODELLING TERMINOLOGY

Modelling units

Unit	Description	Example format
£k	Thousands of £s, in real terms	2,398
nom £k	Thousands of £s, in nominal terms	2,398
flag	Event flag	1
switch	Switch	-
%	Percentage	22.00%
% pa	Percentage per annum	22.00%
factor	A factor	1.2500
index	An index	1.0560
date	Date	28-Mar-2010
check	A model check	
ratio	A ratio such as a cover ratio	1.1700

Glossary

£k: Thousands of pounds

Accounting amortisation: The decreasing of an amount over time for accounting purposes

Accrued: An account that has occurred but as yet remains unpaid

Active periods: Time periods when the event in question is active, often the concession or project itself

Actual historic values: The achieved values describing the finances of a company or entity emanating from the past

Add: Used to denote that summation formula will add this line-item

Addbk: Used to denote that summation formula will add back this line-item

Additive: Subject to addition

Admin sheet: Sheets dedicated to administrative purposes

ADSCR: Annual Debt Service Cover Ratio, the ratio of cash available for debt service over an annual period

Analysis: Calculations using the primary results (the financial statements) of a model

Annualised: Over the period of a year

Asset: A resource that gives rise to future business benefit

At-source referencing: Using cell references that refer to the unique and initial instance of a value

Audit phase: The third phase in a model build, arriving at the construction of the greater part of logic with correct inputs and sign-off from the model auditors

Auto_code: Lazuli code attributed to line-items in FAST + 2

Backward-looking: References that look back in time

Balance corkscrew: Building block used to calculate starting and ending balance

Balance sheet: The financial statement describing the financial balances of a company at an agreed moment in time

Bankers / lenders: A lending entity such as a bank

Banking covenants: Levels and ratios imposed on a borrowing entity or company by a bank in order to assure repayment of the loan

Banking cover ratios: Calculations imposed on borrowing corporations by lenders in order to evaluate the availability of cash to cover debt service

Base rate: The rate associated with a loan often equal to the inter-bank rate at which the lender can itself be funded

BEG: Beginning

Best-practice: The generally accepted best way of doing something

Boolean: A value of 1 or 0

Budget: Detailed operational targets agreed and set by company directors for the year ahead

Budget financial modelling: Where the model contains annual budgets as agreed upon by the board of directors of the company or entity

Build sequence: The order in which the build process is carried out

Building block: An individual, self-sustaining and contiguous set of Excel calculations fed by values and producing values; a modelling component used to build models.

Business modelling: Generic term covering all modelling for business purposes

Calculation sheet: Sheets dedicated to calculations

Cap: Maximum value

Capital: The wealth used to fund infrastructure and other projects

Capitalised development costs: Costs incurred during the development of a project that are capitalised as assets rather than expensed in the profit and loss statement

Cash: Currency or currency equivalents

Cash flow: The financial statement describing the cash movements of a company over an agreed period of time

Cash flow waterfall: A cash flow arranged in priority of payments

Cell dependents: Cells referred to in an initial cell's formula

Cell precedents: Cells that refer to an initial cell's value

Cell references: The names of cells referred to in a cell

CFADS: Cash Flow Available For Debt Service, used to calculate banking cover ratios and available for senior debt service

Checks: Tests carried out to ensure logical and arithmetic accuracy

Conditional formatting: Excel formatting defined by one or many conditions

Construction expenditure: The capital costs required to build a project

Control panel: A sheet dedicated to the temporary control of high-level inputs and results

Control sheet: Sheets dedicated to high-level control purposes

Corollary: A statement that follows from a previous statement, usually a theorem

Corporation tax: Tax on companies or corporations

Counter flow: The direction of information if contrary to the model flow

Credit agreement: Contract defining the rights and obligations of the lender and the borrower of capital

Creditor: Party that is owed money

Daisy chain: When cells use references that are not at-source but random instead

Data book: A compilation of data normally used in a model for use at transaction

Debt finance: Financing by means of bank debt

Debt service: The aggregate of interest and repayment associated with a tranche of debt

Debtor: Party that owes money

Deferred tax: A balance sheet item accounting for temporary differences between accounting and tax value of assets, tax losses and other items that give rise to deferred tax assets or liabilities

Denominator: The bottom part of a fraction

Deposits: Cash deposits to a reserve account

Deterministic modelling: Where the model derives one set of results

Distributions to shareholders: All cash payments to the owners of company shares

Dividends: Payments to shareholders

Double entry: A set of rules for bookkeeping by which financial accounts are logged in two ledgers

DSRA: Debt Service Reserve Account, the cash reserve dedicated to the payment of future debt service

Econometric modelling: The results vary but the main content is of an econometric nature including any or all of:

- Elasticities to derive volume, supply or demand of goods or services
- Regression analysis or other statistical means to forecast volume, supply or demand of goods or services

Effective tax rate: The tax rate of a company calculated over a period of time by taking aggregate corporation tax and dividing by aggregate PBT

Equity finance: Financing by means of risk capital that is subordinate to all other forms of finance

Error-trapping: Wrapping Excel formulae to prevent errors

Event flag: An on/off switch used to control events in a model

Excel: The current spreadsheet software brand name

Expensed: Expenditure that is not capitalised but rather allowed to be fully accounted for in the profit and loss statement as it occurs

External links: References to cells in external workbooks

FAST: Modelling standard

FC: Financial close

Finance debtor: Recognition of the PFI/PPP asset as a finance asset rather than a fixed asset

Financial close: Milestone when a project achieves bank and investor financing

Financial controller: Position in a company with responsibility for the quality and delivery of financial information

Financial modelling: The PFI model is a financial model and a financial model has a P&L (profit & loss), CF (cash flow) and BS (balance sheet) as main results

Financial statements: The profit & loss, the cash flow and the balance sheet

First forecast period: The first period of time in the forecast part of the model

Fixed asset depreciation: The decreasing of an amount of fixed asset over time for accounting purposes

Flag: See Event flag

Floor: Minimum value

Forecast assumptions: Inputs used to forecast the future of a company or entity

Forecast inputs: Inputs used to forecast the future

Forward-looking: References that look forward in time

Growth factor: A value, normally expressed as a decimal that is either greater, equal or less than 1.000, used to multiply other values in order to create a product of higher, equal or lower value

Hard-coded: A raw value within a cell reference

Hierarchy: The organisational arrangement of items in a pre-agreed order

i/o system: Input and output system, the base functionality of a software program

Indexation: The adjustment of income and expenditure by way of a price index relating to the passage of time

Inflation rate: The rate of change in prices over an agreed period of time

Infrastructure: The base physical elements needed to run a modern society

Input: Data used in calculations

Input sheet: Sheets dedicated to the collection of inputs, usually forecast inputs

Inputs: Values used to feed a calculation

Interest: The fee paid by the borrower of an asset for the use of those assets

Interest earned on cash balances: The fee earned by a company with cash deposits

Investor return: The measure of cash return for an investment taking all cash flows into consideration

Investors: An entity involved in the financing of a project or company or venture

IPMT: Interest portion of annuity

IRR: Internal Rate of Return, a mathematical calculation to determine the % rate of return on a series of investment cash flows starting with a negative value and followed by positive values

Issues: Practical considerations in the structure, content and organisation of the elements of a model

Junior debt: Debt that has lesser call over assets as compared to a senior debt holder

Keyboard shortcut: A set of keyboard routines to facilitate accurate computer functionality

Keyboard shortcuts: Use of keys on the computer keyboard to carry out specific application tasks

Last actual period: The last period of time in the actuals part of the model

Layout order: The order in which the building blocks are best placed on the sheet, from top to bottom

Legal entities: Companies

Less: Used to denote that summation formula will subtract this line-item

Liability: A debt or obligation

LIBOR: London Interbank Offered Rate, calculated as the average rate used within the banking community of London to lend to each other

Life cycle expenditure: The capital and operating costs required to maintain the assets of a project

Limited company: A company in which the liability of the directors of the company is limited to what they have invested or guaranteed to the company

Line item: Named accounts that take up one line in a model

LLCR: Loan Life Cover Ratio, the ratio of the net present value of cash available for debt service over the life of a loan to debt outstanding in the period of calculation

Logic: Calculations written in Excel (i.e. not the data)

Lookup: Excel formula used to determine a value based upon a specified condition

Lotus 123: A spreadsheet software brand name in the 1990s

Macro-economic: Relating to the economy as a whole

Macros: Routines written in VBA and used to automate Excel and other applications in Microsoft Office

Management accounting actual inputs: Inputs from the company management accounts used to establish past performance

Margin: The fee charged by banks over and above the base lending rate used to reward the banks for the loan

Max: Maximum

Mezzanine finance: Financing by means of capital that is senior only to the equity of an entity or company

Min: Minimum

Model audit: Third party detailed review and sign-off of a financial model

Model build: The construction of a model

Model checks: The set of all model checks

Model control: The controlled distribution and changes of a model

Model delivery: The handing over of a model to the user

Model flow: The direction of information flow in a model, usually from top to bottom and left to right

Model review: Third party detailed review and sign-off of a financial model

MRA: Maintenance Reserve Account, the cash reserve dedicated to the payment of future life cycle expenditure

Multiplicative: Subject to multiplication

Multi-tasking: Computer term defining ability to perform many tasks at once

Navigation: Getting around the model up and down and across sheets

NEG: Negative

Nom: Nominal

Nominal: Money of the day

Non-time dependent: Not dependent on time

Non-trading income: Income generated from sources not defined as trading – interest income for an infrastructure project is a good example

NPV: Net Present Value, the present value of a discounted stream of future cash flows

Numerator: The top part of a fraction

ONS: Office for National Statistics in the UK

Operating model: A model used to operate the finances of a company or entity in the short and possibly medium term

Operational modelling: Where the model uses management accounting and other actuals to forecast and where the actual updating process happens at regular intervals

Operations: The revenues, costs and capital expenditure of a modelled company or entity

Opex: Operating expenditure

Output sheet: Sheets dedicated to high-level outputs

Output track: One set of aggregate results of a model

Payback: Financial term defining the time when an investment is repaid in nominal terms

PBT: Profit Before Tax, found on the P&L and used to start the tax calculation

PD LK BK: Period look back

PD LK FW: Period look forward

Period: A single time length in a model, normally on one column of an Excel sheet

Periodicity: The definition of a length of time in a model, normally monthly, quarterly, semi-annual or annual

Place-holding: Often colour-coded shading used to allocate rows or columns to results, calculations or inputs that have not yet been completed

PLCR: Project Life Cover Ratio, the ratio of the net present value of cash available for debt service over the life of the project or concession to debt outstanding in the period of calculation

POS: Positive

PPF: Partial period factor

PPMT: Principal portion of annuity

PPP: Public-Private Partnership, a service which is funded by means of a partnership between public and private companies

Pre-payment: Cash payments in advance of their occurrence – insurance payments often take this form

Pre-tax: Before tax

Probabilistic: Models with results in the form of probability distributions

Probabilistic modelling: Where the model can derive a distribution of the set of results

Profit and loss: Financial statement describing the profits and losses made by a company over an agreed period of time

Project developers: Entity responsible for the initial creation and organisation of a project

Project finance: Financing of infrastructure projects based upon the long-term cash flows of the project

Project return: Measure of cash return for an investment calculated on only operational cash flows

Project tail: Normally refers to the periods at the end of a project concession after the senior debt has been repaid

Publicly listed company (PLC): A company that offers its shares to the public through a stock exchange

PV: Present value

Qtrly: Quarterly

Quick start sheet: A compilation of navigational links into the model for use by a manager

RAM: Random Access Memory, fast computer memory

Real: Money as at a set base date

Repayment: The partial or entire repayment of a borrowed amount

Reserves: Cash deposits put aside by a company and excluded from the reward of shareholders and other subordinated finance

Results: The output values of a building block that achieve the specified result

RPI: Retail Price Index, a measure of inflation for all items as defined by the ONS in the UK

RPIX: Retail Price Index, a measure of inflation excluding mortgage interest payments as defined by the ONS in the UK

Seeding: Values given to calculations at the initial stage

Semi: Semi-annual

Senior debt: Debt that has the highest call over assets

Sensitivity analysis: The analysis of change in specified model results by means of change in specified model inputs

Shadow phase: The first phase in a model build, in essence to arrive at the construction of the greater part of logic without considering the complete correctness of the inputs

Shareholder returns: A measure of the cash return to the owners of company shares

Simulation modelling: Where the model can be run a number of times, while changing one or more variables across a pre-determined range, to derive a distribution of the set of results

Software development: The design, build and testing of software

Specification: Explicit list of properties and methods associated with a model build

Spreadsheet: A grid, built in software, allowing the user to carry out calculations usually arranged over a limited number of sheets

SPV: Special Purpose Vehicle, the name given to the private consortium engaged in offering the public authority the designated services

Standardised: Built to a specified standard

Statements & reports: Sums and compilations of results in the form of financial statements or reports

Steps: Collections of sensible and balanced tasks from specification, design, build, test or deliver

Strategic financial modelling: Where the model provides the company's top management with answers to the possible direction of the company's future finances

Strategic model: A model used to create a long-term forecast of the future finances of a company or entity

Structured finance: Sector of finance used to organise and prioritise cash payments in order to value or securitise lending

Subordinated debt finance: Financing by means of capital that is subordinated to other finance, typically the senior debt from a bank

Suppliers: Entities or companies engaged in delivering products or services to other entities or companies

Swapped rate: The fixed interest rate that has been swapped for a variable rate for most of project finance loans

Switch: An Boolean value used to turn events off or on

Syntax: Ordered construction of logic and formulae

Target balance: The balance for a cash reserve account used as a target, often changing over time

Tasks: Actions from any of specify, design, build, test or deliver

Tax depreciation: A tax deduction allowed by the use of business assets

Tax loss balance: The balance of tax losses accumulated by a company or entity

Tax losses: Accumulated losses belonging to a company that can be used to reduce future tax profits

Tax-deductible: Expenditure that is allowed for tax purposes, expenditure that is deductible from taxable profits

Time-dependent: Dependent on time

Timeline: The stream of dates across the top of a model sheet

Top level outputs: Outputs such as IRR, cover ratios and NPVs

TRA: Tax Reserve Account, the cash reserve dedicated to the payment of future tax expenditure

Trace dependents: The definition of the dependents of a cell by means of Excel auditing

Trace precedents: The definition of the precedents of a cell by means of Excel auditing

Transaction: The final act of sale and acquisition associated with an entity or company or a merger between two or more entities or companies

Transactional modelling: Modelling used in the process of concluding a business transaction such as an acquisition or a merger between enterprises

Tree analogy: The visual representation of a financial model as a tree

UK PFI: The Private Finance Initiative in the UK

Unesc: Unescalated

Unitary charge: The amount paid by the public authority to a project company for the delivery of designated services

Units: The standard measurement of a physical quantity

Update phase: The second phase in a model build, arriving at the construction of the greater part of logic with correct inputs

Uplift: Factor used to increase (or decrease) a value

VAT: Value Added Tax in the UK

VisiCalc: A spreadsheet software brand name in the 1990s

W / ERROR: With error

WACC: Weighted Average Cost of Capital, a corporate finance term defining the weighted average interest rate (cost) at which an entity or company has financed itself

Withdrawals: Cash withdrawals from a reserve account

Working capital: A measure of the liquidity of a company or entity based on the amount of cash it actually has to operate at any given moment in time – this is a function of the speed at which debtors pay and creditors are paid

APPENDIX 3
KEYBOARD SHORTCUTS

Keyboard Shortcuts  **Lazuli** Solutions

Calculate / Save

Action	Keystrokes
Sheet only	Shift + F9
Entire Workbook	Ctrl + Alt + F9
Save Workbook	Ctrl + S

Moving Around

Action	Keystrokes
Up / Down Sheets	PgUp / PgDn
Across Sheets	Alt + PgUp / PgDn
Between Sheets	Ctrl + PgUp / PgDn
Across Rows	Right: Ctrl + →
	Left: Home
Sheet Beg. / End	Ctrl + Home / End
Among Windows	Ctrl + Tab
Among Applications	Alt + Tab

Auditing

Action	Keystrokes
Precedent (GO)	Ctrl + [
Last Location (COME BACK)	F5 Enter
Display Formula	Ctrl + ¬
Find / Replace	Ctrl + F / Ctrl + H
Trace Arrows	Alt + T + U, plus:
Precedents	T
Dependents	D
Erase Arrows	A
Quick Graph	Select, F11

Editing - General

Action	Keystrokes
Copy	Ctrl + C, Enter
Move	Ctrl + X, Enter
Copy Across	Ctrl + C,
	Shift + Ctrl + →
Paste Special	Alt + E + S, plus:
Formats	T
Formulas	F
Values	V
Format Cells	Ctrl + 1
Formats	Ctrl + U (underline)
	Ctrl + B (bold)
Undo / Redo	Ctrl + Z / Ctrl + Y

Editing - In Cell

Action	Keystrokes
Edit Mode	F2 (toggles in / out)
Anchoring ($)	F4 (toggles 4 levels)
Skip to Next	Ctrl + → / ←
Line Beg. / End	Home / End

Editing - Row/Col

Action	Keystrokes
Select	Shift / Ctrl + Spacebar
Insert New	Alt + I + R or C
Delete	Alt + E + D

VBA

Action	Keystrokes
Open VBA	Alt + F11

Lazuli Solutions
Tel: +44 20 7450 3318   dominic.robertson@lazulisolutions.com
Tel: +44 7974 147 458   www.lazulisolutions.com

Page 1 of 1
lazuli_keyboard_shortcuts_01f.docx
©2013 Lazuli Solutions

APPENDIX 4
EXCEL FUNCTIONS

LIST OF SIMPLE EVERYDAY FORMULAE

- +/-
- *
- SUM
- MAX
- MIN
- IF
- AND
- OR
- IFERROR
- ISNA
- ABS
- AVERAGE
- EOMONTH
- ROUND
- LEFT
- LEN

LIST OF MORE COMPLEX FORMULAE TO CONSIDER BEFORE USING

- / - division can create the error #DIV/0! This can be either avoided by wrapping in an IF function or by error trapping in a subsequent line of code
- INDEX
- MATCH
- VLOOKUP
- HLOOKUP
- LOOKUP
- SUMIF
- SUMPRODUCT

LIST OF FORMULAE TO AVOID

- OFFSET

APPENDIX 5
BUSINESS MAP OR QUICK START SHEET

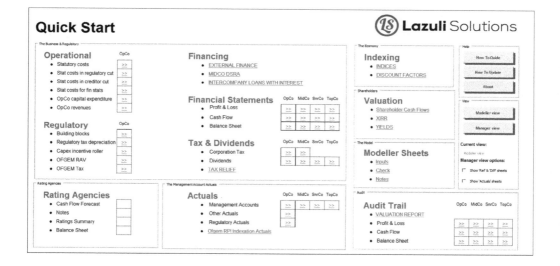

APPENDIX 6
THE TREE ANALOGY

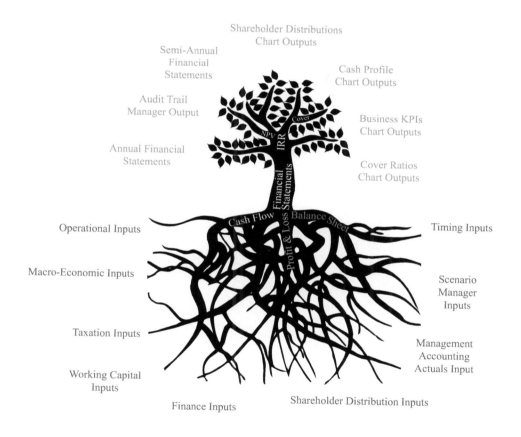

Shareholder Distributions
Chart Outputs

Semi-Annual
Financial
Statements

Cash Profile
Chart Outputs

Audit Trail
Manager Output

Business KPIs
Chart Outputs

Annual Financial
Statements

Cover Ratios
Chart Outputs

Cover

NPV

IRR

Financial
Statements

Operational Inputs

Cash Flow

Profit & Loss

Balance Sheet

Timing Inputs

Macro-Economic Inputs

Scenario
Manager
Inputs

Taxation Inputs

Management
Accounting
Actuals Input

Working Capital
Inputs

Finance Inputs

Shareholder Distribution Inputs

Lazuli Solutions

Lazuli Solutions provides business modelling services across a range of industries. It was founded by Dominic Robertson and is based in London.

Dominic has a long modelling experience. He has been modelling since the early days in the mid-nineties – first with the Henley Centre For Forecasting and Arthur Andersen's Business Modelling Group and then later with Babcock & Brown's Infrastructure Team.

Lazuli is not big on compromise and jargon; instead two principles define us:

1. We keep things simple and clear without creating complications.
2. We say what we think in a direct and forthright manner.

In summary, our approach is about clarity and straightforwardness.

Approach

We start by listening and understanding the client's business. We then design the optimal solution for the client's business by drawing on our past experiences – these may not be in the same industry but may be structurally similar. If the challenge is a new one then we most often revert to the two-dimensional approach as this best suits Excel.

As a rule of thumb, we often find that 'keeping things simple' is the best solution. This is because complex formulae and big logical constructs require higher levels of maintenance and technical understanding. Instead, the objective is to create see-through modelling solutions that allow access at all levels of your organisation as well as achieving your commercial goals.

Good modelling requires flexibility, as the first solution might not be the best and re-modelling is sometimes necessary – sometimes only by 'seeing' and 'touching' can human beings properly understand a problem.

We see our role as primarily 'organisational'. In order to forecast the future with clarity it is necessary to understand the here and now – our models do just that, and we have strong opinions on this. We believe that to get to a deeper level of understanding of your business it *is* important how your business is modelled. For example, indexation causes no end of confusion. So we have elevated indexation to a single sheet and present it in a simple and intuitive manner. This means that each time the user goes back to it there is no need for a new learning process.

A see-through model aims to portray information in the best and most intuitive way, and we are always striving to find new ways of doing this.

Experience

LAZULI SOLUTIONS

- High speed rail operating and strategic models in UK
- Container and bulk port multi-company strategic model in EU
- Media finance slate transaction model in EU
- Regulatory electricity distribution strategic model in UK
- Regulatory gas distribution strategic model in UK
- PFI operating models in UK
- PFI secondary market fund modelling in UK

- Project finance development & analysis in UK
- Project finance bridge model in France
- Software company operating model in UK
- Project finance offshore wind development model in UK
- PFI MOD water and waste water project transaction in UK
- Telecoms data gathering and strategic reporting model system in EU
- Transport strategic acquisition modelling in UK.

PFI

Enterprise Stoke Mandeville Hospital, Aquatrine A PFI, Exeter Courts, Baglan Moor Healthcare, Sussex Police Authority Centralised Custody PFI Project, Genesys Telecommunications Ltd, Buxton Health & Safety Laboratory PFI, North Swindon Schools, British Transport Police, North Birmingham Mental Health Unit, Walsall Street Lighting, Highlands School, London, Greater Nottingham NHS LIFT, Southern Derbyshire NHS LIFT, MaST NHS LIFT 1, MaST NHS LIFT 2, North Nottinghamshire LIFT, Leicester NHS LIFT, Sandwell NHS LIFT, Avon and Somerset Courts, Manchester Street Lighting, Wakefield Street Lighting, Edinburgh Schools, Cleveland Police HQ, Newham Hospital, Newham Housing (Canning Town), Bentilee Regeneration, Kingston Hospital, Enfield Schools, Newham Schools, South Lanarkshire Schools, M6, Scotland, South East London Police Stations, Cleveland & Durham Police Tactical Training Centre, Sirhowy Enterprise Way, Kinnegar Wastewater (Coastal Clearwater), Severn River Crossing, Project Red Dragon - DARA, Ministry of Defence Main Building (Modus), A130, England,

Greater Manchester Police Stations, LUL Connect (Citylink), Glasgow Schools, M40, England, Metropolitan Police Training Centre (Gravesend), A55, North Wales, Newcastle Hospitals, Queen Elizabeth Hospital (Greenwich), Norfolk & Norwich University Hospital, City Greenwich Lewisham Rail Link plc (CGL) , Leisureplan Investments - Bexley Leisure Limited, Leisureplan Investments - D4E Mulberry School Limited, Leisureplan Investments - Penzance Leisure Limited, Dalmuir Wastewater, Sheffield Family Courts, Tay Wastewater, Highland Schools, Scotland, Bishop Auckland Hospital, Criterion Healthcare, South Hampshire Rapid Transit light railway PFI project, CAE Helicopter Aircrew Training Facility, Milton Keynes STC Project

Get in touch with Lazuli Solutions

Call Dominic Robertson at Lazuli Solutions on +44 20 7450 3318 or +44 7974 247 458 or send him an email at **dominic.robertson@lazulisolutions.com**

Index

Lightning Source UK Ltd.
Milton Keynes UK
UKHW051214231118
332781UK00003B/17/P